This groundbreaking work by Dr. Pet [barcode: C000182288] rs for decades to come. Yun spent mo: r-viewing and evaluating Muslim Back 1g equipped him to prepare forms in Bengali, which he used to probe the tensions MBBs face in conversion, relationships with family, and interaction in general after they have left the tight sociological cohesion of Islam. Yun's insights into the subject of identity are some of the best written.

This book is a must-read for workers engaged with Muslims throughout the world because I've seen these same conflicts among MBBs in many countries. Yun's bibliography is excellent. It serves as a guide to much of the current literature that is available relating to MBBs as they struggle to engage in cataclysmic religious and societal upheavals in their lives.

Phil Parshall
Retired SIM Missionary to Bangladesh

Social connection is one of the critical elements formulating one's identity in society. This book researches not only the way of understanding the new identity of MBBs, it also reconstructs how the new identity connects and impacts the neighboring majority society. As a seasoned academic researcher in this field and an experienced field practitioner, Dr. Yun is an outstanding Christian scholar for many scholars and believers to read.

Daniel Shinjong Baeq
Former Director, Hiebert Global Center
Senior Pastor, Bethel Korean Presbyterian Church, Ellicott City, Maryland, USA

Loving one another is a vital marker of Jesus's disciples. Peter Yun's in-depth study takes us beyond the work of Tim Green and Jonas Jorgensen, helping us understand the new, hybridizing, and at times shifting social identities being formed among Bangladeshi Muslims who have become followers of Jesus – and who are learning to truly love one another. A very significant contribution!

David Greenlee, PhD
Director, Missiological Research and Evaluation, Operation Mobilization
Editor, *Longing for Community: Church, Ummah, or Somewhere in Between?*

I want to thank Peter K. Yun for this work which focuses on the problems of Muslim Background Believers in Bangladesh and especially for his in-depth research into our culture and the social status of MBBs. In this book, Dr. Yun heightens the MBBs everyday social problems, identity and persecution. It will help all the MBBs of Bangladesh and definitely will raise awareness of their situation throughout the rest of the world.

Pastor Anwar Hossain
Chairman, Prime Evangelistic Church (PEC)
Executive Director, Heed Bangladesh

Peter Yun's research on Bangladeshi Muslim Background Believers' social identity is much more than a theoretical academic exercise. Dr. Yun's extensive on-the-ground presence while conducting community-based research has resulted in a granular study that aims to build healthy, self-sustaining MBB communities. The insights gained from extensively interviewing Bangladeshi MBBs encourages them, as well as the rest of us who follow Jesus, to live and speak as effective witnesses who are deeply rooted in our communities. Yun's combination of theoretical rigor and real-life struggles of human beings is a welcome and contemporary study of living as faithful and relevant representatives of Jesus.

J. Nelson Jennings, PhD
Mission Pastor, Consultant, and International Liaison,
Onnuri Community Church, Seoul, South Korea
English Editor, *Global Missiology*

Dr. Yun's research is a production written by his heart, head, hands and feet from a glocal perspective. I highly appreciate his wrestling with the many complicated and challenging issues of social identity of Muslim Background Believers (MBBs) in Bangladesh. He successfully analyzes these issues and applies them in useful discovery, conclusions, and implications through multidisciplinary lenses, such as sociology, anthropology, theology, missiology, Islam, and Christianity. Readers will be challenged and encouraged by the findings in this book and will agree with his practical suggestion about the need for more Barnabas's for MBBs in God's harvest fields today. I feel his heartbeat, and I journey with the MBBs from Asian backgrounds through this book.

Keung Chul Jeong (Matthew)
Servant of the Least Community, Pakistan

This book provides readers with critical and profound missiological insights regarding the issue of contextualization in a Muslim society. Using a qualitative research methodology, the author excellently exposes the socio-religious identity of Muslim Background Believers in Bangladesh, which for decades has been a highly critical issue among missiologists and theologians. Through extensive interviews and observations, the author provides enormous information about the new socio-religious identity among MBBs in Bangladesh. I highly recommend this precious book for those who have a strong concern for planting a sound Christian community among Muslim countries.

Hark-Yoo Kim, PhD
President, Hapdong Theological Seminary, Suwon-si, South Korea
President, Asia Theological Association – Korea

How do Muslim Background Believers in Jesus understand their new identity in light of the surrounding Muslim beliefs and practices? In this carefully researched and thoughtful study, Dr. Yun probes the issues of social and religious identity among Bangladeshi followers of 'Isa, showing the sometimes surprising connections as well as breaks with the broader Islamic contexts. Dr. Yun brings together a sound grasp of theoretical literature and issues with a sensitive understanding of the lived realities from his years of ministry in Bangladesh. This is an important contribution to ongoing discussions of religious identity and contextualization.

Harold Netland, PhD
Professor of Philosophy of Religion and Intercultural Studies,
Trinity Evangelical Divinity School, Deerfield, Illinois, USA

Peter Kwang-Hee Yun's research provides an important new contribution to our understanding of how Muslim believers in Jesus self-identify and the implications of that identity for their social life. He then provides sound guidance on ministry in such settings.

Craig Ott, PhD
Professor of Mission and Intercultural Studies,
Trinity Evangelical Divinity School, Deerfield, Illinois, USA

Peter Yun draws on an impressively broad range of interdisciplinary approaches to MBB identity, developing new original thinking which pushes the boundaries in our thinking. Equally important are his qualitative interviews with a large sample of MBBs, allowing us to hear their voices directly. These two strengths of the book, along with its perceptive conclusions, make it a really important contribution in what is still a little-explored field. I commend it warmly.

Tim Green, PhD
Researcher on MBB Identity
Director, Word of Life

Journeys to New Life, Identity, and Community

Empowering Jesus Followers and *Jamaats* in Bangladesh

Peter Kwang-Hee Yun

Langham

MONOGRAPHS

© 2021 Peter Kwang-Hee Yun

Published 2021 by Langham Monographs
An imprint of Langham Publishing
www.langhampublishing.org

Langham Publishing and its imprints are a ministry of Langham Partnership

Langham Partnership
PO Box 296, Carlisle, Cumbria, CA3 9WZ, UK
www.langham.org

ISBNs:
978-1-83973-211-9 Print
978-1-83973-537-0 ePub
978-1-83973-538-7 Mobi
978-1-83973-539-4 PDF

All Scripture quotations, unless otherwise indicated, are taken from the Holy Bible, New International Version®, NIV®. Copyright ©1973, 1978, 1984, 2011 by Biblica, Inc.™ Used by permission of Zondervan.

Scripture quotations marked (NRSV) are from the New Revised Standard Version Bible, copyright © 1989 National Council of the Churches of Christ in the United States of America. Used by permission. All rights reserved.

British Library Cataloguing-in-Publication Data
A catalogue record for this book is available from the British Library

ISBN: 978-1-83973-211-9

Cover & Book Design: projectluz.com

A dedication to the Lord,
and three women who love me and whom I love:
Choohwa, my mother,
Selly, my wife,
and Yebin, my daughter.

Contents

List of Figures

List of Tables

Abstract

The main purpose of this research[1] is to explore the social identity of Muslim Background Believers (MBBs) in Bangladesh. Three research questions address the following subjects: (1) Bangladeshi MBBs' formation of new social identities after belief in 'Isa, (2) MBBs' social integration with Muslims and participation in their religious activities, and (3) MBBs' perception of four important issues (Allah, 'Isa, Muhammad, and the Qur'an). To answer these questions, qualitative research methodology – interviews in particular – was employed. Forty-eight local MBB respondents from diverse believers' communities (jama'ats) and ten experienced foreign respondents were interviewed and observed for one year.

The major findings of this study are presented in response to the research question. First, after developing a commitment to 'Isa, primarily through cognitive and affective factors, MBBs generally became part of one of three social identity groups: Christian/Isai, Isai/Isai Muslim (uboi; both), or Isai Muslim/Muslim. They usually move within these boundaries. Second, all three groups differ from majority Muslims in their approach to social activities such as marriage and children's education. Levels of participation in Muslim religious activities range across the identity groups from no participation to regular participation. Each social identity category has certain benefits and shortcomings. While Christian/Isai MBBs have spiritual benefits such as radical separation from majority Muslims, self-identified Isai Muslim/Muslims face theological and practical ambiguities such as, whether the Qur'an is one of the divinely inspired books and whether to participate in Muslims' formal

---

1. The dissertation was originally entitled *An Exploration of the Social Identity of Muslim Background Believers in a Muslim Majority Community in Bangladesh.*

prayers (*namaz*). *Isai/Isai* Muslims who identify themselves both ways need careful guidance in developing a transparent identity.

This research draws several suggestions and implications from its diverse findings. It recommends the following: (1) accept the reality which divides MBBs among three social identity groups and focus on Christ-centeredness, not Christianity-centeredness, (2) encourage the *Isai* Muslim/Muslim group to focus more on the Bible than the Qur'an to eliminate syncretic factors while respecting their initiative and decision, (3) pursue true partnership beyond money and hierarchy between foreign missionaries and local believers to empower MBBs to form a harmonious, healthy community, and (4) study the whole three-layer identity of MBBs and study Bangladeshi Muslims and Islam comprehensively.

Acknowledgments

Doing research work and writing in English are not easy tasks for a foreign student whose first language is not English. This study might not have been possible without the generous persons who helped me finish it. First, I deeply express my thanks to my research mentor Dr. Harold Netland who allowed me to proceed with my research and writing and kindly supported me. I also appreciate the thoughtful comments and encouragement about my research that I received from Drs. Priest and Ott. Second, I am especially indebted to my local supervisor Dr. Saifur Rashid at the University of Dhaka. When I was struggling to change my research topic, his advice helped me to decide on this subject, and his generous concern for me encouraged me to stay in Bangladesh. Third, I am grateful to my research respondents who kindly showed great hospitality to me. I am also thankful to my proofreader, Hilary Guth, who also gave me good suggestions and encouraging comments. Last, I would like to thank my family – parents, wife, and children. Without their continuous support and sacrifice, I would not have finished this project properly.

CHAPTER 1

Introduction

Research Problem

This research focuses on the social identities of Muslim Background Believers (MBBs) in Bangladesh with relation to contextualization. To begin with my personal journey, holistic poverty alleviation was the concept that motivated and drew me to come to Bangladesh. Since my initial short-term visit in 2008, the vision of fulfilling both the physical needs of one of the poorest countries in Asia and the spiritual needs of the people there (90% Muslim, 9% Hindu, and 0.3% Christian) has made me eager to learn and travel through this country.[1] During several years in Bangladesh as a cultural learner and researcher, I focused on friendship and participation in the real life of MBBs in this country. The context of spiritual hardship due to pressure from the Muslim majority combined with physical need is the starting place for the contextualization discussion in Bangladesh, which is one of the most fruitful but also controversial fields among Muslim majority countries.[2]

---

1. According to the most recent data from the CIA World Factbook, Bangladesh's population consists of 89.5% Muslims, 9.6% Hindus, and 0.9% other religions (2004 estimate). The remainder 0.9% is divided almost equally between Buddhists, Roman Catholics, and Protestants (0.3% each). Central Intelligence Agency, "Bangladesh Religious Population."

2. Bangladesh was the first field of Phil Parshall, one of the most prominent pioneers in the contextualization discussion. He has written several books based on his experience in Bangladesh such as *Muslim Evangelism* (2003). Edward Ayub, an MBB leader in Bangladesh, reveals his unpleasant feeling that Bangladesh has been used as "the laboratory and parade ground" of insider ideology. Ayub, "Observations," 21.

"The Word became flesh and made his dwelling among us" (John 1:14). Since God's incarnation in Jesus and Pentecost, the gospel of Jesus Christ has been carried across cultures. The gospel, which has been conveyed beyond cultures, also "must be expressed from within culture."[3] Due to the two characteristics of the gospel – translatability (across cultures) and indigeneity (within cultures) – the tension between the universal truth of the gospel and these two characteristics has always existed and continues in the current globalized mission era.[4] Andrew Walls also discusses this tension in terms of the "indigenizing" and "pilgrim" principles of the gospel. The "indigenizing" principle stressed that God accepted us "as we are" in our indigenous uniqueness, while the "pilgrim" principle reminds us that God asks us to be different from culture in order to become universal children of God.[5]

The term "contextualization" reveals this tension, as well as the effort for the gospel to break through cultural boundaries.[6] Contextualization has been defined by various theologians and practitioners. Applying to the tension of the gospel and context, contextualization refers to "the dynamic and comprehensive process by which the gospel is incarnated within a concrete historical or cultural situation."[7] Contextualization has become one of the most significant concepts and practices for the understanding and development of modern missiology and mission works.

Contextualization as both concept and practice brings many kinds of questions from different contexts to the surface. Darrell Whiteman introduces three functions of contextualization: (1) to communicate the gospel within a

---

3. Gilliland, "Contextual Theology," 28; Hiebert, *Gospel in Human Context*, 31.

4. The translatable character of the gospel was popularly introduced by Lamin Sanneh's books (2003, 2008, and 2009). Sanneh argues that the translatability of the gospel as it spreads through cultures enables Christianity to become a world religion. Sanneh, *Disciples of All Nations*, 25–28.

Indigeneity is the noun form of "indigenous." The indigenous church reflects the cultural distinctiveness and avoids any duplication of other cultural dominances such as Western churches. Terry, "Indigeneous Churches," 483.

Harvie M. Conn discussed the relationship between translatability and indigenization, saying, "indigenization is a term describing the 'translatability' of the universal Christian faith into the forms and symbols of particular cultures of the world." Conn, "Indigenization," 481.

5. Walls, "Gospel as Prisoner," 136–39.

6. Moreau, "Contextualization," 321. Scott Moreau historically surveys related terms of contextualization such as accommodation, adaption, indigenization, and inculturation and their relationship with it. Moreau, 325–29.

7. Fleming, *Contextualization*, 19.

local context by presenting the gospel in a manner consistent with the needs of the people in the context, (2) to critique culture by exposing previous sinful cultural patterns and behaviors in light of the gospel, and (3) to create a new community by developing "contextualized expressions of the Gospel . . . [for] expanding our understanding of the kingdom of God."[8] We must consider then how to determine what is appropriate contextualization. Questions such as the following need to be addressed in discussions of contextualization discussions: In establishing churches or Christ-centered communities in a new context, to what extent should the expression of the gospel build upon local linguistic, cultural, and religious patterns? In coming to faith in Christ, must one entirely reject one's past cultural and religious markers? How do we decide what is acceptable and what is not?

In practical current missions, "the need for contextualization" by MBBs, inquirers, and mission practitioners has been reported.[9] Reports indicate that growing numbers of Muslims around the world have been drawn to faith in Christ through Bible reading (sometimes Qur'an reading as well), dreams or visions, the witness of faithful friends, or the power of prayer in the name of 'Isa (Jesus). The range of ways in which MBBs express their faith is as diverse as the ways and means through which MBBs have dedicated their lives to Christ. But a central issue for MBBs is their identity.

Problem Statement

The problem that this study addresses is that of the identity of MBBs in Bangladesh, and, in particular, their social identity with respect to the sur-rounding Muslim communities in which they find themselves. Thus, this research focuses on the social identity of MBBs in a broader Muslim com-munity in Bangladesh, seeking to determine the degree to which MBBs are integrated within the Muslim community in terms of their activities and social life, and also exploring MBBs' perceptions regarding the degree of continuity between their own belief and practices and those of the Muslims around them. The research also examines social dynamics that allow for changes in identity from Muslims to followers of 'Isa and scrutinizes social

---

8. Whiteman, "Contextualization," 2–4.
9. Woodberry, "Contextualization among Muslims," 283.

boundaries between the Christian and Muslim religions and cultures. We will also consider some missiological issues regarding indigenous four-self dynamics among believers' communities.

Research Questions

The following research questions and sub-questions guide this study:

1. What factors were involved in MBBs coming to identify themselves as followers of 'Isa? Have the ways in which MBBs identify themselves religiously changed since their conversion?

    SQ1a. What factors were involved in their conversion and what were the responses from others?

    SQ1b. What factors were involved in their mental (inner), behavioral (outer), and identity change?

2. To what extent and in what ways are MBBs integrated into the social, religious, and cultural fabric of the broader Muslim community life?

    SQ2a. How do MBBs live out the four family/social issues regarding marriage, funeral, children's education, and finance?

    SQ2b. What social activities and roles within the larger Muslim community do MBBs participate in? If they do not participate in some activities, why not?

    SQ2c. What are the determinant factors that they use to decide to stay in their social identity and patterns of life?

3. To what extent and in what ways do MBBs think there is continuity and/or discontinuity between their own beliefs and practices and those of Muslims around them? Do their views affect whether, or how, they share the gospel with Muslims? Do they also pursue a self-standing (four-self) faith community in the long run?

    SQ3a. Do MBBs think differently from the majority Muslims regarding core concepts such as Jesus ('Isa), the Bible, Muhammad, and the Qur'an?

SQ3b. Are MBBs actively sharing their faith with Muslims? If so, do they build upon the perceived commonalities between Islam and Christianity in sharing their faith? Or do they avoid using Islamic terms, beliefs, and practices? Do MBBs want to build contextualized communities adapting Islamic terms and practices or more Christianized communities excluding previous Islamic patterns of life?

SQ3c. What are the realities and possibilities of four-self dynamics (self-propagating, supporting, governing, and theologizing) in the Bangladeshi MBB community?

Methodology

This research employed a qualitative field research method to answer the research problems and questions by exploring the social identity of MBBs in Bangladesh and their integration with Muslim neighbors and their faith communities. The research relied especially on the use of interviews as a research tool, alongside various qualitative data collection methods focused on observing the interviewees' lives and backgrounds. While I did not write detailed ethnographic field notes, I observed the social and religious life of MBBs, using the strength of relatively long-term stay (three and a half years) in the research field to visit two major research fields as often as possible. Whenever I visited the fields, I tried to stay in MBBs' houses in the village unless doing so would threaten their security. But, I majorly employed a full range of interview methodology from conversation and informal interviews to semi-formal and formal interviews. After finishing the research between August 2014 and May 2015, I organized and analyzed the data with Nvivo 10.

Contextualization among Muslims

Responding to recent issues in contextualization with diverse groups of MBBs, John Travis, a Christian mission scholar and practitioner, published a wide range of perspectives on Christ-centered communities in Muslim contexts called the C1–C6 spectrum.[10]

> C1 – Believers in traditional Christian fellowships where worship is not in the mother tongue
>
> C2 – Same as C1, but worship is in the believers' mother tongue
>
> C3 – Believers in culturally indigenous Christian fellowships that avoid Islamic forms
>
> C4 – Believers in culturally indigenous fellowships that retain biblically permissible Islamic forms, but not identifying as Muslims
>
> C5 – Muslim followers of Jesus in fellowships within the Muslim community, continuing to identify culturally and/or officially as Muslims, though a special kind
>
> C6 – Muslim followers of Jesus in limited, underground fellowship.

The spectrum sets out various views about the degree to which followers of Jesus can make use of linguistic, cultural, and religious forms associated with Muslim communities while living as disciples of Jesus. Among the six categories, C4 and C5 are the most controversial, and among the three types of distinguishing lines, the issue of religious identity is the most crucial.[11]

The kind of highly contextualized approach involving Muslims who remain within an Islamic context has been practiced by evangelicals since the 1970s. According to Sam Schlorff, Charles Kraft introduced the term "a Muslim church" by his defining "Muslim" as a cultural term a few decades ago.[12] He developed this idea in an article named "Dynamic equivalence churches in Muslim society."[13] In "Some reflections on possibilities for people

---

10. Travis, "C1 to C6 Spectrum," 407–8; Travis and Woodberry, "When God's Kingdom Grows," 30.

11. Parshall, *Muslim Evangelism*, 71–73; Green, "Identity Choices," 62.

12. Schlorff, "Translation Model"; Kraft, "Dynamic Equivalence Churches."

13. Charles Kraft began by defining "church" in the biblical sense of *ekklesia*, as the people of God away from the "prevailing sociocultural patterns." Kraft, "Dynamic Equivalence Churches," 115. He posits the "existence of grouping of God's people within so-called 'Muslim' cultures (1) that are committed in faith allegiance to God in accordance to biblical revelation and (2) that function within their own sociocultural matrix in ways equivalent in their dynamics

movements among Muslims," John Wilder proposed two forms of a people movement among Muslims based on his research of early Hebrew Christianity and the Messianic Jewish Movement:

1. A people movement to Christ which remains within Islam.
2. A people movement constituting a new church of Muslim cultural orientation.[14]

The first one of the two forms proposed by Wilder is very similar to the C5 approach – a movement remaining within Islam. The second is similar to the C4 (or C3) approach – a movement differentiating the churches of believers from a Muslim background from the churches of believers from other religious backgrounds. The appropriateness of the C4 and C5 approaches has been the source of much contemporary debate.

Unlike the C5 grouping, which approaches the issue through the categorical and ecclesiological lens of Christ-centered community, some proponents of C5 such as Kevin Higgins and Rebecca Lewis define this as an "insider movement."[15] They define this as a movement that takes place beyond religious boundaries, and involves people moving – "to Jesus that remain to varying degrees inside the social fabric of Islamic, Buddhist, Hindu, or other people groups."[16] Dudley Woodberry closely connects C5 believers to insider movement among Muslims: "C5 expresses a group of persons who accept Jesus as Lord and Savior but remain within the Muslim community to lead others to follow Christ in an 'insider movement.'"[17]

Rebecca Lewis, taking insights from the New Testament and Acts, points out that there are two essential elements in any insider movement: continued community and retained identity. She explains these two elements of the insider movement in detail:

---

to biblically recommended examples." He also suggested the possible use of the terms "Muslim Christians" or "Christian Muslims" to describe people who are dedicated to God through Jesus and at the same time remain culturally Muslim. Kraft, 119–20.

14. Wilder, "Some Reflections," 310.

15. On the frontier mission side, such as a magazine like *Mission Frontiers*, insider movement is also called as Jesus movement.

16. Higgins, "Key to Insider Movements," 155. David Garrison signifies insider movement as "popular movements to Christ that bypass both formal and explicit expressions of the Christian religion." Garrison, "Church Planting Movements," 151. Some others such as Gavriel Gefen call this as Jesus movements beyond religious boundary. Geven, "Jesus Movements," 7.

17. Woodberry, "To the Muslim?," 23.

1. The gospel takes root within *pre-existing communities* or social networks, which become the main expression of "church" in that context. Believers are not gathered from diverse social networks to create a "church." New parallel social structures are not invented or introduced.

2. Believers *retain their identity* as members of their socioreligious community while living under the Lordship of Jesus Christ and the authority of the Bible.[18]

While Woodberry almost equates C5 with the insider movement among Muslims, Lewis tries to differentiate between the two because some C5 believers do not remain in the Muslim community or exist away from their natural social networks.[19] In practice, some C5 believers exist away from their hometowns in order to do evangelistic activities following their own or an organization's vision and strategy. In this study, I will use both terms. I will use the term "C5" or "C5 believers" from the C-spectrum to designate the specific community of believers as Muslim followers of 'Isa, and the term "insider movement among Muslims" to refer to the movement which demonstrates the two characteristics of continuing natural community and retaining religious identity. The distinction is worth noting because an important issue in my research is how and why individuals change and/or retain their social identity among the Muslim majority communities after coming to believe in 'Isa.

The concept of "social identity" is directly connected to contextualization in a Muslim-majority context – indeed, social identity and contextualization are like two sides of the same coin. While the term "contextualization" is more familiar to foreign practitioners seeking to understand the indigenous believers and their community than it is to locals, "social identity" is a more practical term for use in discussing the complex reality faced by MBBs. Nevertheless, contextualization is not simply for outsiders who try to "make the gospel relevant" within a particular culture. It is also something that believers within a culture ought to be engaged in and which missionaries should do together with communities of local believers. The term "social identity" reflects the social reality of local believers. This study addresses the ongoing reality of MBBs' social identity focusing on contextualization from

---

18. Lewis, "Insider Movements," 16.
19. Lewis, "Promoting Movements," 76.

the individuals' new formation of social identity by faith on 'Isa and social integration with the majority to its application in the collective level of MBB community. To understand the reality and problems of MBBs in Bangladesh, we must start with a historical survey of MBBs in Bangladesh.

Social and Historical Context of Bangladeshi MBBs

The constitution of Bangladesh states that "the state religion of the Republic is Islam, but the State shall ensure equal status and equal right in the practice of the Hindu, Buddhist, Christian and other religions."[20] Among the religions, Christianity ranks fourth with 0.3 percent in contrast to the dominant religion of Islam, with around 90 percent Sunni Muslims. The government of Bangladesh follows the principle of "secularism" by eliminating "any discrimination against, or persecution of, persons practicing a particular religion" in its constitution.[21] According to Bangladesh 2012 International Religious Freedom Report, however, persecution of religious minorities by Islamic fundamental groups is frequently reported despite these constitutional provisions. Also, in Article 41 on freedom of religion, the constitution of Bangladesh addresses freedom of preaching and establishment of religious institutions as follows: "(a) every citizen has the right to profess, practice or propagate any religion; (b) every religious community or denomination has the right to establish, maintain and manage its religious institutions."[22]

Moreover, Bangladeshi citizens have to indicate which of several religions they belong to when they register their ID cards, even though religious information does not show up on the ID cards themselves. They automatically follow their father's religion unless they register for a change of religion. Once Muslims decide to follow 'Isa, they can decide whether to go to the court and change their official religion or live without legally changing their religion to Christianity. One of the MBB respondents interviewed for this research expressed that the Muslim majority community began persecuting his family when he changed his legal identity from Muslim to Christian.

---

20. *Constitution of Bangladesh*, 2012, 2A, 5.
21. *Constitution of Bangladesh*, 12d, 13.
22. *Constitution of Bangladesh*, 32.

Bangladesh had very few Muslim converts to Christianity until the 1970s. This was because most local Christians came from a Hindu background due to the legacy of William Carey's outreach and translation of the Bible for Bengal Hindus. These Hindu converts had a strong adhesion to their former religion and culture.[23] Because the initial formation of Christian identity in Bangladesh took on a distinctly Hindu cultural shape, Muslim converts were sometimes required to adopt Hindu cultural forms and regulations as a verification of genuine conversion; these forms included changing their names, using Hindu-dialect Christian terminology, and even eating pork.[24] Muslim converts to Christianity who adopted these kinds of behaviors met a hostile reception from their families and communities, often resulting in expulsion. These "exiles" wandered among churches and foreign missionaries for their survival.[25]

This pattern has diminished since the 1970s due to a few local converts resisting the pressure to follow previous examples and several foreign missionary organizations passionately reaching out to Muslims from outside the existing Bangladeshi churches majorly from Hindu background. Despite the goal to build culturally relevant and spiritually sincere communities, the gap between cultures of the existing churches and Muslim converts was too great. For this reason, several foreign mission agencies have tried to build an MBB community that is separate from the traditional Hindu background churches so as to allow for Islamic cultural forms and encourage MBBs to remain within the boundaries of family and community. This was not an insider movement or C5 community, but rather an effort of contextualization among Muslims similar to a C4 community, carried out by evangelical mission organizations trying to find more appropriate ways to engage local Muslims with the gospel.[26] Meanwhile, beginning in the mid-1970s, local leaders from

---

23. Croft, "Muslim Background Believers," 39.

24. An interview respondent from a Muslim background shared an experience with the "pork" issue from around thirty years ago. While he was staying in a traditional (Hindu-background) Christian leader's house temporarily, his younger brother (a Muslim) came from his hometown and visited him. The Christian leader said, "I made a special dish for you." But, it was a pork dish. Even though he had thought that he could bring his brother to 'Isa slowly, after this incident his brother returned to his village after showing much anger. They still have not restored their relationship.

25. Johnson personally asked me (the author) to use a pseudonym for his name. Johnson, "Training Materials," 25.

26. Johnson, 27–31.

Muslim background and several missionaries tried to encourage new followers of *'Isa* to stay within their community and preserve their religious identity in order to reach out to their family and friends in their pre-existing networks. This was the beginning of the insider movement in Bangladesh.

Another crucial reason for the formation of separate communities of traditional Hindu-background Christians and MBBs was the birth of a new Bible translation in *Mussolmani* (Muslims') Bangla, the *Kitabul Mokaddos* ("Holy Books"). This new version has been published and distributed since the late 1970s with the assistance of a foreign organization with a passion for reaching out to Muslims in their heart language.[27] Along with the use of the Muslim-friendly Bible, *jama'ats* (house churches or small gatherings of MBBs) have been started from the mid-1970s.[28] However, because of the lack of knowledge and experience of *jama'at* leaders they have not been built up to maturity.[29]

It is also worth mentioning that another turning point in Muslim evangelism is the initiative of local MBBs outside of direct involvement of foreigners. After realizing the influence of foreign missionaries' outreach, the government of Bangladesh has started to restrict missionary outreach to local Muslims by minimizing the direct evangelistic activities of foreigners and limiting development work through registered NGOs. Contrary to the government's intentions, however, this has helped local MBBs own their responsibility to reach out to their Muslim neighbors and made them more proactive in thinking about how locals and foreigners can work together.[30]

However, after around forty years of history in the Bangladeshi MBB community, things have not gone entirely smoothly for two major reasons. First, MBBs have been struggling with their social/cultural positioning and identity in the local Muslim-majority society. Some Muslim converts moved directly into the established Christian church by adopting Christian names and existing Christian cultural patterns. Some wanted to remain within the

---

27. Jennings, "Muslim Background Believers," 24.

28. The term *jama'at* is an Arabic word referring to Muslims' large groups or gatherings. MBBs are using the term following the Muslims' usage, but usually MBBs' *jama'ats* are small. Recently, some MBBs are beginning to use the word *mondoli* ("assembly, church" in Bangla) instead of *jama'at* due to the negative nuance of the term *jama'at* as used by Islamic political groups such as *Jamaat-e-Islami*. *Mondoli* is a relatively neutral term, unlike the term *girja* (a traditional Hindu background term for "church").

29. Taher, "Society of Bangladesh," 1.

30. Johnson, "Training Materials," 27–31.

majority community, retaining their religious identity for fear of persecution and sometimes for the continued ability to reach out to their Muslim neighbors, whether by their own choice or due to a foreigner's encouragement. Others are located somewhere between these two margins.[31] These MBBs have strived to find appropriate social positions and cultural behaviors such as the use of religious language, religious forms, and participation in important social activities and festivals according to their new faith and identity. The issue of social identity is directly connected with contextually interpreting the gospel by deeply considering local religious and cultural forms and context. For these MBBs, social identity regarding contextualization has become a significant issue.

Second, considering the economic situation in Bangladesh which is relatively poor, even by world standards, financial factors have always been "a stumbling block" in the MBB society's path to maturity. In their day-to-day life, MBBs have faced economic disadvantages, such as difficulty getting a job, diminished access to promotions, or losing customers when their conversionis revealed. More importantly, indigenous MBB evangelists have tended to depend on the financial support of foreign missionaries and organizations for their livelihood.[32] However, funds from outside are not always certain, consistent, or stable. For example, if a church (or several house churches) is planted and a pastor is supported by foreign funding, sudden stoppage of funds means loss of livelihood for the pastor and local MBBs lose their shepherd. From time to time disputes among local organizations have occurred regarding financial support in evangelistic work. This tendency toward dependency has occurred across the spectrum of MBBs, from open converts (close to C1–C4) to insider believers (close to C5). For MBBs then, becoming a self-sustaining faith community is another significant issue.[33]

---

31. Abu Taher, one of the MBB leaders, mentions that the believers from a Muslim background did not know what kinds of identity they should have: "Somebody is Christian, *Isai*, *Isai* Muslim, or directly call themselves Muslim" in their present society. Taher, "Society of Bangladesh," 1.

32. Jennings, "Muslim Background Believers," 59.

33. In addition to Johnson's research and conversations with various MBBs and foreign workers, I am specially indebted to two persons for my understanding of these two major issues. One is an Asian kingdom worker, Lee, and the other is a Bangladeshi MBB, Akbar (pseudonym). I learned much about the history and difficult situation of Bangladeshi MBBs in a lecture for new workers in Bangladesh given by Lee, who has worked in Bangladesh for more than twenty years and knows the context well. Sometimes one rural MBB group is a member of multiple

After several decades of history of the Bangladeshi MBB community, practitioners generally agree that several situational realities exist in which MBBs are immersed in terms of collective application of social identity. In his presentation for new practitioners, one veteran worker in Bangladesh, Musa Lee, describes the situation of MBBs in Bangladesh.[34]

1. Evangelism: The gospel has normally been spread to rural and low class first rather than urban and mid-upper class. Many more converts are evangelized by local people than by foreigners.

2. Living: Most local MBBs pastors and evangelists are dependent on foreign funds.

3. Leadership: There is very little organized biblical training for building up the new generation of leaders. Also, because most MBB evangelists only focus on evangelism, leadership is less likely to be nurtured for local MBBs.

4. Conflict: Conflict frequently occurs over the extent of contextualization and differing amounts of foreign funds received.

5. Community: It is very hard to find a self-sustaining community and leadership.

6. Network and Partnership: Indigenous partnerships and networks often stop or are severely hampered after only a few meetings due to conflict.

Lee's description of the situation of MBBs in Bangladesh addresses three areas: evangelism, funding, and leadership. Also, Abu Taher mentions that MBBs' lack of biblical knowledge and application hampers the development of MBB community in Bangladesh.[35] In this sense, these four areas are directly connected to the social application of three-self formula first introduced by Venn and Anderson[36] and the four-self model discussed by Paul Hiebert.[37] Three-self model looks for churches to be self-propagating (evangelism),

---

organizations in order to secure more funding and raise the number of believers for each foreign mission organization. Akbar has worked with Christian organizations and a foreign MBB-majority development organization; he shared his own stories regarding the above issues.

34. This material was introduced on 3 May 2014, at an orientation meeting for new foreign practitioners. It was in another language and was translated by the author. Lee, *Orientation Paper*.

35. Taher, "Society of Bangladesh."

36. As cited in Shenk, "Rufus Anderson," 168–72.

37. Hiebert, *Anthropological Insights*, 193–224.

self-supporting (funding), and self-governing (leadership); Hiebert adds the fourth self, self-theologizing (application of the word of God in their own context). Hirsch and Catchim use the term "four-self dynamics" to discuss the application of this concept to an autonomous missional church movement capturing the "God-given right of all peoples to have their own distinct cultural identity."[38] Robert Priest researched each principle and its relevance for missions.[39] By researching these four-self dynamics in the context of Bangladeshi MBBs, we can diagnose the present social dynamics of MBB community and forecast their future development. Researching MBBs' intentions and understanding of the self-propagating principle helps establish the possibility of enhancing the gospel movement continuing beyond the life of paid evangelism. The self-supporting and self-governing dynamics connect to the continuity of the next generation of the MBB community by minimizing the effect of the uncertain involvement of missionaries while maximizing the local initiative of the movement. The self-theologizing principle touches on how MBBs respond to their own particular Muslim-majority context in light of the Scripture.

As mentioned above, the major problems related to social identity and self-sustaining faith communities that Bangladeshi MBBs are facing are ongoing and not easily answered. However, these two problems cannot be considered separately; they are interwoven for historical and situational reasons. The present study focuses on the first issue – social identity and social integration of MBBs within a Muslim-majority community – but it also deals with the second issue through the lens of four-self dynamics in order to offer a present diagnosis and prospective view of the future of MBB community.

A number of questions regarding social identity must be addressed. First, what do we mean by "social identity" of MBBs? How are MBBs' new social identities formed and changed? In what kinds of social activities do they participate or not participate? What do they think and do differently from majority Muslims? What are the similarities and differences between them? Do they share the gospel with Muslims by focusing on commonalities between the two religions or not? Do they not only intend to share the gospel, but also build a self-standing (four-self) community at the same time? In this

---

38. Hirsch and Catchim, *Permanent Revolution*, 230.
39. Priest, "Researching Contextualization," 299–318.

study, we explore MBBs' social identity as it develops from the beginning of their faith journey, examining their social interactions with their Muslim neighbors and their perceptions regarding continuity between the two religions. We also extend this research to address questions about four-self issues affecting the Bangladeshi MBB community's ability to be self-propagating, self-supporting, self-governing, and self-theologizing while they seek to co-exist with the Muslim majority.

Significance of Research

This topic has not received much attention in research-based studies, yet it has crucial implications for missions worldwide. The issue of MBBs' conversion was discussed by the authors of *From the Straight Path to the Narrow Way: Journeys of Faith*, edited by David Greenlee. Due to the recent rise in the number of MBBs in various areas, the issue of MBBs' identity has been popularized by many practitioners in Muslim-majority countries. For example, the book *Longing for Community: Church, Ummah, or Somewhere in Between?* is one of the outcomes of growing attention to MBB identity by the academic community.[40] My research focuses primarily on the social identity issue. This intensive, community-based research also has significant implications for how to build healthy, self-sustaining MBB communities, as well as insights for Bangladeshi MBBs who are seeking to become good witnesses that are deeply rooted in the culture of their communities.

Delimitations

This research was conducted through mainly interviews. The research took place primarily in two local communities in Bangladesh, but also involved several other communities. Because of the limited quantity of research fields in a South Asian country, the research findings may not be applicable to all MBBs in the world, such as those in the Middle East (Arabic countries) and South East (or Central) Asia. Also, because this research focused mainly on certain social groups of MBBs such as Christian or *Isai* groups (C2 or C3 on the C-spectrum), it does not cover the whole spectrum of MBB groups

---

40. Greenlee, "Introduction."

equally, although the research did include several more contextualized re-spondents and groups. Further, the research was not intended to be a direct comparative study of Christian/*Isai* groups and *Isai* Muslim/Muslim groups; nevertheless, it included several comparative analyses of different socially identified groups of MBBs.

CHAPTER 2

Research Methodology

This chapter addresses research procedure by describing this study's research methodology and the field research setting. The qualitative methodological approach of the research and background information about the field will be included here.

Research Questions Restated

The primary research questions guiding this study are as follows:

RQ1. What factors were involved in MBBs coming to identify themselves as followers of *'Isa*? Have the ways in which MBBs identify themselves religiously changed since their conversion?

RQ2. To what extent and in what ways are MBBs integrated into the social, religious, and cultural fabric of the broader Muslim community life?

RQ3. To what extent and in what ways do MBBs think there is continuity and/or discontinuity between their own beliefs and practices and those of Muslims around them? Do their views affect whether, or how, they share the gospel with Muslims? Do they also pursue a self-standing (four-self) faith community in the long run?

Research Methodology

This research employed qualitative field research method to explore social identity and social integration of MBBs, extending to MBBs' small gatherings called *jama'at*. One of the strengths of this research method is that by going "directly to the social phenomenon under study and observing it as completely as possible, researchers can develop a deeper and fuller understanding of it."[1] Moreover, this method's inductive approach enables researchers to go "back and forth from data collection and analysis to problem reformulation and back."[2]

Among the various data collection methods available for qualitative research, I made full use of one research tool – *interview*. This research used the full range of interview styles, from conversation and informal interviews to semiformal and formal interviews. For the informants, I did not try to conduct interviews in haste. After unofficially meeting with them and developing "considerable rapport," I asked informal questions relating to the topic.[3] Instead of using a fixed set of questions, I pursued an approach in which "new questions emerge as the conversation continues, and we are open to proceeding in new directions as information is gathered."[4] This informed interviewing, considered as a "useful strategy for discerning different viewpoints held by insiders," helped me listen to informants' opinions toward the followers of 'Isa in the community.[5] For MBBs – the main focus of the research – I conducted semi-structured and structured interviews after building long-term "sufficient rapport."[6] Though I prepared an interview protocol with a structured series of questions, I gave "the respondent considerable freedom to wander from the topic."[7] I also gave respondents freedom to share long or detailed answers or stories.

In forming interview questions, I tried to avoid judgmental questions that directly asked interviewees for their opinion. Rather than asking about their own thinking about some sensitive issues, I asked them what others think or do.[8] In addition to the interview questions, Russell Bernard notes

---

1. Babbie, *Practice of Social Research*, 286.
2. Creswell, *Research Design*, 183.
3. Jorgensen, *Participant Observation*, 88.
4. Hiebert, *Gospel in Human Context*, 167.
5. Jorgensen, *Participant Observation*, 88.
6. Jorgensen, 89.
7. Hiebert, *Gospel in Human Context*, 167.
8. Hiebert, 168.

the importance of the interview language.[9] To the best of my ability, I conducted all of the interviews with Bangladeshi respondents in Bangla (a native language of MBBs in Bangladesh) by myself. I did not start the interview process until I felt ready enough to communicate with local MBBs – in fact, I waited for two and a half years to develop sufficiently my ability to communicate in Bangla. I conducted one interview in English, by the Bangladeshi interviewee's own choice. I did not have many problems communicating with the respondents, but I asked questions when I felt that I did not completely understand them.

The Field Research

I conducted the field research for this study. I did all the interviews and informal observations myself, though I received help in translating one-third of interview recordings from Bangla to English from three master's and honors level student assistants at Dhaka University. The items of the field research include the researcher, the place, plan, and length of the research, observation, and interviews.

The Researcher

I came to Bangladesh in February 2012. Since that first year, I have developed friendships with MBBs in Bangladesh, in addition to learning the local language. I had certain advantages in learning the Bangla language quickly because my mother language, Korean, shares a similar sentence order and structure with Bangla. I took a number of classes at an intensive Bible college with Bangladeshi MBBs from across the country and also sometimes took part in teaching them when they asked me to do so. After my first year of language study at a private language institute in Dhaka, I took a position as an affiliated PhD researcher in the anthropology department at the University of Dhaka. This was a three-year position, corresponding to my three-year research plan. In the first year of the plan (my second year of Bangladeshi residence), I focused on mastering the language; in the second year, I began my field research; and in the third year, I wrote and finished my research thesis. During those periods, I improved my Bangla communication skills

---

9. Bernard, *Research Methods*, 224.

with the help of master's-level students at the university and by studying with MBBs at a Bible college. Beginning in 2014, I sometimes taught local MBBs on how to meditate on the Bible (*Kitab*) when they asked me to do so.

Since my third year of residence in Bangladesh, I have often been invited to speak for occasions such as Christmas festivals and family seminars, and to teach inductive Bible study (for example, the book of Mark) at local *jama'ats*. After gaining the ability to conduct the research myself without a translator through teaching MBBs and interacting with university students for two and a half years, I started to conduct field research interviews along with informal observations. After recording the interviews, I translated two-thirds of the interviews myself. The rest of the interviews were translated by three Dhaka University master's and honors students. But, I rechecked all their English translations after receiving transcripts from them. Translations of Bangla articles written by MBB leaders were done by two additional Bangladeshi MBB helpers who could translate Bangla to English.

Place of Research

The majority of this research was conducted in the *Jamuna* district (pseudonym) of Bangladesh. I chose two large Muslim-majority communities with a population of over ten thousand, where around fifty MBBs co-exist with Muslims. Two research fields (*jama'at* H and U) were small cities in this large rural district. The people of the district are employed in farming, run their own businesses, or work for the government and companies. The majority are mid-low class people. In the urban side of the district, there are public and private universities and several English medium schools – meaning most communication between teachers and students take place in English – run by private schools or NGOs. Most of the schools in the region, however, are Bangla medium schools run by the government and NGOs, and some students in these areas go to Madrassas run by the government and private Islamic authorities, which offer low tuition fees and qur'anic teachings. Most families in these villages have TVs and electricity in their houses, but they love to gather together to talk and have fellowship with their neighbors in the evenings. Another reason they gather together almost every evening is that electric power goes off for several hours at almost the same time every day. In contrast to the men, who freely visit their neighbors' houses and public areas in the evening, women were hardly seen in these places.

Both *jama'ats* (H and U) registered with the Bangladeshi government as a type of Christian religious organization called a Trust so that they can do religious activities and even preach the gospel to Muslim neighbors without worrying about interrogation from police about their activity. Based on the constitution's provision regarding freedom of religion, people and organizations with a clear Christian identity can engage in propagation activity. If, however, MBBs did not register as a Christian organization (Trust) or change public identity, the government and police could doubt and interrogate them. Because the Muslim *somaj* (religious community) and fundamentalists do not like Muslim converts' evangelistic activities, MBBs want to prove their new identity and get help from police to protect them from Muslim fundamentalists and *somaj*. Social judgment by the Muslim *somaj* often occurs in the village when a Muslim converts to faith in 'Isa (or Christianity) or MBB evangelists preach when a conflict happens.[10]

The styles of the two *jama'ats* are different. *Jama'at* U covers a larger area and has several regional sub leaders in place. Also, while *jama'at* H members gather together regularly on every Friday morning at an MBB leader's house (a group of around 10–20 believers), *jama'at* U members do not strictly gather together in one place regularly, but rather they often gather with one or two other believers' families when a leader visits believers' houses. This is because the believers do not all live near each other. *Jama'at* U has around thirty possible small group leaders. They often participated in training and seminars when teachers from outside of this area came. I visited and participated in both *jama'ats'* activities when they held family seminars, Bible seminars, and in 2014 I visited the Christmas festivals of each *jama'at*. On Christmas day in 2014, I visited the Christmas celebration of two *jama'ats*.' For the Christmas festival at *jama'at* H, believers from Muslim background and believers' friends were invited, including ten police officers. Actually, the police officers have been invited for ten years to protect the festival from Muslim fundamentalists. But, the leader of the *jama'at* has the intention to let them hear the gospel

---

10. I visited the home of one MBB belonging to *jama'at* U upon his invitation. After I stayed one night at his house, there was a rumor around the village saying "one foreign Christian gave 3,000 taka [around $40 US] to them." He has been a revealed believer for the past three years, but people of the village restarted their discussion about his change of faith to 'Isa from a general Muslim. The Muslim *somaj* met and discussed whether a Muslim convert could stay in the village and *somaj*. The MBB had to defend his faith in the Qur'an and the *Kitab* in the face of social judgment.

and enjoy the special meals. I was also invited as a speaker at the festival of *jama'at* H (there were three speakers at that time). I did not fully participate in the Christmas festival of *jama'at* U due to a schedule delay and needed to leave early. When I was present, there were thirty believers from Muslim background waiting for the festival, and I heard around eighty believers from this *jama'at* network came to the festival, three preachers preached, and those who attended were treated to good food. Information on the two *jama'ats'* is given below (Table 1).

Table 1. Two *Jama'ats'* Information

	***Jama'at* H**	***Jama'at* U**
Village population	100,000	500,000
Believers from the *jama'at* and their large network	200	300 (covering a larger area)
Weekly attendance	10–20 believers	Gathering irregularly in different places
Way and places of gathering	Central way: in a leader's house. Training and festivals in a leader's house	Spreading way: in each house for family gatherings, or Trust office for training or seminars
Christmas invitations	100	80

Plan of Research

After deciding on specific local communities to research, I regularly visited the communities. For interview, I visited the two *jama'ats* and their surroundings around ten times during one academic year, and visited them many times for informal friendship and preaching opportunities before this period. For semi-formal and formal interviews, twenty-one of the forty-eight Bangladeshis I interviewed are from these two *jama'ats* (thirteen interviews from *jama'at* U and eight from *jama'at* H). The remaining twenty-seven interviews were conducted among MBBs around Bangladesh, regardless of their *jama'ats* and community observation (six more *jama'ats* and individuals from different *jama'ats*).[11]

---

11. I have had relationships with several *jama'ats* (N, I, and E) for a year, but the *jama'ats* M, S, and N/L groupings actually have individuals from different *jama'ats* who closely network with one another.

Interviews

I selected forty-eight MBBs for individual formal and recorded interviews. Most of these interview respondents were drawn from among the network of believers with whom I had naturally formed friendships over the preceding two and a half years. For example, I met believers' group leaders in various ways, such as through the MBBs' Bible college or through my participation in the Isai Fellowship in Bangladesh. After I began having fellowship with the leaders of a particular believers' group, I wasoften invited to their village, where I would stay for several days and participate in their weekly *jama'at* fellowship. In this way, I built a trusting relationship with the leaders and their Muslim background congregations, and most of my interviews were done after several meetings that focused on building relationships. While this was a typical pattern, there were also several other cases. I was introduced to several believers by foreign missionaries or local believers with whom I had already established friendship. In the case of respondents who did not want me to visit their villages for security reasons, I met with them in urban areas within their district but away from their village. For these reasons, eleven of my forty-eight local respondents were interviewed at our first meeting.

Most of the interviewees were first-generation MBBs; three were second-generation MBBs. In terms of the respondents' gender, most of the MBBs chosen for interviews were male, because a male researcher was not culturally allowed to interview a female respondent. In order to get some females' point of view, I chose three couples so that these women could give responses together with their husbands. In terms of my own judgment, although the number of female respondents was low, it sufficed because these women were very open and bright and were transparentin the presence of their husbands.

For the purpose of reviewing the validity and reliability of the data from the forty-eight formal interviews of Bangladeshi MBBs, I added another interview protocol to obtain foreign workers' and indigenous MBB leaders' views regarding the issue (Appendix 3). Ten individual foreign workers from diverse organizations were selected to help back up and verify the MBBs' interview data, as well as provide some foreign practitioners' views of MBBs' social identity. Six MBB leaders in Bangladesh (in terms of their current ministry position) were selected in order to reveal indigenous leaders' thinking on the history of Bangladeshi MBBs, the social identity issue, and a possible diagnosis and prescription. Moreover, two focus group interviews – one with a group of three foreign workers and the other with a group of three *Isai* MBBs – were conducted following the same interview protocol as the foreign and indigenous leaders' interview protocols. The purpose of the two focus group interviews was to provide a free environment for discussion about the issue based on the second interview protocol's summarized version of the issue. Because all but one of the respondents in the focus group interviews are included in the list of forty-eight interview respondents, the contents of the focus group interviews are mentioned using the same file name, without distinguishing from the formal interview. Ten foreign workers – three Asians and seven Westerners (including both Europeans and Americans) – were interviewed face to face, by telephone, or by email. Three MBB leaders (included among the six MBB leaders mentioned above) helped obtain further information about the history of MBBs in Bangladesh and the identity issue beyond the scope of the interview protocol questions. The total number of respondents, then, was fifty-eight: forty-eight MBBs, including six indigenous leaders, and ten foreign workers. Demographic details of foreign respondents are displayed below (Table 2).

Table 2. Demographic Outline of the Foreign Interview Respondents

File name	Age	Gender	Ethnicity (home background)	Years working in Bangladesh	Interview method
F01	60s	M	Westerner	30+	Phone
F02	60s	M	Westerner	30+	Phone
F03	60s	M	Westerner	30+	Phone
F04	50s	M	Asian	20+	In person
F05	40s	M	Westerner	10+	Email
F06	40s	M	Westerner	10+	Email
F07	40s	F	Westerner	10+	Email
F08	50s	M	Westerner	10+	Email
F09	40s	M	Asian	10+	In person
F10	50s	M	Asian	20+	In person

Demographic Outline of the Interview Participants

Members of more than eight different *jama'ats* participated in individual interviews (Table 3). For the security of the respondents and their *jama'ats*, the names of the *jamaʿats* are shortened and anonymized. Each respondent has an individual number such as N01 or E04. While a larger number of interviewees belong to *jamaʿats* H and U, only a small number of interviews – three to five respondents – are from each of the other *jamaʿats*. In the table below, *jamaʿat* S represents separated respondents – that is, those who were the only interviewee from their *jamaʿat* – and N/L signifies national leaders of MBBs.

Table 3. Demographic Outline of the Interview Participants

Jamaʿat name	File name	Age	Gender	Years since bapt-ism	Social identity	Jamaʿat name	File name	Age	Gender	Years since bapt-ism	Social identity
H	H01	40s	M	20+	C/I	I	I01	50s	M	20+	C/I
	H02	20s	M	10+	C/I		I02	50s	M	20+	C/I
	H03	20s	F	3+	C/I		I03	40s	M	10+	C/I
	H04	60s	M	20+	I/IM		I04	40s	M	10+	IM/M
	H05	60s	M	5+	I/IM	E	E01	20s	M	N/A	IM/M
	H06	30s	M	Not yet	I/IM		E02	30s	M	5+	I/IM
	H07	20s	M	5+	IM/M		E03	40s	M	10+	IM/M
	H08	40s	M	Not yet	IM/M		E04	40s	M	10+	IM/M
U	U01	50s	M	20+	C/I	M	M01	30s	M	10+	IM/M
	U02	60s	M	3+	C/I		M02	50s	M	15+	IM/M
	U03	40s	M	3+	C/I		M03	40s	M	20+	IM/M
	U04	20s	M	2+	C/I		M04	40s	M	N/A	I/IM
	U05	40s	M	3+	C/I		M05	40s	M	15+	IM/M
	U06	40s	M	20+	C/I	S	S01	40s	M	15+	C/I
	U07	40s	M	5+	C/I		S02	40s	M	3+	C/I
	U08	40s	F	5+	C/I		S03	50s	M	20+	C/I
	U09	20s	M	5+	C/I		S04	40s	M	15+	C/I
	U10	40s	M	3+	I/IM		S05	40s	M	20+	C/I
	U11	40s	M	7+	C/I	N/L	L01	50s	M	20+	C/I
	U12	40s	M	10+	C/I		L02	50s	M	20+	C/I
	U13	40s	F	7+	C/I		L03	50s	M	20+	IM/M
N	N01	40s	M	5+	C/I		L04	60s	M	20+	C/I
	N02	60s	M	5+	C/I		L05	60s	M	20+	C/I
	N03	40s	M	5+	I/IM		L06	60s	M	20+	I/IM

Although the N/L respondents are not the official representatives of MBBs, I tried to listen to the voices of leaders of MBB organizations or NGOs in Bangladesh. Age, gender, and years since baptism are provided to describe the background of interview participants. Finally, the social identities of each interviewee – mostly based on the interviewee's own indication – are indicated using the abbreviations C for Christian, I for *Isai*, IM for *Isai* Muslim, and M for Muslim. Most of the respondents could not identify themselves in terms of a single social identity – most indicated two. Also, some respondents – such as I01 could not describe their social identity clearly, so I classified their social identities according to my own judgment, based on the interview results and their activities. Detailed information about each category, based on Tim Green's former research and categorization, is presented in chapter 3. All the respondents voluntarily participated in formal interviews and gave me their own names.

Length of Research

One of the strengths of this research was my long-term stay in Bangladesh, which gave me the benefit of being a long-term resident in the field. By the time I began my research, I had already formed friendships with the people who live in the field of the research for over a period of about two years. Before the formal research period, I visited the village for the sake of friendship, sharing spiritual fellowship and biblical teaching at events such as *jama'at* gatherings and biblical seminars run by MBBs. Finally, I conducted regular research in the field for almost one academic year (August 2014–May 2015), in addition to the two and a half years of informal fellowship and observation before my formal research. Alex Stewart comments that a long period of residence in the field is "the single most potent tactic that ethnographers have to enhance veracity."[12] He adds that longer periods of research "increase variation both in what could be observed and in the capacities to notice."[13] During the first several months of the formal research, I primarily observed the community and built rapport with community members through informal conversations and interviews with community members from diverse

---

12. Stewart, *Ethnographer's Method*, 20.

13. Stewart, 21; Ottenberg, "Changes over Time."

religious backgrounds. Following observation and rapport-building, I proceeded to participant observation and formal interviews.

Informal Observations

I tried to maintain good relationships with both MBBs – including interview respondents – and their Muslim neighbors in the research areas. In addition to interviewing individuals, I informally observed two *jama'at* communities (U and H) that consist mostly of MBBs who identify themselves as Christian and *Isai* (follower of *'Isa*), albeit without writing ethnographic field notes in detail. These observations helped me understand my interviewees' backgrounds and experiences. In these two communities, several individuals identifying as *Isai* Muslims (close to C4) participated in interviews. Also, outside of these two *jama'ats*, several respondents came from a group of Muslim insider believers who identify as *Isai* Muslims or Muslims (close to C5). This large spectrum of respondents helped this research include rich descriptions and discussions of various kinds of MBBs' social identities and communities.

Representatively, I observed several festivals and special gatherings, such as the *Qurbani* (sacrifice) *Eid* festival (one of the biggest festivals in Bangladesh), Christmas, and a gathering of the National MBB Fellowship (organized by the Isai Fellowship in Bangladesh and funded by a foreign organization). In order to participate in the four-day and three-night meeting of five hundred members of the National MBB Fellowship, I visited the general secretary's office and got permission to participate as long as I would sleep and eat in the same condition as other attendees. This gathering is an occasion for new believers to experience assurance of salvation in *'Isa* and be encouraged by sermons, praying together, and sharing fellowship with other MBBs. At *Qurbani Eid*, I observed what MBBs and Muslims were doing at this big *Eid* festival. On the day of sacrifice activity, I observed the festival while asking local Muslims questions about the meaning of the activity and visiting Muslim homes before and after their animal sacrifices for remembering Abraham's obedience to the Almighty. Most of all, during several days of the *Eid* festival, I observed MBBs' participation in Muslims' social/religious activities. During the Christmas festival, I participated in worship time by preaching a sermon in Bangla and my family members after the worship time (or Christmas celebration) enjoyed Bangla food and fellowship with MBBs and their guests, such as the police who had been invited for security.

My informal observations of the general life of MBBs, including these three activities, enabled me to understand more fully the context in which the respondents live and to use what I learned from the observation to illuminate what I heard from the respondents. My observation provided me with a discerning eye toward the credibility of what they said.[14]

Data Collection and Analysis Tool

My main data collection method was interview. Interviews were conducted to gain information about the social identities of MBBs and their social integration, particularly through narratives. Interview data included respondents' theological views and understandings, as well as their examples and stories of personal and social experiences. My informal observations helped check the validity of interview data such as by observing interviewees' *jama'at* gatherings and interactions with majority community members.

In terms of the data analysis, Nvivo 10 was employed to assist in data analysis by helping me manage and organize the data I gathered. The key themes of the research were displayed and organized by certain codes. After I translated the recorded data from Bangla into Korean myself and into English (by me and my Bangladeshi helpers from Dhaka University), I imported the data into Nvivo10 and coded it, categorizing the emergent themes and analyzing important issues and details. In addition, these Dhaka University students helped with the translation of several Bangla articles and small booklets into English to illustrate Bangladeshi MBB society and social identities.

---

14. The lack of trust is another common problem in Bangladesh. It is often said that it is possible to lie and exaggerate the facts to others for the sake of one's own survival and interests. I needed to be careful in discerning the genuineness of what was said by the respondents.

CHAPTER 3

Precedent Literature

This chapter reviews four areas of precedent literature that provide a theoretical and practical base for this study. The first section considers the concept of the dual religious belonging and its application. The second section examines the insider movement, addressing both theological/biblical and missiological/anthropological issues. The issue of the C4/C5 identity debate is also dealt with in this section. The third section explores MBBs' identity focusing particularly on Tim Green's writings on the subject of social identity theories and practices for understanding MBBs. The fourth section provides a survey of the MBBs' community in Bangladesh based on Bangladeshi literatures and MBB research in Bangladesh. The four-self issue (self-propagating, supporting, governing, and theologizing) is also examined in the fourth section.

Dual Belonging and MBBs' Insider Approach

Muslims cannot separate their culture and society from their religion. In addition, their religious identity cannot exclude a sociocultural dimension. Martin Goldsmith describes the wholeness of religion, society, and culture within Islam:

> Islam is within the whole warp and woof of society – in the family, in politics, in social relationships. To leave the Muslim faith is to break with one's whole society. Many a modern educated Muslim is not all that religiously minded; but he must, nevertheless, remain a Muslim for social reasons, and also because it is the basis for his political belief. This makes it almost unthinkable

for most Muslims even to consider the possibility of becoming a follower of some other religion.[1]

The Issue of Dual Identity (as a Muslim and a Follower of 'Isa)

On the basis of Goldsmith's statement, John and Anna Travis argue that in this inseparable society of culture, religion, and politics, "changing religions [is] a total break with society."[2] This means that conversion to Christianity is "not just a spiritual birth . . . [but] a clean break with family, culture and society as a whole."[3] They agree that in Islam there is an inseparable mixture between religion and culture.[4] After Travis and Travis define contextualization as maintaining continuity between culture and faith in Christ, they concur with Kraft's suggestion: "view religion [such as Islam] as an integral part of one's culture, allowing God to work through it rather than against it."[5] Charles Kraft held that Muslims will be saved if their primary allegiance is to Christ, regardless of religious boundaries.

> If Muslims replace their previous primary allegiance with a commitment to as much of Christ as they can grasp, that is saving, even if they remain in their previous cultural (including religious) structures. Those structures are their "place to feel at home," and the structures serve well as a secondary or tertiary allegiance. It is *within the structures, not extracted from them,* that God wants to meet people.[6]

Religion scholars and sociologists have been able to capture some people's dual religious belonging and dual identities. In his empirical study, Gideon Goosen asked two main research questions regarding whether dual religious belonging exists in practice, and, if it does exist, what its nature is. After interviewing thirty-three people who are involved in two religious traditions, Goosen concluded that dual religious belonging exists and those who

---

1. Goldsmith, "Community and Controversy," 318.
2. Travis and Travis, "Appropriate Approaches," 403.
3. Travis and Travis, 403.
4. Travis and Travis, 403.
5. Travis and Travis, 403; Kraft, *Anthropology*, 210–14.
6. Kraft, 212, (italics in original).

experience it have a tendency to adhere to "one main religion while having a second" as a secondary.[7] Catherine Cornille agrees with Goosen's two findings regarding the existence of dual religious belonging and the primacy of one religious belonging. She observes that most cases of dual religious belonging that include Christianity are made possible when other religious teachings do not contradict with Christian faith, or can be reinterpreted within the framework of Christian faith, symbols and rituals.

> In most cases, the encounter with other religions is framed by one's primary religious identity. Only those beliefs and practices of the other tradition are endorsed that are not in contradiction with the Christian faith, and the meaning of symbols and rituals that may be adapted is usually altered to fit the Christian ritual and doctrinal tradition.[8]

Cornille extends her discussion of complexity of dual religious belonging after conversion, because conversion involves the process of shifting. A person's religious conversion may occur in the form of a radical shift to another religion, or may involve lingering between two religions due to social attachments of a previous religion.

> This may go all the way to conversion, or to a shift from belonging to one religion to identifying with a different religious tradition. While some may give expression to this shift through a formal process of initiation, others may linger between traditions, unable to let go of deeply ingrained social and symbolic attachments, while clearly understanding the old tradition from the normative perspective of the new one. In both cases, one may speak of "changed" rather than a double religious belonging. But the loss of one's original or primary religious commitment may also lead to a genuinely intermediate position in which one tradition is normative in certain areas of belief and practice and another tradition in other areas.[9]

---

7. Goosen, "Empirical Study," 173.

8. Cornille, "Introduction," 4.

9. Cornille, "Double Religious," 46.

Cornille also discusses the challenge of dual religious belonging to identity. In her view, "identity seems to depend more on some practices and beliefs than on others."[10] After presupposing the difficulty of judging which of these are more fundamental, Cornille posits that the cultural and historical context and religious self-understanding of an era determine which aspects of a religious tradition are seen as the most important.

> The question of the essential core of a religion seems to be the subject of much debate within each religion, as well as part of the process of contextualization and change. When discussing the issue of conflicting fundamental beliefs, one cannot but accept a certain cultural and historical relativity. But there is no other starting point than the relative religious self-understanding of each age as it is expressed not only in concrete beliefs, but also in ritual and ethical life.[11]

Claude Geffre permits this kind of movement to become Christian without changing one's former religious identity because of the close correlation between culture and religion.[12] He says,

> Since Christianity encounters not only cultures but also the religions to which these cultures are directly related, it not only exercises a critical function with regard to cultural and religious totalities but also undergoes a process of assumption and transformation. Hence, to become Christian after belonging to a non-Christian tradition does not necessarily mean alienation from either the previous cultural and ethnic identity or from one's previous religious identity.[13]

Evangelical scholar Kang-San Tan offers two critiques of multiple religious belonging: it assumes a pluralistic theology of religions, and it can

---

10. Cornille, 49.

11. Cornille gives an example of Buddhists who have heard of the death and resurrection of Christ. "This belief [death and resurrection of Christ] would seem to be radically incompatible with a Buddhist worldview and analysis of sin and suffering. Some individuals involved in the dialogue might wish to deny the centrality of this belief or reinterpret it in Buddhist terms. But to do this might itself indicate a Buddhist rather than Christian primary religious identity." Cornille, 49.

12. Geffre, "Double Belonging," 99.

13. Geffre, 99.

be sustained only as a liminal stage.[14] Despite these criticisms of multiple religious belonging, Tan agrees with Geffre's distinction between multiple religious belonging "which is a postmodern form of syncretism" and dual belonging "which is the fruit of inculturation."[15] Tan does not forget the overlapped nature of culture and religion in the formation of Asian identity. He warns us not to fall into the temptation of "judging indigenous expressions of Christianity that look foreign as being syncretistic."[16] Tan also calls for Christian theologians to consider Asian realities of multi-religious belonging and converts' need for time to synthesize their previous faiths.

> Previously, Christian theology has tended to treat non-Christian religions as tight and separate religious systems. Such a treatment is increasingly problematic as it does not reflect the multireligious realities in Asia whereby influences and cross fertilization of religious beliefs are daily faith experiences. In particular, there is a need to take into account the experiences and struggles of Christian converts from Asian religions, namely, the convert's own relationship with their previous faiths. Often, most converts outwardly reject their past faiths in the process of conversion to Christianity. However, as some argue, it is unrealistic to expect new converts to terminate previous faith suddenly and radically. The tensions of liminality and inter-identity of dual belonging are hurriedly glossed over rather than given due space for analysis and synthesis. Over time (second or third generations), some Asian Christians may begin to rediscover their past religious roots and may re-appropriate aspects of their past religious traditions.[17]

Tan continues to consider the insider movement as a "current contextualization model of dual belonging"[18] that is unlike multiple religious belonging, which he sees as religious pluralism, in four senses: retaining identity and

---

14. Tan, "Dual Belonging," 27–28.
15. Tan, "Can Christians Belong?," 257.
16. Tan, 261.
17. Tan, "Dual Belonging," 54.
18. Tan, "Can Christians Belong?," 257.

culture, avoiding Christian label, including conservative Christian mission groups, and connection to people movement.

> Rather than a pluralist appreciation of other religions, dual belonging stems from a growing recognition that Muslims and Hindus need not leave behind their past identities and cultures. Tan added, "It calls for ultimate loyalty to Jesus Christ without necessarily changing one's religious identity."[19]

> Promoters of the insider movement seek to avoid the negative connotations of "Western Christianity" – labels such as imperialism, anti-nationalism and foreign influences. For Asian converts to Christianity, Jesus could be the centre for their faith while they identify culturally and socially with their past religious belonging in Islam or Hinduism.

> Unlike the first radical proposal of combining two or more religious systems, many of the proponents of insider movements include conservative Christian mission groups who are firmly in the exclusive camp, with regard to their theology of religions.

> While the first two models [a radical pluralism in a pluralist theology of religion and an internal multi-religious identity within an inclusivist framework] tend to consist of *individuals* without an identifiable community, insider movements tend to consist of *mass movements* of Hindus or Muslims toward Christianity.[20]

Tan concludes that the insider movement is acceptable to evangelicals as long as insiders screen themselves by the Christian Scripture. This is because the highly contextualized church of the insider movement consists of "largely local Islamic forms to which are attached Christian meanings. The meanings come neither from the sending nor receiving societies but primarily through a contextual interpretation of the Christian Scripture."[21] Moreover, Tan advises observers of the movement to look at this issue from both insider (emic)

---

19. Tan, "Dual Belonging," 30.

20. Tan, "Can Christians Belong?," 257–58.

21. Tan, 262. The relationship between form and meaning with foreign and local dynamics will be illustrated in page 85 (@@) in Anthropological View of Contextualization vs. Syncretism.

and outsider (etic) perspectives, for insiders to become "a hermeneutical community," and for evangelicals to develop a theology of the kingdom.[22] My assessment is that Tan's observation, coming from an Asian theologian of religion, is true in terms of the Asian religious context's tendency of dual belonging. His suggestion to pursue Asian Christianity deeply rooted in the Asian context and reflecting Asian previous religious forms different from the Western Christian tradition is also valid. Tan's argument of the insider movement as a proper dual belonging model is theoretically acceptable, but it needs to be practically verified in a real context.

Negative Effects of Muslims' Conversion and the Insider Approach

A Muslim who converts to Christianity lives in a state of social confusion and is emotionally drained. In addition, the shame culture in Muslim society imposes the constant pressure of being marked as betrayers or enemies of their nation.[23] Both negative effects – extraction and anomie – are interwoven on the personal and public levels. The significance of leaving Islam is similar to losing one's identity and becoming culturally isolated after being connected to a local community and the world of Islam (*dar al-Islam*). It is seen as becoming part of the world of war (*dar al-harb*).[24] This phenomenon of cultural isolation can be called deculturation. As an example of anomie, Kathryn Ann Kraft's dissertation explains the situation of Arab MBBs as disappointment due to the loss of expectation. When Muslims come to faith to Christ, they do so "with high hopes for their possibilities and the expectation that this will give them fully realizable lives, as well as for many a sense of relief that after a long time of thinking and studying, they have finally decided."[25] In contrast, one convert woman whom Kraft interviewed found that the reality did not reach her expectation, even feeling that nobody was beside her or available to share her new faith.[26] These negative effects are mainly because a

---

22. Tan, 258–64.

23. Meral, "Conversion and Apostasy," 510.

24. Meral, 510.

25. Kraft, "Community and Identity," 180.

26. Kraft, 180.

Muslim's conversion concerns not only the individual, but the entire family and the family's place in their community and culture.

Moreover, converts might find it difficult to adjust to their new life due to negative reactions from the Christian community.[27] A huge distinction between church and Islamic culture also makes it difficult for converts from Islam to be resocialized to Christian culture. This primarily results from anti-Islamic attitudes expressed by local Christians (sometimes driven by Western Christian missionaries) who prefer Western Christian forms of rituals and spiritual disciplines. This strong reaction against Islam causes MBBs to experience more cultural alienation. Baig mentions that MBBs face three forms of opposition when they choose to follow Christ: (1) opposition from government structures; (2) banishment from the Muslim *ummah* (community); and (3) suspicion from Christian community.[28] In seeking to avoid the negative effects of extraction, the "insider movement" tries not to "extract believers from their families and pre-existing networks of relationships, significantly harming these relationships," in contrast to the Western "aggregate-church" model.[29] Because they retain their socioreligious identity, Muslim insiders can avoid losing their identity and breaking away from society.

Due to the negative effects of conversion to Christianity, the insider movement is growing naturally in Muslim-majority countries, especially Asian Muslim-majority countries. The defenders of the movement support the positive effects of using preexisting networks, retaining socioreligious identity, and eliminating the negative effects of conversion. Other cautious observers worry about the possible bad effects of remaining within an Islamic religious context and the problem of syncretistic identity. The next section deals with key issues in debates over the insider movement.

Insider Movement Discussions and Debates

The insider movement has been hotly debated for around thirty years and remains controversial today. Many journal articles, books, and dissertations about the movement have been written by theologians and practitioners from

---

27. Baig, "Ummah and Christian," 71.

28. Baig, 71.

29. Lewis, "Promoting Movements," 75.

diverse backgrounds, but the essential issues in recent debates are similar to the issues being discussed several decades ago. The key discussions and debates narrated in this section can be considered in two parts: theological/biblical and missiological (anthropological/ethical) debates.

Introduction of C4 vs. C5 Debate

The insider movement among Muslims has raised diverse and highly debated issues since the 1980s. During thirty years of discussions, the term C5 – the category of Christ-centered community that is most closely aligned with the insider movement among Muslims – was used in this discussion for around twenty years, but recent practitioners of the insider movement hesitate to use this term because the C5 category does not intentionally emphasize natural social networks and indigenous movement characteristics.[30] In order to examine the history and issues of the insider movement discussion, however, it is necessary to use the C-scale – especially C4 and C5 – in this study. Moreover, while many mission thinkers and practitioners point out its limitations, I believe the C-spectrum is still helpful for understanding the reality of MBBs in a Muslim-majority country like Bangladesh.

In a December 2009 article in *Christianity Today*, Joseph Cumming summarized the C4 and C5 debates. Cumming's description of the debates looks at two types of issues: theological and missiological.[31] Cumming described the C4/C5 debate and reactions to it, which have been received both positively

---

30. Another analysis of the differences between the two is that while C5 is a typological distinction of Christ-centered community, the insider movement among Muslims shows a Christward (kingdom) movement, even though the two categories overlap. Kim also comments that though C5 is the closest model to the insider movement within Muslim communities, because C5 insiders need to have initiatives, if the movement arises, the two are not the same. Kim, *Jesus Coming*. Kevin Higgins mentions a current tendency to avoid the C5 label, saying, "Most practitioners are moving away from the C-Scale, including Travis himself, or at least distinguish between C-5 and 'insider movement.'" Higgins, "Inside What?," 76. Higgins does not explain the reason for this, but in my view, while the C5 category posits a static ecclesiological type with only a synchronic view – some C5 practitioners try to put MBBs in the category – the insider movement contains movement characteristics such as being active, directional, and kingdom-oriented as it works through existing networks, and has both a synchronic and diachronic view.

31. Cumming first explained that just as messianic Jews follow Jewish customs from the Torah and *Halakha* (the collective body of Jewish law) while confessing Jesus as the prophesied Messiah, so a similar movement among Muslims existed, called messianic Muslims. Cumming, "Muslim Followers?," 32.

and negatively in Christian and Muslim circles.[32] After a brief display of Travis's C1–6 scale, Cumming categorizes the C4/C5 debates in terms of the sides' positions on eight points: syncretism, comparisons with Judaism, opinions of Muslim community, views of Muhammad, views of Christ, views of the church, persecution, and ethical issues. His description of the debates is summarized in Table 4 below.[33]

After tracing the evangelical awareness of religious identity, Cumming explains that evangelicals have generally valued relationship with Christ more than religious boundaries, saying "Since the Wesleyan revival and the Great Awakening of the 18th century, evangelicals have insisted that what matters most to God is not one's identity as 'being a Christian,' but rather whether one has a life-transforming relationship with Jesus Christ."[34] Finally, Cumming points out the absence of the insiders' voices, and carefully supports their human rights and cautiously considers them to be a part of the universal body of Christ.[35]

Table 4. Cumming's Description of the C4 vs. C5 Debates and His Comments

Issue	C4 Concern	C5 Response	Cumming's Comment
Syncretism according to Scripture	Scripture condemns syncretism. Trying to be both Muslims and followers of Jesus is syncretistic.	This is not the syncretism Scripture condemns. C5 believers live under the authority of the Bible, reinterpreting or rejecting anything contrary to Scripture.	Suggested to look at both sides of the discussion in IJFM, EMQ.

---

32. While some Muslims have persecuted these believers, others allow messianic Muslims to live discreetly within their communities. Also, while Christian defenders of the movement consider both messianic Muslims and messianic Jews as brothers in Christ, critical observers argue that "Islam and Judaism are different, that Muslim identity cannot be reconciled with biblical faith." Cumming, 32.

33. All contents and descriptions used in Table 4 are in the original. Cumming, 34–35. The chart is mine.

34. Cumming, 35.

35. Cumming, 35.

Comparison with Judaism	Islam and Judaism are different: one cannot compare "Messianic Islam" with Messianic Judaism. The Hebrew scriptures are recognized by Christians as inspired; the Qur'an is not. The mosque is pregnant with Islamic theology that explicitly denies biblical truths.	Islam and Judaism are different, but both are monotheistic. Islam recognizes the Torah and New Testament as scripture alongside the Qur'an. Rabbinic Judaism sees as authoritative not just the Hebrew scripture (*Tanakh*) but also the *Talmud*, which, like the Qur'an, contains a mixture of material compatible and incompatible with the New Testament.	Term messianic Islam is unhelpful. Muslims recognize Jesus as Messiah but raise other objections to Christian beliefs about Christ. C5 affirms the Bible as God's word.
Ethical issue/Is it deceitful?	C5 approach is deceitful. How would you feel if Muslims showed up at your church claiming to be Christians, then tried to convert your people to Islam?	It is not deceitful if C5 believers are transparent with the Muslim community about who they are and what they believe. C5 believers honestly see themselves as Muslims, not as Christians pretending to be Muslims.	Travis's scale describes how believers born and raised as Muslims see their identity.
Opinion of Muslim Community	The Muslim community won't tolerate such aberrant Muslims within their ranks.	It's too soon to be certain of that.	The Muslim community can speak for itself. Their primary concern has been whether C5 continue to practice Muslims' requirements.
Muhammad	To call oneself Muslim is to affirm Muhammad as a true prophet of God. That is incompatible with the Bible.	Actually, Muslim means different things to different Muslims. C5 believers have a variety of views about Muhammad, including: (1) one can be culturally Muslim; (2) Muhammad was a prophet; (3) Muhammad was a prophet for Arabs; (4) Muhammad was a true prophet; and (5) this question is unimportant either way.	The prophethood of Muhammad is non-negotiably essential to Muslim identity. "Muslim" means different things in different contexts.
Persecution	C5 MBBs retain Muslim identity to avoid persecution for the cross of Christ.	That's an unfair judging of motives. The issue is religiocultural identity, not the cross of Christ, which C5 believers affirm.	It is wrong to say that C5 avoid persecution. They were persecuted.

Issue	C4 Concern	C5 Response	Cumming's Comment
Church (*Ecclesiology*)	What about the church? Do C5 believers see themselves as part of Christ's body?	C5 believers form Christ-centered fellowships in which they study the Bible, pray, and celebrate baptism and the Lord's Supper. These are *ekklesia* in the NT sense, though they may look very different from what Christians usually call "churches."	Scripture calls fellowships to recognize the unity and universality of the worldwide body of Christ.
Christology	I have heard some C5 groups have sloppy Christology. This alarms me.	Some C5 believers do have fuzzy Christology, but so do many ordinary Christians everywhere. What matters is C5 believers' direction of movement: toward Christ. They pray in his name, worship him as Lord, and experience his supernatural working in their lives. Their Christology keeps moving higher.	As this movement grows, one hopes those leaders will understand sound Christology. Sensitivity to the direction of movement is right.

Theological/Biblical Debate

This section deals with biblical and theological issues involved in the C4 vs. C5 debates. After a brief overview of the key points of the C4/C5 debate, we will examine the following biblical and theological issues: mosque attendance, the *shahada* [Islamic creed], comparison to Judaism, and the biblical cases of Naaman and the Jerusalem Council's case.

In his article "Followers of Jesus (*'Isa*) in Islamic mosques," Timothy Tennent summarizes three key arguments regarding the insider (or C5) movement among Muslims: biblical/exegetical, theological, and ethical. First, Tennent examines biblical and exegetical points, surveying key verses which determine whether it is a biblically supportable movement or not. Second, Tennent addresses C5's theological issues regarding the question of the relevance of historical Christianity. Finally, he addresses ethical issues that are significant to practical missions.[36] Tennent rejects the insider movement and

---

36. Tennent, "Followers of Jesus," 104.

submits counterarguments to the movement's defenders. Like Tennent, Phil Parshall and Gary Corwin also oppose the movement while observing it cautiously. However, some missiologists and practitioners such as Kevin Higgins, Rick Brown, Joshua Massey, and Rebecca Lewis support this movement and have published many articles to explain it. Table 5 shows proponents and characteristics of both sides of the debate.

Table 5. Two Different Opinions Regarding Insider Movement among Muslims

	C5 supporters	C4 supporters and cautious observers or opponents of C5
Characteristics	Kingdom Circle; focus on high contextualization, remaining in preexisting community; retaining indigenous identity; centered set	Historic Christianity; concern about syncretism; believers change their identity from Muslims to Christians; centered and boundary set
Proponents	John Travis, Kevin Higgins, Joshua Massey, Rebecca Lewis, Rick Brown	Phil Parshall, Timothy Tennent, Bill Nikides, Gary Corwin, Dick Brogden

Phil Parshall vs. John Travis

In 1998, Phil Parshall, renowned for his contextual approach to Muslims, published an article called "Danger! New directions in contextualization." His greatest concern is the remaining religious identity of Muslims who attend mosque regularly and are surrounded by Muslims reciting the *shahada*, an Islamic creed confessing that God is one and Muhammad is the messenger (prophet) of God. His worries about the movement are based on his personal meetings with the movement's advocates and his own evaluations of data, gathered through interviews with seventy-two key people in the movement. The interviewees are representative of around five thousand MBBs from sixty-eight congregations in sixty-six villages. In Table 6, Parshall himself reveals the pros and cons of this movement.[37]

---

37. Parshall, *Muslim Evangelism*, 69–70. The text in Table 6 has been taken directly from the original.

Table 6. Phil Parshall's Interview Data from 72 Key Muslim Insiders

Pros (up sides)	Cons (down sides)
66% read or listen to the gospel daily. 55% say God is Father, Son, and Holy Spirit. 97% say Jesus is the only Savior. 93% say, "Allah loves and forgives because Jesus gave His life for me." 100% say, "People can be saved from evil spirits through faith in Jesus." 100% pray to Jesus for forgiveness of sin 97% say they are not saved because of Muhammad's prayer. 100% feel peace and close to God when reading the New Testament.	50% go to the traditional mosque on Friday. 31% go to the mosque more than once a day. They do standard Arabic prayers, which affirm Muhammad as a prophet of God. 96% say there are four heavenly books, namely, *Torah*, *Zabur*, *Injil*, and Quran (This is standard Muslim belief, i.e. Law, Prophets, Gospels, and Quran.). 66% say the Qur'an is the greatest of the four books. 45% feel peace or close to Allah when listening to the reading of the Qur'an.

Parshall argues that, in contrast to the clarity found in C1–C4, the C5 category lacks consistency.[38] This point is also demonstrated by his meeting with two C5 advocates who call themselves Bob and Harry. Parshall believes that Bob "crossed the line into syncretism" because he "affirmed Muhammad as a prophet of God."[39] Harry was expelled from the mosque because he was a Western follower of *Isa* even though he joined the *salat* prayer. These led Parshall to express five particularly concerning features of insider ministry among Muslims:

1. Encouragement for MBBs to remain in the mosque permanently.
2. Affirmation of the *shahada*, either implicitly or explicitly.
3. Use of the term Muslim without a qualifier.
4. Biblical passages used to authenticate C5.
5. "Son of God" becomes "Isa-Al-Masih."[40]

These concerns about C5 practices lead to Parshall's five guidelines for Muslim mission:

---

38. Parshall, 68.
39. Parshall, "Danger!," 409.
40. Parshall, *Muslim Evangelism*, 71–73.

1. We must be acquainted with biblical teaching on the subject of syncretism.
2. Islam as a religion and culture must be studied in depth.
3. An open approach is desired.
4. Contextualization needs constant monitoring and analysis.
5. Cross-cultural communicators must beware of presenting a gospel which has been syncretized with Western culture.[41]

Following these guidelines, he concludes by calling for multi-disciplinary discussions regarding the issue of the C5/insider movement among Muslims.

As an initial response to Parshall's invitation to discussion, John Travis wrote an article titled "Must All Muslims Leave 'Islam' to Follow Jesus?" for the same edition of *Evangelical Mission Quarterly*.[42] Travis values statistics taken from interviews and evaluates the insider movement among Muslims positively by comparing it to American Christians: "How many American pastors would be delighted to find these same statistics true of their own congregations?"[43] In terms of the "down sides," he argues that we do not need to be surprised that 45 percent of the respondents feel near to God when they listen to Qur'an reading because the sound and chanting melody, which has moved their hearts for a long time is familiar. Travis also argues that mosque attendance alongside C5 gatherings is not a problem because this practice does not have much meaning and they could stop. Rather, their sudden absence could invite a great threat from Muslim extremists, and the imam forbids them from gathering for C5 meetings on Friday afternoons.[44] The discussion between Parshall and Travis provides a good introduction of the issue. We will now examine some critical issues on both sides.

Mosque attendance

Mosque attendance is one of the most critical issues for opponents of the insider movement because, as Parshall believes, "the Mosque is pregnant with Islamic theology" as the place where "Muhammad is affirmed as a prophet

---

41. Parshall, "Danger!," 410.
42. Travis, "Response to Phil."
43. Travis, 411.
44. Travis, 411.

of God and the divinity of Christ is consistently denied."[45] Though he does not oppose Muslim believers' brief continued attendance after conversion, Parshall questions "whether they should remain permanently within the context of false religious teaching."[46] He fears a possible danger of reversion to Islam due to continuing participation in practices and rituals in mosques.[47]

Responding to Parshall's concern, Travis and Woodberry express their opinions differently.[48] Travis says the frequency of mosque attendance by C5 believers varies. While some C5 believers attend prayers in the mosque, others rarely or never go because there are many nominal Muslims in much of the Muslim society. Also, adopting the terms "process" by Gilliland[49] and "direction" by Hiebert,[50] Travis says "mosque attendance may only be a transitional part of some C5 believers' spiritual journey."[51]. He adds that, besides mosque attendance, affirmation of acceptable Islamic forms is making bridges for witnessing Jesus as Messiah to their family and community, as well as allowing Jesus followers to remain in their local Muslim community.[52]

Woodberry holds that insiders are in a better position to decide whether or not to attend the mosque in their context.[53] He introduces one North African case in which nobody would listen to a convert unless he attended the mosque. Woodberry describes early Jewish Christians who also attended synagogues during times of hostility to Christians. Referencing Romans 14:14, he adds a condition for Muslim insiders who continue to attend the mosque, cautioning them against saying anything against their conscience.[54]

Naaman's plea: 2 Kings 5:18–19

The text of 2 Kings 5:18–19 is used by C5 proponents to legitimize Muslims who worship Jesus and continue to attend mosque. Timothy Tennent critically evaluates movement proponents' use of this passage for support because the

---

45. Parshall, "Danger!," 409.
46. Parshall, "Lifting the Fatwa," 291.
47. Parshall, *Muslim Evangelism*, 71.
48. Travis, "Messianic Muslim Followers"; Woodberry, "To the Muslim?"
49. Gilliland, "Contextual Theology."
50. Hiebert, *Anthropological Reflections*.
51. Travis, "Messianic Muslim Followers," 55.
52. Travis, 56.
53. Woodberry, "To the Muslim?," 27.
54. Woodberry, 27.

text shows contextual ambiguity. He argues two points: First, temple attendance is only allowed in dutiful accompaniment of the frail master. Second,
Naaman's asking for "forgiveness" reflects that Naaman and Elisha knew it
was wrong.[55] Therefore, the prophet does not bless any activity or self-identity
of Naaman "as a follower of Rimmon who actually worships Yahweh in order
to draw other worshippers of Rimmon to the true knowledge of Yahweh."[56]
Tennent concludes that "Naaman sees his bowing as a barrier to his effective witness rather than a stepping stone to a more effective witness."[57] Dick
Brogden agrees with Tennent and considers Naaman's plea as a prophet's
allowance of an exceptional case rather than endorsement, saying,

> Naaman's famous request to "bow down in the temple at the
> hand of my master" is an allowance (an exception), not an en-
> dorsement for daily practice. Naaman himself quickly realized
> that his religious practice would have to drastically change. The
> fact that he asked for an exemption reveals that he knew the
> practice to be wrong.[58]

In an article, Daniel Baeq responds to Tennent's interpretation and opinion
of the text. In response to Tennent's first argument, Baeq interprets Naaman's
temple attendance as a response to "social pressure," which Muslim followers
of *Isa* similarly endure.[59] For the second argument, regarding "forgiveness,"
Baeq distinguishes Namaan's bowing from his master's worship of Rimmon.
With an anthropological explanation of form and meaning, he explains that
Naaman does not commit idolatry because "he is only going through the
motions and has detached spiritual significance from the act of bowing to
Rimmon."[60] Kevin Higgins also understands Elisha's answer of "Go in peace"
as an acceptance of Namaan's remaining inside his religious context after
his conversion to the true God of Israel. Higgins argues that "the text is an
example of a follower of another religion who becomes a believer in the true

---

55. Tennent, "Followers of Jesus," 108.
56. Tennent, 108.
57. Tennent, 108.
58. Brogden, "Inside Out," 35.
59. Baeq, "Contextualizing Religious Form," 204.
60. Baeq, 204.

God and yet continues to worship the true God within the religious life and practices of his prior religion."[61]

This issue raises another question: "Are C5 Muslims committing idolatry?" – or, do they worship a different God? Higgins's judgment of Corwin's assumption is that Corwin believes that C5 believers worship a different God,[62] saying "he [Corwin] is concerned that the C5 or 'insider' paradigm is promoting the worship of a different god, in the ontological sense."[63] Higgins answers that insider movements, which he is acquainted with, teach that "Jesus is Lord and Savior, that Jesus as God's Word is also God," and they are not the case.[64]

Shahada

The mosque attendance issue relates to the issue of reciting the *shahada* (an Islamic creed of God's oneness and Muhammad's prophethood) in the mosque. This creed is "a central foundation upon which all of Islam rests" and affirms not only that God is one, but also that Muhammad is the messenger of God (*Allah*).[65] Parshall questions that "if one affirms the 'prophet' of the creed, doesn't it follow that one must therefore believe his prophecy? . . . my conclusion is that I cannot affirm the Qur'an as the Word of God."[66] Roger Dixon expresses his sadness for some Western missionaries who say the *shahada* to become official members of Islam.[67] Waterman also worries that this practice results in unhealthy discipleship in C5 believers, saying, "making (or encouraging others to make) untrue statements does not constitute a healthy form of gospel witness or discipleship."[68] Waterman questions the statement of brother Yusuf, one of the indigenous C5 movement leaders, that "affirming

---

61. Higgins, "Key to Insider Movements," 158.

62. Corwin, "Humble Appeal," 17.

63. Corwin, 17.

64. Higgins as quoted in Corwin, "Humble Appeal," 17.

65. This study presupposes that Allah is neither an idolatrous term, nor a solely Islamic term. Higgins says, "For hundreds of years all Arabic-speaking Christians and Arabic Bibles have used Allah as the only possible word for God." Higgins as quoted in Corwin, 17. Also, many Bangladeshi MBBs are using this term to refer to the Almighty God in the Bible. Parshall, "Lifting the Fatwa," 291.

66. Parshall, 292.

67. Dixon, "Moving on," 14.

68. Waterman, "Do the Roots?," 59.

Mohammad does not in fact affirm a body of doctrine."[69] Waterman argues that affirming Muhammad as God's messenger implies "affirmation of the contents of the Qur'an and perhaps some of the *hadith*."[70]

Gary Corwin assumes that participating in *salat* prayer in the mosque is the beginning of harmful Islamic theology for C5 believers. His assumption is that affirming Muhammad connects to all doctrines of Islam.

> Whether one is saying the Lord's prayer while going through the motions of the *salat*, or rationalizing the many meanings of the term "prophet" while one is declaring Muhammad is Allah's prophet in the *shahada*, the message communicated by the very action to all those around is a declaration of adherence to the doctrines of Islam.[71]

Corwin connects this issue to the early church's confession that Jesus, not Caesar, is Lord. He argues that C5 communities seem to lack sole allegiance to the God of the Bible saying, "Likewise, the record of the New Testament and subsequent church history is that those mature in the faith would rather die than allow their testimony to cloud the message that Jesus, not Caesar, is Lord and that the Triune God alone must be the object of our worship."[72]

In his article "Biblical Muslims," Rick Brown stresses the different context and meaning of the early church's confession. Brown explains that, at the time of the first century, "Christians preached that Jesus is Lord, implying that Caesar was not lord, so this brought them into conflict with the law . . . [so] Polycarp and many other Christians died rather than deny that Jesus was Lord."[73] Brown argues that "the *shahada* does not have such implications," since saying *rasul allah* means "one sent on a mission by God."[74] Brother Noah, an indigenous leader of C5, makes the following comments about Muhammad's mission:

> Muhammad called his people to repent and turn away from sin and turn to the true God, the God of Abraham. He also said

---

69. Yusuf, "Response to Gary," 12.

70. Waterman, "Do the Roots?," 59.

71. Corwin, "Humble Appeal," 11.

72. Corwin, 16.

73. Brown, "Biblical Muslims," 72.

74. Brown, 72.

there is only one true God, the God of Abraham . . . Saying that Muhammad is a prophet does not mean that Jesus is not the Messiah and the Lord. It also does not mean that Muhammad is Messiah or Lord. Muhammad never claimed that. So, someone can say the *shahada* and at the same time can believe in Jesus as his Savior and Lord.[75]

Brown explains that he knows some C5 believers who would willingly die in order to defend Jesus's identity as Lord, but not in order to deny Muhammad's identity as *rasul allah*, saying, "I know Muslim followers of Jesus who are prepared to die before they would deny that Jesus is Lord, but they are not willing to die for the sake of denying that God had a mission for Muhammad."[76]

Brown also illustrates that the refusal to recite the *shahada* leads to believers' expulsion from most Muslim communities. This is because such a refusal means "a shameful rejection of their customs and heritage,"[77] and it brings a curse from God on the family and community when a member apostatizes. For C5 believers, however, saying the *shahada* means various things depending on context. Brown presents examples of circumstances under which Muslims and C5 believers say the second part of *shahada*. These range from speaking it as a "traditional interpretation of Muhammad's mission" or "a customary sign of social solidarity rather than as a conviction" to speaking it "only under duress" or choosing "not say the *shahada*" at all.[78] Brown introduces brother Noah's comments about saying *shahada* in Muslim culture in his article, saying "Normally a Muslim will not say the *shahada* out loud at any time. A Muslim will not ask another Muslim to say the *shahada*. So this is not a Muslim question; it is a Christian question to a Muslim who believes in *Isa Al-Masih*."[79]. Brown advises that C5 believers minimize or omit the second half of the *shahada*, saying that the second part "should be avoided whenever possible and said only under duress with an interpretation

---

75. Noah as quoted in Brown, 73.
76. Brown, 72.
77. Brown, 70.
78. Brown, 70.
79. Noah as quoted in Brown, 70.

that is compatible with the Bible."[80] He concludes with his preference to emphasize keeping the movement going rather than refusing to say the *shahada*: "I would not withhold the Gospel just because those proclaiming it did not refuse to say the *shahada*."[81]

Comparison with Judaism

C5 opponents argue that it is not reasonable to compare messianic Muslims with messianic Jews in the same way because they are different. The messianic Jews are using only inspired Scripture (the Old Testament), while messianic Muslims are using the uninspired Qur'an. The mosque, which is pregnant with Islamic theology, also denies biblical truths.[82] L. D. Waterman strongly rejects the application of messianic Jews' case to messianic Muslims, saying "Nothing suggests that Muslims (or any other religious group) might have a status similar to Jews, based on formal or cultural similarities between their religion and that of the Jews. Messianic Jews themselves reject claims that C5 ministry is 'similar to the messianic Jewish movement.'"[83]

However, C5 proponents find similarities between Islam and Judaism in their monotheistic character. Another similarity is that Islam acknowledges the *Torah* (Pentateuch), *Zabur* (Psalms), and the *Injil* (the gospel or NT) as among the four main books of Scripture, along with the Qur'an.[84] Cumming adds an argument for the validity of comparisons between the two, saying,

> Rabbinic Judaism sees as authoritative not just the Hebrew scripture (*Tanakh*) but also the Talmud, which, like the Qur'an, contains a mixture of material compatible and incompatible with the New Testament. Traditional synagogue liturgy also seems to repudiate New Testament teachings, but both liturgies can be reinterpreted, and attendance at prayer does not necessarily mean affirming every word of liturgy.[85]

---

80. Brown, 73.
81. Brown, 73.
82. Parshall, "Danger!," 409; Cumming, "Muslim Followers?," 34.
83. Waterman, "Do the Roots?," 57.
84. Brown, "Biblical Muslims," 65.
85. Brown, 34.

This issue is not simple to judge. It also relates to whether a Jewish case is applicable to other cultural and religious background believers. C5 proponents find some principles to apply to the insider movement among Muslims and other diverse cultures and religions in Acts 15.

Jerusalem Council: Acts 15

In his article "To the Muslim I became a Muslim?," Dudley Woodberry investigates Acts 15 as one of the incarnational models of mission beyond cultural barriers in the Bible.[86] Woodberry mentions seven criteria for connecting this text to the insider movement among Muslims: how God is working, the call of God, reason, theology, Scripture, guidance of the Holy Spirit, and the essentials. First, just as Paul and Barnabas "reported the conversion of the Gentiles" (Acts 15:3–4 NRSV), Woodberry explains that there are many reported signs that God is working among Muslim insiders in many regions. Second, just as Peter announced that "God make a choice among you . . . Gentiles would hear the message of the good news" (v. 7), so Jesus's followers among Muslims believe that they are "called to break the traditional barriers between communities to incarnate the gospel in the Muslim community."[87]

Third, Peter and the Council used their own reasoning alongside the guidance of the Holy Spirit, saying "it seemed good to the Holy Spirit and to us" (Acts 15:22–23, 28). Woodberry points out that our own reasoning is needed for acceptance or rejection in the case of the insider movement. He firstly calls us to consider the Muslim context, including features such as the complex binding of society and religion and the negative connotation of the term "Christian." He adds that the fundamental question of "whether Muslims may accept Jesus as Savior and Lord while remaining socially and legally Muslim" must also be examined reasonably.[88] Based on this question, he reasonably tries to think through the advantages and drawbacks of the movement. While the movement brings about one of the greatest opportunities to share the gospel in Islamic culture, unless we are alert it might create syncretistic believers who do not discard the non-biblical teachings of Islam. Woodberry states,

---

86. Woodberry, "To the Muslim?," 25.
87. Woodberry, 25.
88. Woodberry, 25.

An advantage of insider movements is that they can provide an opportunity for the gospel to be incarnated into a Muslim culture with a minimum of dislocation of those elements of Muslim societies that are compatible or adaptable with the gospel. And, although they have aroused intense opposition, sometimes instigated by members of traditional churches, they have frequently allowed more opportunity and time for ordinary Muslims to hear and see the gospel lived out than when the new disciples of Christ are expelled upon conversion or join a traditional church with a different ethnic and cultural constituency that has little rapport with the Muslim majority. Likewise, insider movements allow faith and spiritual maturity to develop in a context relevant to the new disciples' background and probable ministry.

On the other hand, there can be drawbacks. There is not a clear break with non-biblical teachings of Islam. Discipling raises greater challenges as does building bridges with traditional churches, if there are any.[89]

Fourth, Woodberry deals with the theological part of the movement based on Peter's statement that "We believe it is through the grace of our Lord Jesus that we are saved, just as they are" (Acts 15:11). Woodberry comments that this soteriological issue – by grace alone, not by law – should be included in the insider movement discussion. Fifth, in James's speech, the whole Scripture points toward the inclusion of the Gentiles in salvation. Sixth, in Peter's speech, Peter announces that the Holy Spirit guides the Gentiles just as the Jews. Woodberry states that "many of those whom I have met in insider movements have manifested the indwelling the Spirit of God by their spiritual fruit, wisdom, and devotion."[90] Lastly, the Council requires some "essentials" beyond salvation (vv. 28–29). Woodberry explains that these "essentials" deal with fellowship and morality. In Kevin Higgins's article, this issue is examined in detail.

In his article "Acts 15 and insider movements among Muslims: Questions, process, and conclusions," Kevin Higgins argues that the main issue in Acts

---

89. Woodberry, 26.

90. Woodberry, 27.

15 is "not simply whether Gentiles must become culturally Jewish to follow Jesus," but is soteriological in nature.[91] He connects Acts 15 to the insider movement, saying in both cases "the fundamental issue is not about culture and forms, but about salvation."[92] Higgins notices that just as Acts 15 reveals the process of solving the issue of a Gentile movement for salvation, so the issue of insider movement among Muslims is not resolved by a one-time action, but through a process. The process includes three criteria: questions, process, and conclusions. First, Higgins digs deeply into two questions with which Woodberry also deals in his application of Acts 15 to the C5 discussion. These two questions are:

1. What is necessary for a Muslim to be saved?
2. What is necessary for unity between believers in a movement to Jesus among Muslims and believers from other backgrounds (for example, Western Christian)?

As for the process of discussing the insider movement, Higgins offers five suggestions: remember that it is a long-term process; be careful and open-minded in consideration; listen to the experiences of hardship by insiders; continually wrestle with Scripture; and maintain the necessary spirit of brotherhood.[93] In this part, Hyun-Mo Lee agrees with Higgins regarding the need for process. Lee also advises him to add a historical research to his approach. Lee says that the insider movement among Muslims has many debatable issues. He concludes, however, that the insider movement needs to go through a correcting and supplementing process through diverse discussions and evaluations rather than be impetuously discarded without careful field observations.[94]

In a concluding part of his article about Acts 15, Higgins answers the question about what is necessary for Muslims' salvation, arguing that Acts 15 gives us some clues.[95] As the Gentiles had received the Holy Spirit (v. 8), been cleansed (v. 9), experienced the grace of Christ (v. 11), and were asked to refrain from idolatry (v. 20), the salvation of the Muslim insiders can be

---

91. Higgins, "Acts 15," 30.
92. Higgins, 30.
93. Higgins, 33.
94. Lee, *Response to Kevin Higgins*.
95. Higgins, "Acts 15."

understood in the same way. However, Higgins points out that the measurement of salvation is not the cognition-centered measurement of Western Christianity, but is a matter of a life transformed by works of the triune God. Also, most arguments about the insider movement focus on sanctification – ongoing discipleship and cognitive development of salvation – not concerns of salvation (justification) itself. Higgins answers from his own experience, encouraging "regular 'disciples' gatherings" and "a lifelong process of soaking in the Scripture together."[96] He understands this is a process under the guidance of the Holy Spirit working within insiders by insiders' initiative.[97]

The second question Higgins addresses in terms of Acts 15 is about "the essentials for unity" and fellowship, including "ethical/theological 'minimums' and cultural concessions."[98] Higgins maintains that these matters are crucial, but not a prerequisite for salvation.[99] Rather, he presents three essentials for obtaining salvation based on Jesus's words in Luke 24:44–49: (1) to believe in Christ, (2) to repent of sins, and (3) to receive the Holy Spirit.[100] According to Higgins, the Jerusalem Council in Acts 15 required four minimums, only two of which (idolatry and fornication) are still important today for ethical (fornication) and theological (idolatry) reasons.[101] For Higgins, the other two requirements represented cultural concessions meant to advance unity and fellowship in Christ between Gentile and Jewish believers. Higgins judges that these four essentials are not preconditions for salvation at all times, but were used to achieve unity and fellowship in that time and culture. He concludes with a suggestion of giving the same opportunity of contextual decision to MBBs: "What then will we 'require' of Muslim followers of Jesus? Will we (non-Muslims) trust them to make the same type of contextual decisions that we ourselves make?"[102]

---

96. Higgins, 35.

97. Higgins, 35.

98. Higgins, 35.

99. Higgins, 35–36.

100. Higgins, 36.

101. The other two, concerning food "from the meat of strangled animals and from blood," are no longer required as minimum essentials; for example, the eating of blood sausage in Spain. Higgins, 37.

102. Higgins, 37.

On the other hand, Timothy Tennent believes that it is not appropriate to use this text as a biblical ground for the C5 movement. Unlike Higgins, who emphasizes the question of salvation, Tennent argues that the purpose of Acts 15 is finding a new identity in Christ and requiring Gentiles' separation from their pre-Christian religious identity.[103] After distinguishing between religious identity and cultural identity, Tennent argues that the four requirements of the Jerusalem Council for Gentiles meant separation from their religious identity "since all four of these prohibitions are linked to common pagan practices of the time."[104] In this sense, he asserts that the text of the Jerusalem Council supports a C4, not a C5, strategy. He states,

> It seems evident that Acts 15 does provide powerful and com-
> pelling support for C-4 strategy in the Muslim world since the
> Gentiles were not asked to sacrifice their social and national
> identity. However, in order for this text to be used as a basis for
> C-5, one must also argue that the Gentiles were not asked to
> abandon their *religious* identity.[105]

Tennent adds that the argument that separation between religion and culture is impossible for Muslims ignores the former work of C4 believers.

> Those who say that Muslims cannot separate religion and culture
> are ignoring over thirty years of successful C-4 contextualiza-
> tion throughout the entire Islamic world which has proved that
> MBBs' new identity in Christ is so powerful that it does, in fact,
> provide a new religious identity without one having to sever
> their former cultural identity.[106]

Dick Brogden agrees with Tennent's argument of calling for religious change.

> The Acts 15 passage is quoted rightly in defense of Insider
> Movements to show that Gentiles (Muslims) do not have to
> become Jews (Cultural Christians) to follow Jesus. An attending
> truth, however, that is often overlooked is that religious change
> was directly asked for. "Abstaining from things offered to idols,

---

103. Tennent, "Followers of Jesus," 105.

104. Tennent, 105.

105. Tennent, 105.

106. Tennent, 106.

blood, things strangled and from sexual immorality . . ." (Acts 15:29) were all direct socio-religious practices of the Gentiles in Antioch, Syria, and Cilicia. There had to be a turning, a ceasing from these socio-religious elements.[107]

In a 2009 article in *Korean Mission Quarterly* (*KMQ*), Steve Sang-Cheol Moon evaluates the theology of the insider movement. He argues that evaluating only soteriological issues in the insider movement is not enough. This debate needs to take a more comprehensive view by including the task of sanctification after salvation and considering authentic ecclesiology. He says that "the view of churchless Christianity stands on the very destructive position of the biblical ecclesiology."[108] He also cites John Calvin's statement that a congregation without preaching of the word of God and practice of the sacraments is not a church.

Moon is critical of Higgins's exegesis of Acts 15, arguing that his interpretation argues from a self-centered angle. According to Moon, Higgins misses the point that the decision of the Jerusalem Council is a theological agreement that prohibits mixing foreign moral, behavioral, and ritual religious activity with the gospel. Moon argues that Higgins's interpretation is an example of eisegesis based on the biased simple logic that the Council did not require any legal condition except faith. He finally argues that this radical contextualization has no ground as a legitimate theological viewpoint.

In conclusion, while Woodberry and Higgins both use the Jerusalem Council text to support C5 believers regarding salvation, Tennent, Brogden, and Moon argue that this text is relevant for C4 believers only, as it concerns identity issues. For my assessment, it is hard to judge that one side of the argument is perfectly correct. These discussions call for a deeper investigation of missiological identity issues.

Missiological/Anthropological/Ethical Issues

This part of the chapter investigates the insider movement among Muslims in view of practical missiology. We will examine discussions about C4 vs. C5 identity, the remaining Muslim community, C5 as a frontier mission strategy,

---

107. Brogden, "Inside Out," 34.
108. Moon, "Critical Review," 21.

and syncretism. In addition, the section on the anthropological viewpoint helps explain the insider movement through the use of various charts.

C4 vs. C5 Identity Issue

In his article "Misunderstanding C5," Joshua Massey raises a question about the C4 identity. Generally, C4 advocates agree that entering the kingdom of God is not tied to Christianity alone because the connotation of the term "Christian" is irreparably damaged among Muslims. The problem is, however, that C4 attitudes push MBBs into Christianity and out of Islam. Massey asserts that while this works well theoretically, things are not so neat sociologically. The religious identity of C4 believers is hard to define.[109]

Moreover, Massey argues that many C4 believers go back and forth between Christian and Muslim communities "like a sociological chameleon, trying to maintain acceptance in two different worlds."[110] He argues that the "C4 identity (being neither Christian nor Muslim) is a very difficult position for MBBs to maintain. The more they behave like Gentile Christians, the more they will be trusted by C1–3 believers, but distrusted by Muslims."[111] Unlike the theoretical appropriateness of C4 believers, they have a tendency to cross categories, especially toward the process of Christianization, which unavoidably leads them out of the local Muslim community and into Christian community.[112]

Massey argues that, unlike C4 believers, C5 believers do not confuse their socioreligious identity between the two categories. While they identify as Muslims, they recognize that the Spirit of God has transformed their life. They practice reading the Bible regularly, so that they have some ability to judge what is biblically acceptable or not. Missionaries – cultural outsiders, can bring C5 leaders "back to prayer and the Bible for answers, confident that the Holy Spirit will 'guide them into all truth' (John 16:13)."[113]

Unlike Massey, Timothy Tennent argues that "retaining Islamic *religious* identity, not just Islamic *cultural* identity" is not ethical. In his view,

109. Massey, "Misunderstanding C5," 300.
110. Massey, 301.
111. Massey, 301.
112. Massey, 301.
113. Massey, 301.

"one's religious identity with Jesus Christ creates a necessary rupture with one's Islamic identity. Otherwise, our identity in Jesus Christ would mean nothing."[114] In that sense, Tennent argues that the discontinuity between the two identities is desirable.

> It is unethical to pretend this discontinuity does not exist or to act as if it is merely a matter of cultural forms. Rather, [arguing having dual identity] creates such a strong negative reaction that it inadvertently damages the credibility of Christians and feeds further distrust towards those who follow Christ. A more open witness in a straightforward, but contextually sensitive way seems to hold the greatest promise for effective and ethical Christian penetration into the Muslim world.[115]

Finally, Tennent proposes the C5 approach as "a temporary or transitional bridge by which some Muslims are crossing over into explicit Christian faith, hopefully to one of a C3 or C4 character." While C3 and C4 believers have long sustained historic Christianity without major cultural conflict, he argues that C5 believers do not have the long historical and empirical evidence to verify them as an independent movement.[116] John Travis[117] and Kevin Higgins[118] respond critically to Tennent's argument. Travis criticizes Tennent's comment about C5 as an unethical movement. Travis recalls Tennent's comment that "The real question is if it is ethical for a Muslim follower of Jesus Christ to retain their identity as Muslims even after they have become devoted followers of Jesus Christ."[119] Travis responds that Tennent's view that "if a Muslim follows Jesus and does not renounce Islam, he is unethical" is an "extremely biased statement, spoken by an outsider."[120] This ethical question, Travis argues, "can really only be answered by Muslims who claim to follow Christ," for "only they can say whether or not their conscience is violated."[121] Travis

---

114. Tennent, "Followers of Jesus," 113.
115. Tennent, 113.
116. Tennent, 113.
117. Travis, "Response to Tennent."
118. Higgins, "Identity, Integrity."
119. Tennent, "Followers of Jesus," 112.
120. Travis, "Response to Tennent," 125.
121. Travis, 125.

asserts that the Muslim insiders whom he knows are sincere. He says "The Muslims I know who have accepted Christ are not hiding, are not lying, deceiving or being unethical. They say to Christian and Muslim alike, "We follow Christ and uphold the Old Testament, Psalms and New Testament as the Word of God."[122]

Responding to Tennent in an article titled "Identity, integrity and insider movement," Kevin Higgins argues that "one can maintain a dual identity and be a fully biblical disciple of Jesus."[123] He argues that this dual identity consists of Identity one: *Follower of Jesus and a Member of the Church*,[124] and Identity two: *Follower of Jesus and a Muslim.* As a basis of his dual identity argument for Muslim insiders, he brings up the case of the early church. In Acts, Higgins argues, the Jewish believers as "the member of 'the church' continued to attend Temple and synagogue *as well as* meeting in homes and in public places."[125] According to Higgins, the New Testament church was a movement

> within social and religious life of the Jewish people. This movement took structural or formal expression as it met in separate homes or public gatherings *and* as its members continued in the Temple and synagogue. They did not cease to be the church in the Temple worship, and they did not cease to be Jewish in the home meeting. There was a dual identity.[126]

Higgins argues that this dual identity is "like two circles that overlap to a great degree (though not fully)."[127] This concept is explained in greater detail in the discussion of Kingdom circles under anthropological viewpoints below. The identity issue leads to another ethical issue of remaining within the Muslim community from both the Muslim and Christian side.

---

122. Travis, 125.

123. Higgins, "Identity, Integrity," 117.

124. His meaning of church here does not signify Western-style aggregate church, but rather the universal body of Christ gathering beyond any limited building or space.

125. Higgins, "Identity, Integrity," 118. Italics in the original.

126. Higgins, 118.

127. Higgins believes that it is possible to apply this Jewish case in the early church to a Muslim context unless one holds one of two extreme views of Islam: "Islam is a demonic and deceptive lie conceived by Satan" or "Islam is the final truth from God, or an equally valid expression of truth." Higgins, 120.

Remaining Muslim Community

To Tennent's challenge regarding the ethics of remaining in the Muslim community after deciding to follow Christ, Travis argues that there are many
cultural Muslims who have differing beliefs or know almost nothing about
Islam.[128] The purpose of C5 communities, however, is not just to remain
within their context, but to live as witnesses of Christ in their native communities. Travis considers reinterpretation of the role of Muhammad and
the Qur'an as the most challenging task facing C5 believers, because some
qur'anic verses do not support the historical fact of Jesus's crucifixion.[129] These
perspectives can help place C5 MBBs in non-heretical seats without forcing
them to immediately move toward C4 or other points of the spectrum, and
also help them find common ground on which to witness to Jesus in their
local Muslim communities.[130]

Joshua Massey supports Travis's opinion and the insider movement as a
whole. In the article "His ways are not our ways," Massey describes various
ways to find Jesus as the true Savior and Lord within many different contexts.
He points out that God's ways are unpredictable and amazingly diverse as
people come to Christ, especially in the Muslim context. Growing numbers
of C3–C5 believers represent a surprising progression of God's diverse action
in drawing Muslims to Christ.[131]

Comparing them to first-century Gentiles who were not required to convert to Judaism to follow Jesus, Massey argues that Muslims do not have to
convert to "Christianity" to follow Jesus. Massey believes that C5 believers are
certainly real disciples of Jesus. They just do not want to identify themselves
with "that godless Western institution called 'Christianity,' where (from a
Muslim perspective) homosexuals enter the clergy, immodest women worship in scantily clad summer dresses, and people put their Holy Scriptures

---

128. Travis, "Response to Phil Parshall," 413.

129. Travis, 414; Accad, *Building Bridges*, 144.

130. Travis recommends Accad's book *Building Bridges* as a starting point to reinterpret
Muhammad and the Qur'an, which denies the crucifixion of Christ. There are several Qur'an
verses, which clearly support Jesus's crucifixion. Accad also displays some examples of Muslims
who have successfully remained in the community of Islam after receiving Christ, some referring
to themselves as "Muslims who are truly surrendered to God through the sacrifice of Messiah
Isa." Accad, 35.

131. Massey, "His Ways," 189–90.

on the floor right next to their dirty shoes."[132] Because the meaning of the term "Christian" is too negative in a Muslim context, C5 believers want to call themselves Muslims even though they disagree with common Muslim beliefs such as the Bible's corruption and an uncrucified Jesus. Therefore, C5 believers would like to identify themselves as "Muslim" followers of Jesus. Massey speaks for a C5 believer:

> I don't pray like a Christian, with Western pants and collared shirts; I dress like a Muslim. I don't talk like a Christian, with all their strange terms to describe God and his prophets; I talk like a Muslim. I don't eat like a Christian, consuming pork chops and haram meats (i.e. from animals not butchered in the "kosher" way); I prefer halal meats, like a Muslim. I don't have a Christian name, like John, Tom, or Paul. I have a Muslim name.[133]

The ethical question of whether it is possible for Christians to become Muslims to reach Muslims is very significant. Travis generally agrees with Parshall's concern about Christians' conversion to Islam to win Muslims. He normally advises his Christian-background coworkers, "especially the expatriates, to take on a C4 expression of faith, and not enter Islam to reach Muslims."[134] Travis believes, however, that God might specially call certain Christian workers to do precisely this.[135] He states,

> I could imagine that in some instances God may call uniquely gifted, well-prepared individuals, whose ministries are firmly backed by prayers, to C5 outreach and religious identity. These C5 missionaries would be Muslims in the literal Arabic sense of the word (i.e. "one submitted to God") and their theology would, of course, differ from standard Muslim theology at a number of key points. They would have to be ready for persecution, and it would be best if these believers were of Muslim background.[136]

---

132. Massey, 191.
133. Massey, 192.
134. Travis, "Response to Phil Parshall," 413.
135. Travis, 412–13.
136. Travis, 413.

If they make their belief clear and are permitted by local Muslims, Travis counterquestions, "should we not praise God for the opportunity they have to share the Good News in a place few would dare to tread?"[137]

To Parshall's ethical objection about "how Muslims would feel about such an approach," Travis answers that the question is not relevant.[138] Travis argues that this approach is better in terms of not inducing Muslims to convert to Christianity. He notes,

> The majority of Muslims that I have talked to object to any activity they perceive as an attempt to attract Muslims to Christianity. However, *the C5 approach, which communicates the message of salvation in Christ without the intent to persuade Muslims to "change their religion," might in fact be the one most appreciated by Muslims.* By separating the gospel from the myriad of legal, social, and cultural issues implied in changing religious camps, a more straightforward, less encumbered message can be shared and (we hope) embraced.[139]

Evaluating the C5 Movement as a Mission Strategy

Steve Sang-Cheol Moon criticizes the insider movement as a frontier mission strategy. He is concerned with the movement for three reasons.[140] First, Moon questions the excessive expectation for self-theologizing on the part of the insiders. He mentions Woodberry's preference regarding insiders' final decision of where they situate themselves in the position of contextualization or social identity.[141] Though he agrees that self-theologizing should ultimately be pursued, he questions whether we should expect immature self-theologizing in situations where theological and ecclesiological foundations are lacking. Second, Moon believes it is not good to prioritize Muslim insiders' identity over Christians' identity. Moon argues that if a faith confession brings about expulsion, it is worth enduring the situation. The reason he says this is that the MBBs he has met outwardly try to express their faith at all costs, just like

---

137. Travis, 413.

138. Parshall, "Danger!," 410; Travis, 413.

139. Travis, "Response to Phil Parshall," 413; Italics added.

140. Moon, "Critical Review," 18–25.

141. Woodberry, "To the Muslim?," 23–28.

the martyrs of the early church. He states that "sometimes, God's wisdom was a faith of martyrdom. The insider movement is not God's wisdom even though it seems to be good for man's strategy."[142] Third, Moon argues that the insider movement is the result of excessive attachment to the idea of people movement. He argues that

> God's strategy may be converting individuals of a small number of chosen people. Group conversion is not always effective, and we cannot pursue it without considering the context. In the situation of many places of strong Islamic fundamentalism, the possibility is even rare. In many parts, the logic of the insider movement is the logic of hanging up the numbers. Rather than pursuing on a large scale mass conversion, it is better for having a simple goal of making disciples one by one and helping them to live by biblical faith in the field of frontier mission.[143]

His view is that frontier mission requires patience to learn God's wisdom and pursue traditional path.

From a different critical perspective, Gary Corwin worries about the involvement of Western money in the C5 movement, as it might lead to cultural imperialism. This movement, he argues, "advocates – in the name of cultural appropriateness – a new form of western missiological imperialism into contexts where local believers are already believing, living, and applying the Gospel."[144] Bill Nikides extends this argument, saying that the C5 movement is not an indigenous movement, but a movement by Western money. He insists that "C5 is a reflection of intentional western missiology, western training, and often a great deal of western money."[145] Nikides explains the process of the movement involving Western missionaries and criticizes it as another imposition on indigenous communities:

> This is how it works: *westerners are trained and indoctrinated to prefer C5 as an advisable methodology.* They go into the mission field and indoctrinate nationals. Leaders emerge among

---

142. Moon, "Critical Review," 23.
143. Moon, 23.
144. Corwin, "Discussion with Ralph Winter," 18.
145. Nikides, "Evaluating 'Insider Movements,'" 5.

nationals who then often are employed by westerners to evangelize and form communities of believers. Bible study methods, such as Manuscript Bible Study are taught by parachurch organizations that help the nationals love Jesus without having to give up Islam. Missionaries return home with stories of breakthroughs, omitting uncomfortable details, to raise more funds that fuel the growth. At least in its more extreme expressions, *it smacks of a new kind of neo-colonialism imposed on the "natives."*[146]

Nikides also criticizes a tendency to remain stuck in the C5 category. "Missionaries and C5 national leaders have used seemingly every means (seniority, theology and sometimes money) to keep believers from leaving C5. C5ers are often not encouraged to attend seminars or other forums where alternative understandings might be suggested."[147] This part of his criticism needs to be clearly answered by C5 movement proponents. In my own judgment, in some sense, we cannot claim that any of the C-scale categories (C1–C5) are free of the influences of Western missionaries and money.

Syncretism

Dick Brogden warns of the tendency of the insider movement to become syncretic unless theology directs "anthropology when determining missiology."[148] Brogden thinks highly of the overseeing role of theologians "who objectively question whether Insider Movements are straying toward syncretism."[149] In response to Brogden's statement, Rebecca Lewis identifies the role of missiology as "seeing what God seems to be doing and evaluating that in the light of scripture."[150] Her point is that the discussion of syncretism needs to fully consider the context of what is really happening and whether what is happening distorts the biblical truth.

Scott Moreau defines syncretism as "the replacement or dilution of the essential truths of the gospel through the incorporation of non-Christian

---

146. Nikides, 6; italics added.
147. Nikides, 5.
148. Brogden, "Inside Out," 36.
149. Brogden, 36.
150. Lewis, "Response to Brogden," 36.

elements."[151] He values highly the role of indigenous actors in deciding which activities are syncretic. Moreau states,

> The local community must be empowered to biblically evaluate their own practices and teachings. Missionaries must learn to trust that indigenous peoples are able to discern God's leading and trust God to develop and maintain biblically founded and culturally relevant Faith and Praxis in each local context.[152]

In his article "Contextualization without syncretism," Rick Brown states that "biblical Christianity is a worldview but not a culture"[153] and argues that most C5 believers are cultural Muslims. He also asserts that "syncretism (as commonly understood) is a parameter of worldview, whereas contextualization is a parameter of enculturation."[154] His definitions imply that C5 believers are properly contextualized and are not contradicting biblical Christianity because they have a biblical worldview that is culturally adaptable but does not to fall into syncretism. He argues that all of the categories, from C1 to C6, have the potential to support a syncretic worldview. Brown not only holds that C5 does not wander into syncretism, but also considers it to be an effective and "well-contextualized" missional movement.

> The C1 to C6 communities differ in their degree of enculturation, yet each of them could have any degree of syncretistic worldview. The ideal is for all of them to have a Biblical worldview. . . . Messianic Muslim fellowships are more feasible and more effective. They are brave, well-contextualized, open in their testimony, effective in outreach, and capable of multiplying rapidly.[155]

Agreeing that there is some danger of syncretism in the C5 movement, Travis suggests seven guidelines that may help believers avoid slipping into syncretism:

1.   Jesus is Lord and Savior, there is no salvation outside of him.

---

151. Moreau, "Syncretism," 924.
152. Moreau, 924.
153. Brown, "Contextualization without Syncretism," 132.
154. Brown, 133.
155. Brown, 133.

2. New believers are baptized, meet regularly with other believers.
3. New believers study the *Injil* (and *Torah* plus *Zabur* if available).
4. New believers renounce and are delivered from occultism and harmful folk Islamic practices.
5. Muslim practices and traditions are done as expressions of love for God and/or respect for neighbors, rather than as acts necessary to receive forgiveness of sins.
6. The Qur'an, Muhammad, and traditional Muslim theology are examined, judged, and reinterpreted in light of biblical truth.
7. New believers show evidence of the new birth and growth in grace.[156]

Parshall is also concerned about syncretism and C5, though his definitions differ from Travis's. In his editorial writing, Massey introduces his discussion with Parshall and his concern with the ideas of some advocates of C5 that he met.[157] They insisted that "it is okay to affirm Muhammad as a genuine prophet of God; that Muslim background believers should attend the mosque perpetually; and that Christians should consider legally converting to Islam to win Muslims as Muslims."[158] Massey, however, answers that it is not C5. Travis answers Massey's request to define C5 more practically. "A C5 believer will certainly have different beliefs from other Muslims (e.g. *Isa* did die on the cross, Muhammad is not a prophet in the biblical sense, salvation is in *Isa al-Masih* and not in works)."[159] In the next part, the proponents of C5/ insider movement among Muslims anthropologically explain that the movement is not syncretic.

Anthropological Viewpoint

Some anthropologists and mission practitioners who support the insider movement have tried to explain what is happening in Muslim society anthropologically. Rick Brown illustrates the insider movement using Paul Hiebert's concept of Bounded Set and Centered Set.[160] Rebecca Lewis uses a Kingdom

---

156. Travis, "Response to Phil Parshall," 414.
157. Massey, "Editorial," 2.
158. Massey, 2.
159. Massey, 2.
160. Brown, "Biblical Muslims."

Circle to explain the difference between spiritual and socioreligious identity.[161] Frank Decker and Darrell Whiteman use a form and meaning table to distinguish contextualization from syncretism.[162]

Bounded sets or centered sets

In his article "Biblical Muslims," Rick Brown introduces Paul Hiebert's two missiological points of view in terms of "bounded sets" (BS) and "centered sets" (CS).[163] While BS Christians define themselves in terms of a recognizable socioreligious category, which involves criteria such as agreeing on the same doctrines and practicing the same religious rituals, CS Christians define themselves in terms of closeness to the center or model – Jesus Christ.[164] Brown argues that this difference may lead to misinterpretation and conflicts in missiology.[165] These two different mindsets result in two different missionary approaches. While BS is focusing on the expansion of socioreligious boundary, CS is pursuing the growth of a Christ-centered kingdom. Both support contextualized ministry, but they practice it differently.

> One group is seeking to contextualize their brand of Christian religion, while the other is seeking to contextualize collective discipleship to Christ. So each sees the other as deficient and sometimes as threatening. Personally, I think there is a place for both in God's plan, but the boundary-set approach often leads to conflict and recrimination between socio-religious groups and to suffering and shame within families. Even extracted, long-standing converts feel the pain of this competitive socio-religious approach.[166]

Brown, influenced by Hiebert's theory, asks which criteria decide whether some Muslims are saved or not? Is Christianity a boundary or is Jesus in their heart? A Kingdom Circle displayed by Rebecca Lewis tries to answer this question.

---

161. Lewis, "Insider Movements," 18.
162. Decker and Whiteman, "White Paper," 7.
163. Brown, "Biblical Muslims."
164. Hiebert, *Anthropological Reflections*, 110–35.
165. Hiebert, 69.
166. Brown, "Biblical Muslims," 69.

Kingdom circle

Rebecca Lewis and other C5 practitioners are trying to demonstrate whether someone can enter the kingdom of God regardless of socioreligious boundaries. Figures 1, 2, and 3 below include the circle of the kingdom of God. The other circles and arrows reveal correlations for entering the kingdom drawn from the implications of the book of Acts beyond diverse socioreligious identities.[167]

Figure 1 indicates the relationship between Judaism and the kingdom of God. From the book of Acts, we find that early Jewish disciples could enter the kingdom of God with a new spiritual identity (A), even though they held onto their socioreligious identity by, for example, observing their law and preserving their worship style at the Jewish temple (B).

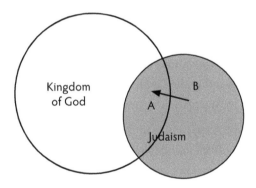

Figure 1. Kingdom Circle 1

Figure 2 shows that some Gentiles, who were dedicated to Christ as the Lord and Savior in Acts, entered the kingdom (C), even though many non-believers still remained (D). As seen in Acts 15, the Jerusalem Council announced that Gentile believers could enter the kingdom without converting to Judaism and passing through the Jewish socioreligious boundary (E).

---

167. Lewis, "Insider Movements," 18.

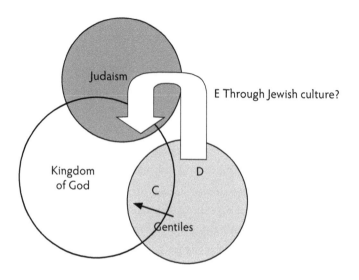

Figure 2. Kingdom Circle 2

Figure 3 illustrates the contemporary situation. The term "Christianity" is considered as a socioreligious system characterized by Western religious forms and cultures, rather than faith in Christ itself. Lewis applies principles found in Acts 15 to this case:

> While many people who call themselves Christians have truly believed in Christ and entered the Kingdom (F), others have not, though they may attend church (G). The Acts 15 question is still relevant today: Must people with a distinctly non-Christian (especially non-Western) identity "go through" the socio-religious systems of "Christianity" in order to become part of God's Kingdom (H)? Or can they enter the Kingdom of God through faith in the Lord Jesus Christ alone and gain a new spiritual identity while retaining their own community and socio-religious identity (I)?[168]

Lewis's argument indicates that Muslim followers of Jesus can enter the kingdom of God without passing through Christianity.

---

168. Lewis, 18.

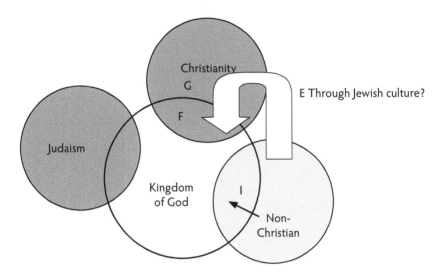

Figure 3. Kingdom Circle 3

Anthropological view of contextualization vs. syncretism

An anthropologist Darrell Whiteman and mission practitioner Frank Decker discuss the insider movement anthropologically. They argue that "Insider movements of Muslim followers of Jesus are not syncretistic," but they are "dynamic examples of radical biblical contextualization."[169] They draw a chart of correlation between meaning and form (Figure 4).[170] Decker and Whiteman put "form" on the horizontal axis, with Western forms on the left and Indigenous forms on the right. They put "meaning" on the vertical axis, with Christian on the top and Pagan on the bottom. Decker and Whiteman argue that this chart, which produces four combinations of form and meaning, illustrates the significant difference between syncretism and indigenous followers of Christ.[171]

---

169. Decker and Whiteman, "White Paper," 6.
170. Decker and Whiteman, 7.
171. Decker and Whiteman, 7.

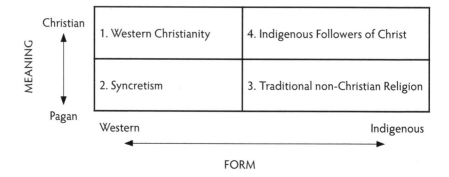

Figure 4. Form and Meaning

In Quadrant 1, we see Western Christianity, where Western form and Christian meaning meet. The authors assert that this was "one of the consequences of mission in the age of colonialism, and we find expressions of Western Christianity all over the world today."[172] In Quadrant 2, we find syncretism, where Western forms and pagan meanings converge. They argue that the problem of pagan meaning results in religious syncretism as seen in "folk Catholicism," which seems Christian outwardly but is bound up with many pagan beliefs, and the American "health and wealth gospel," which retains Christian forms but is united to sub-Christian meanings. Quadrant 3 indicates that traditional pagan religion exists where indigenous forms accompany pagan meanings.[173]

Most importantly, Quadrant 4 represents indigenous followers of Christ, positioned where Christian meaning and indigenous forms combine to produce culturally appropriate forms of genuine faith in Christ. The authors give a few examples: Methodist Church in Fiji, where traditional Fijian cultural forms are used; E. Stanley Jones's application of the concept of the ashram in India; and the seeker-sensitive worship model developed by Bill Hybels in the United States. They also consider Muslim followers of Christ to fit in the fourth quadrant because the forms are culturally appropriate and they preserve biblical meaning. Therefore, the authors argue, the insider movement among Muslims is "not slippery slope to syncretism," but

---

172. Decker and Whiteman, 7.
173. Decker and Whiteman, 8.

"contextualization that produces indigenous followers of Jesus is the best hedge against syncretism."[174]

History of Recent Development of Discussions and Key Discussions

Since the publication of major discussions from prominent authors such as Phil Parshall, Tim Tennent, John Travis, and Kevin Higgins in the mid-2000s, the insider movement discussion has continued in missiological journals such as *International Journal of Frontier Missiology* (IJFM) and *St. Francis Magazine*.[175] While most of the relevant IJFM articles – alongside *Mission Frontiers* – tend to promote the insider movement, *St. Francis Magazine* has mostly criticized the insider movement. The gap between these two has hardly narrowed up to the present. Meanwhile, the "Bridging the Divide" (BtD) consultation began in 2011 to promote understanding of each side of the issue. BtD is an annual meeting consisting of "a committed group of missiologists, theologians and church leaders from those who promote Insider Movements and also from those who are critical of them."[176] BtD produced an alternative term for Muslim followers of Jesus, "socio-religious insiders," but two missiologists (Daniels and Waterman) prefer the term suggested by an insider leader, Abu Jaz, who describe himself and his colleague as "cultural insiders, but theological outsiders" (CITO).[177] BtD's respectful discussions have helped bring a softer tone to the continuing debates. BtD has also produced several academic and practical contributions published in an October 2013 special edition of the *ERT (Evangelical Review of Theology)* and in *IJFM* and *EMQ*.

Muhammad, Christian and Biblical Theology of Islam, and Shahada

Among the various issues addressed in recent discussions, three deserve particular attention here due to their critical implications for my research:

---

174. Decker and Whiteman, 9.

175. *Mission Frontiers* published a special edition in May–June 2011, changing the name of the movement from Insider Movement to Jesus Movement (*Insider Movement to Jesus Movement: Discovering Biblical Faith in the Most Unexpected Places*). The edition covered the Jesus movement, in which people are following Jesus without converting from their previous religions to Christianity in diverse religious backgrounds.

176. Haskell, "Editorial," 291.

177. Jaz, "Clarification," 56; Daniels and Waterman, "Bridging the Socio-Religious," 62–63.

Muhammad's prophethood, a call for the development of a Christian theology of Islam, and *shahada*. These three issues are closely connected with each other and with the reinterpretation of Muhammad and the Qur'an – which, according to Travis, is "the most challenging task of C5."[178]

First, in the title of his research article, Harley Talman raises a bold question "Is Muhammad also among the prophets?"[179]. As an evangelical scholar who does not consider Islam "as an alternative way of salvation apart from personal faith in Christ," his quest to assess Muhammad accurately and biblically was also motivated by the reality of conflict between Christians and Muslims, which he identified as "more of an obstacle to the gospel than a preparation for it."[180] He also finds that qur'anic testimonies about Jesus helped them to encounter him as Savior in their spiritual journey.[181] After reviewing a relatively lengthy study of early Islamic literature regarding Muhammad, he mentions that his purpose for writing is related to "expanding constricted categories of prophethood to allow Christians to entertain the possibility of Muhammad being other than a false prophet."[182] He stresses Muhammad's unique role as "a bearer of God's message in Arabic" by turning people "from paganism and idolatry to monotheism" and as someone who was "preparing a potential bridge to the gospel of Christ."[183]

Second, in response to Talman's controversial article, Martin Accad – a specialist in Islam and Christian-Muslim relations who gained his PhD from Oxford – asks readers not to judge Talman too quickly from our own perspectives, challenging us instead to develop "Christian and biblical theology of Islam."[184] Accad begins his argument by pointing out three major issues in current missiological debates regarding Muslims: (1) the legitimacy of the insider movement; (2) the legitimacy of highly contextualized Bible translation; and (3) the legitimacy of "dialogue as a complementary approach to Christian mission to Muslims."[185] He suggests that disagreements on these

---

178. Travis, "Response to Phil Parshall," 413.
179. Talman, "Is Muhammad Also?," 169.
180. Talman, 171.
181. Talman, 171.
182. Talman, 181.
183. Talman, 183.
184. Accad, "Towards a Theology," 192.
185. Accad, 191.

questions have barely diminished over time due to difference in the debaters' own theologies of Islam. While those who take a positive view of these three issues think "some aspects of Islam's religious culture" are redeemable, critics "tend to have a more demonizing view of Islam," seeing "nothing redeemable in the entire phenomenon."[186] For this reason, Accad calls for historical and scientific research aimed at "making sense of Islam within a Christian worldview," which could help us "increase creative conversation, trigger renewed and honest inquiry, and challenge the historic situation of conflict between both communities."[187] He believes these efforts also need to focus on fulfilling "the mission of God in communities where Christians and Muslims live side by side."[188]

Third, Gene Daniels in a recent article notes that he is concerned about MBBs or Muslim insiders reciting the *shahada* in public, even though he agrees with two characteristics of the insider movement – retaining identity and continuing community. His concern comes from "what is communicated when a follower of Christ recites the *shahada*" rather than the contents of the second part of the *shahada*, which affirms Muhammad's prophethood.[189] While the term "prophet" is used in many ways even in the Bible (see, for example 1 Kgs 13:1–22), his worry concerns receptors' decoding of the message. Because recitation of the *shahada* happens in public, receptors belonging to the Muslim community can have different ideas from MBBs or Muslim insiders, who reinterpret Muhammad's prophethood to mean something quite unlike the understanding held by normal Muslims. This results in miscommunication. Daniels mentions two mistakes made when believers recite the *shahada*:

> One, it completely neglects the context in which such a speech-event takes place – a creed – which by nature implies a fixed understanding of the meaning.

---

186. Accad, 191.
187. Accad, 192.
188. Accad, 192.
189. Daniels, "Saying the *Shahada*," 307.

Two, relying on a reinterpretation of Muhammad places exclusive weight on the meanings *encoded* by the speaker rather than those *decoded* by the receptor, thus causing miscommunication.[190]

Daniels's concern is insightful, pointing to the need for discussions of MBBs' reinterpretation of Muhammad to take into account the views of Muslim receptors as well as the conscience of MBBs.

Overall, these three articles not only challenge us to dig deeper into text and context, but also suggest guidelines and boundaries to aid our navigation. Discussions of Muhammad and the Qur'an in particular would carry different nuances for MBBs than they would for traditional and foreign Christians. MBBs might appreciate it if other Christians were to make more of an effort to understand the place of Muhammad and the Qur'an in MBBs' background and birth communities. Moreover, these MBBs will be able to provide insightful input into, and take initiative in, these discussions. The issues dealt with in these three recent articles are relevant to my research findings and will be discussed further in chapter 5 as part of the analysis of RQ 3.

Conclusion of the Insider Movement Debate

The insider movement among Muslims may move toward syncretism unless carefully monitored and guided. As we conclude this section, it will be helpful to introduce Abdul Asad's well-organized chart illustrating this issue. In his article "Rethinking the Insider Movement Debate," Asad summarizes most of the insider movement discussions with a chart contrasting syncretistic C5 to appropriate C5. He concludes that the movement needs to move toward appropriate C5 (Figure 5).[191]

Asad argues that if the C5 movement moves toward "Syncretistic C5," the movement will be in danger of syncretism, but if the movement adopts "Appropriate C5" principles and strategies, it would be desirable to continue. He states,

The end goal of "Syncretistic C5" is unclear, and thus leaves open dangerous possibilities such as syncretism or Churchless

---

190. Daniels, 310; italics in the original.
191. Asad, "Rethinking the Insider Movement."

Christianity. By way of contrast, the "Appropriate C5" has a clearer set of guidelines that should not be compromised, and a clearer end goal – an indigenous church movement that is well related to the global church.[192]

Asad's appropriate C5 model resolves some of the ethical and biblical/theological problems addressed in the C5 discussion. For example, in category 8, about self-identity, syncretistic C5 emphasizes Muslim identity but appropriate C5 focuses on the believer's identity as a follower of 'Isa. Also, missionaries are not recommended to adopt C5 identities (category 6), the Bible (Injil/New Testament) is elevated above the Qur'an (category 11), and the shahada is reinterpreted while the discussion of Muhammad's prophethood is avoided (category 10).

The insider movement among Muslims is an intentional or voluntary ongoing social movement. It has some strong points in the area expanding the large body of Christ from a kingdom of God perspective, but it also needs to be developed with much caution. The perspectives of multiple disciplines can help here.

Sociologically, the insider movement has an ongoing process of development. It is present in many Muslim-majority countries, and whether it brings conflict or peace, we need to more carefully observe and review this ongoing social phenomenon from a sociological perspective.

Missiologically, the insider movement among Muslims demands a cautious approach, as it may be supported as a foreign mission strategy that replaces the development and encouragement of national/indigenous missionaries. It may also introduce missional and ethical issues.[193] Although attitudes toward the insider movement have tended toward one of two extremes – some proponents say that it gets results, it should be promoted by missionary initiatives in all Muslim countries, while some opponents argue that it needs to be resisted because it contaminates historical Christianity – these simplistic approaches are not enough. From the perspective of missiological anthropology, there is a need for investigation of the interrelation between the insider movement and people movement, as well as a closer look

---

192. Asad, 157.
193. Tennent, "Followers of Jesus (Isa)," 112–13.

Syncretistic C5	Appropriate C5
C-Spectrum Extractionism Contextualization Syncretism 1 2 3 4 5 Enter at 5, always drifting toward syncretism	C-Spectrum Extractionism Contextualization Syncretism 1 2 3 4 5 Enter at 5, always transitioning toward contextualization
1. Methodology: almost always prescriptive 2. Insider primarily means IN mosque 3. Ecclesiology: content with low expression of church, *koinonia* (fellowship) is enough 4. Churchless Christianity a real danger because of ambiguous goal for expression of church 5. Homogenous Unit Principle employed liberally with little or no concern for Kingdom diversity, thus likely to remain homogenous over time 6. Missionaries free to adopt C5 identity 7. Views C5 as a *permanent strategy* and sees little or no need to move toward C4/3 8. Self-Identity: **Muslim** follower of Isa 9. Perceived ID: Muslim 10. Likely to affirm *shahada*, prophethood of Muhammad, problematic qur'anic texts 11. Qur'an and *Injil* seen as equal 12. Susceptible to "reverse-*Taqiyyah*" effect	1. Methodology: chiefly descriptive, prescriptive use is situational 2. Insider moves from IN mosque to IN social/family networks 3. Ecclesiology: move from low expression to higher expression of church, *ekklesia* is goal 4. Churchless Christianity not likely because of clear vision for C4/3 New Testament churches 5. Homogenous Unit Principle recognized, but with end goal as "Ephesians Moment" disciples, reconciled to other expressions of global Christianity 6. Only national MBBs may adopt C5 identity 7. Views C5 as a *temporary strategy* to gain momentum and critical mass for C4/3 8. Self-Identity: Muslim ***follower of Isa*** 9. Perceived ID: Strange kind of Muslim, possibly with deviant theology 10. Re-interpret *shahada*, respectfully avoid discussions about prophethood of Muhammad and problematic qur'anic texts 11. *Injil* elevated above Qur'an 12. "We do not use deception" (2 Cor 4:2)

Figure 5. Syncretistic C5 vs. Appropriate C5

(All contents, including bold, capitals, and italics, are from Asad, 155–56.)

at Muslims' collectivism and identity.[194] Muslim insiders are coming to Christ with whole families or sometimes with whole communities. Comparative research of the insider movement in other cultural and religious contexts – such as Jewish and Hindu – is also needed if we are to understand the essence of the movement.

Theologically, it is necessary to examine the differences between the insider movement and historical Christianity.[195] This connects to the question of theological syncretism. However, the previous discussions of the movement have been limited to comparisons with the Western Christian heritage. Future discussions should focus more on what the Bible really implies regarding the issue and how the theme of the kingdom of God is connected. With Christians' concerns and efforts, Muslim insiders' efforts to study the Bible, and the guidance of the Holy Spirit, I expect that the day will come when world Christians will truly call Muslim followers of Christ our brothers and sisters.

MBBs' Identity and Tim Green's Research on Social Identity of MBBs

The identity of MBBs is a complex issue. Even though MBBs are converted to Christianity, it is hard to simply call them "Christians" because existing Christians have lived in the same area and hold different cultures and beliefs. It is also hard to call them Muslims because they have received Christ as Savior and Lord and have a Christian faith, in spite of the long journey of Islamic belonging in the past and the negative connotation of the term "Christian" among their neighbors. Warrick Farah, a mission practitioner who worked in the Middle East, reveals the difficulty in strictly identifying MBBs as either Christians or Muslims:

> There are twin errors I see being made in mission praxis when it comes to the identity issue. The first error is to ask Muslims who are considering embracing biblical faith to identify as "Christians." The other error is to insist that MBBs continue to

---

194. Lewis, "Promoting Movements to Christ," 75–76.
195. Tennent, "Followers of Jesus (Isa)," 171–76.

call themselves "Muslims." Both errors over-assume the role of the Kingdom worker in local theologizing.[196]

This reality reflects the "socioreligious" complexity of MBBs who pursue a biblical way of life in the Muslim majority context.[197]

MBBs' Self-Identity

In his article "Should Muslims become 'Christian'?," Bernard Dutch investigates self-identity issues among MBBs. Dutch argues that Western Christians have a tendency to overemphasize the MBBs' self-identity, forcing them to have Christian identity and to judge the issue too easily without considering the context. For example, many Western Christians conclude that if an MBB continues to express himself or herself as a Muslim, that he or she "crosses a line from contextualization to syncretism."[198] Dutch, however, argues that the issue of MBBs' identity is "fluid, taking the most appropriate form for the situation."[199] He suggests that, in order to avoid the negative connotations of the term "Christian," MBBs can, for instance, avoid this label and identify themselves using different terms – such as "followers of 'Isa" – in response to diverse views and contexts.[200]

Dutch found that one of the main reasons for avoiding the term of "Christian" in the community where he served was that the term "Christian" effectively means "animist background Christian." For the people in the village, a "Christian" means a follower of "the polytheistic path of animism" and a betrayer of family and community. Dutch continues,

> With such an understanding of the term, who can blame the Muslim community for ostracizing a "Christian" and his family from the life of the community? The "Christian" child will have no playmates, and his marriage will be almost impossible to arrange. A "Christian" identity actually communicates the very antithesis of what it means to be a Christ-follower.[201]

---

196. Farah, "Emerging Missiological Themes," 18.
197. Farah, 18.
198. Dutch, "Should Muslims Become 'Christian'?" 15.
199. Dutch, 15.
200. Dutch, 15.
201. Dutch, 18.

Dutch categorizes seven types of believers in the area in which he worked:

1. Animist background Christian
2. Christian with Muslim culture (most receive outside funding)
3. Neither Christian nor Muslim (there is no supporting community)
4. Jesus Muslims (Muslims regard this as a disguise for Christianity)
5. Mystical Muslims (Sufi background: regarding Jesus as a mediator before God)
6. Muslims with non-mainstream beliefs and practices [202]
7. Full Muslims (remove any trace of difference between themselves and an orthodox Muslim identity).[203]

At the other extreme end of the spectrum, opposed to animist background Christian, full Muslims try to fulfill all the pillars of Islam before coming to faith in Christ. Other believers considered this approach to be syncretistic, and saw it as undermining any effective witness.[204] Finally, Dutch suggests low profile approaches that involve "remaining in society; identifying those who are open; appropriately arousing people's interest; and wooing them toward Christ."[205] He says that this type of approach not only bears sensitive witness to potential believers in any situation, but also maintains good relationships with family and community.

One of the pioneers in the study of MBBs' identity study is Seppo Syrjanen, whose dissertation title was, "In Search of Meaning and Identity" in 1984. Although he primarily deals with conversion narratives from Pakistani MBBs, he extends his research with various theories of identity applied to MBBs' situation. His findings indicate that the conversion process consists of three steps: the period of awareness, the period of decision, and the period of incorporation. The first two steps reflect that the MBBs' motivations for conversion are diversely influenced by supernatural experiences, Scriptural cognition, or friends' or missionaries' guidance. In the third step, these MBBs faced

---

202. While keeping their identity as Muslims, they adhere to "several non-mainstream practices in prayer, celebration of Muslim holidays, and Scripture reading." They try not to lose their chance to share their witness with inquirers about their faith. Dutch, 19.

203. Dutch, 18–19.

204. Dutch, 19.

205. Dutch, 21.

struggles on two sides: the fear of Muslims' reaction and the inhospitality of existing Christians, and they confessed having had "extremely bitter experiences with the Pakistani Christian community."[206] A comment from one of Syrjanen's respondents reflects the difficulty and struggle of MBBs' identity after conversion: "Conversion is possible, but after that it is difficult, most difficult."[207] Syrjanen's research plays an important role as a frontier study of MBBs' identity because he does not limit his study to reasons why they convert to Christianity, but also interacts with conversion experiences, including their inner meaning, and the identity struggles experienced by MBBs in the process of and after changing their religion.

Kathryn Ann Kraft's dissertation research focuses on community and identity among Arab MBBs in Lebanon and Egypt.[208] Her research extends the scope of research to Muslims' *ummah* (community) and *tawhid* (law) as well as Arab MBBs' reality when new identity is formed and challenged. Significant contributions of her research include not only her detailed illustration of her research process – including a discussion of the researcher's position as both "insider and outsider" – but also her prudent analysis of the context of Arab culture and the reality of MBBs. My research and Kraft's deal with several similar points, though the difference of context between Arab countries and South Asia will inevitably bring about different foci and results.

In 2004, missiologists and practitioners from Muslim countries gathered to reflect on the issue of MBB conversion in an event called the "Coming to Faith Consultation" (CTFC). Later in 2006, they published *From the Straight Path to the Narrow Way: Journeys of Faith*, edited by David Greenlee. At their next gathering in 2010 – the "Second Coming to Faith Consultation" (CTFC2) – the presenters and participants focused on MBBs' identity without intentional discussion about this before the meeting.[209] The results of the gathering – edited by David Greenlee and published in 2013 as *Longing for Community: Church, Ummah, or Somewhere in Between* – reflect the shifting focus of mission practitioners from MBBs' conversion to MBBs' identity.

---

206. Syrjanen, *In Search of Meaning*, 180.

207. Syrjanen, 172.

208. Kraft, "Community and Identity." Her dissertation was published with some abridgment and extension in 2012 as *Searching for Heaven in the Real World: A Sociological Discussion of Conversion in the Arab World*.

209. Greenlee, "Introduction," xiv.

Longing for Community is a pioneering book of articles related to issues of MBBs' identities, bringing diverse theories and points of view to the interpretation of this aspect of MBBs' reality. The articles of the book are introduced in the next section with special reference to Tim Green.

Tim Green's Research on Social Identity of MBBs

There is no universal definition of identity, despite the extensive social science literature on the subject.[210] Gillespie discusses identity as answering three questions: "Who am I?" "Where do I belong?" and "How do I fit?"[211] He defines identity simply as "selfhood."[212] However, identity cannot be simply defined by either selfness or otherness. Gillespie supports this idea of distinguishing between identity as "coherent sense of self" and as "the mirrors of others."[213] Hans Mol once mentioned before Gillespie's comments about selfness and otherness of identity that the personal and social characteristics of identity interact dependently and in conflict with each other.[214] In this sense, most scholars agree that identity has multiple levels.

Tim Green, an identity researcher studying MBBs, cites psychologist Benjamin Beit-Hallahmi's book about the three levels of identity: collective, social, and ego-identity.

> At the top I would place *collective identity*, i.e. identity as defined by the group. . . . In the middle I would place *social identity* labels as used by the individual and by others to identify him(self). At the bottom or deepest level I would place *ego-identity*, which is privately or even unconsciously experienced by the individual.[215]

After synthesizing identity theories and considering the contribution of practitioners, Green presents three layers of identity: core (similar to Beit-Hallahmi's "ego-identity"), social, and collective identity (see Figure 6).

---

210. Green, "Conversion in the Light," 43.

211. Gillespie, *Dynamics of Religious Conversion*, 132.

212. Gillespie, 139.

213. Gillespie, 140–41.

214. Mol, *Identity and the Sacred*, 59.

215. Beit Hallahmi, as quoted in Green, "Conversion in the Light," 44.

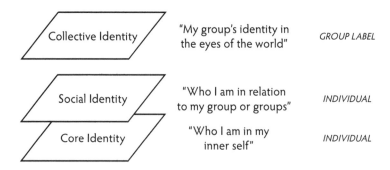

Figure 6. Identity at Three Levels[216]

First, "core identity" – displayed at the bottom of Figure 6 – is an individual level of identity. Core identity, which is also called ego or personal (or, religiously speaking, spiritual) identity, can be defined as "the inner heart of a person's self-awareness and worldview, first formed as young children subconsciously internalize their parents' value and outlook."[217] Green agrees with Beit-Hallahmi's emphasis on the role of religion in forming ego (core) identity, saying, "religion gains its power on the individual level when it becomes tied to one's ego-identity, when it is imbued with high ego-involvement."[218] As Gillespie comments, religious conversion is a key factor in changing and formatting the core (personal) level of identity. "It is personal identity which most closely correlates with the self-integration of religious conversion or return."[219] A follower of *'Isa*, who has new belief in *'Isa* as Lord and Savior, begins to realize who he is in his new relationship with *'Isa* from this core identity level.

Second, "social identity" is also an individual level of identity, but it includes the thinking and influence of one's community, family, and friends. Tim Green defines social identity as "who I am in relation to my group or groups."[220] In the context of Islam, a Muslim's social identity is mostly assumed

---

216. Image taken from Green, 44.
217. Green, 46.
218. Beit Hallahmi, as quoted in Green, 47.
219. Gillespie, *Dynamics of Religious Conversion*, 139.
220. Green, "Conversion in the Light," 44.

rather than chosen. Green comments on the religious social identity which is assimilated with family and community in an Islamic context, saying,

> Religious social identity is initially internalized, like other social identities, within the boundaries of the family. Most people are simply born into a religion, rather than choosing one. Islam as a social identity is more often assumed than chosen, at least in traditional Muslim societies, for it is woven into the fabric of daily life. The Muslim creed is whispered into one's ears at birth and recited over one's corpse in death.[221]

How can we apply these insights to social identity of MBBs in a Muslim-majority context? Hans J. Mol mentions that core identity and social identity are closely related and must be negotiated. "Personal (core) and social identity very much depend on one another, but there are also numerous possibilities for conflict between the two."[222] In this sense, the social identity of MBBs begins with the experience of conversion (or religious change) at the core identity level and applies to the person's belonging among either Muslims or Christians – or in between the two. It is also related to their acquaintance with the specific social group by significant others' or their own decision.

Third, collective identity relates to how others – such as, perhaps, the majority Muslim community – recognize the groups of believers, whether as "Christians," "Muslims," or something in between. This level signifies "our" identity on a group level, "my groups' identity in the eyes of the world."[223]

Kathryn Kraft distinguishes collective identity from social identity by noting that social identity is associated with an individual, while collective identity is associated with a symbolic group.

> Collective identity must be distinguished from social identity. . . . Social identity is merely an individual type of identity whose main influence is interpersonal, or social, relationship. Collective identity is an identity that is rooted in a symbolic group or a social category. In fact, an individual does not necessarily have a relationship with others who share a collective

---

221. Green, 46.
222. Mol, *Identity and the Sacred*, 65.
223. Green, "Conversion in the Light," 45–47.

identity; what matters is a cognitively-based sense of belonging to a group.[224]

She also sheds additional light on Tim Green's three levels of identity by defining and distinguishing core (individual) identity in terms of personal characteristics, social identity in terms of social interactions, and collective identity in terms of group belonging. "While individual identity is usually defined in terms of personality and development, and social identity is defined in social interactions such as a person's job and friendships, collective identity is about the social structures and groups in which a person roots him/herself."[225]

In an article from *Longing for Community*, "Identity choices at the border zone," Tim Green introduces two circles of identity, which illustrate religious boundaries deeply related to social community and cultural activities (Figure 7).[226]

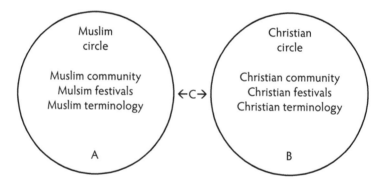

Figure 7. Circles of Identity[227]

As we see in this diagram, these different religious backgrounds have their own communities, festivals, and terminology. Historically in Bangladesh, these two religious communities have hardly shared religious festivals and terminology. If a Muslim in Bangladesh comes to faith to Christ, the person who converts inevitably crosses their former boundaries and moves toward the other. Practically speaking, however, many new MBBs are hard to place

---

224. Kraft, "Community and Identity," 165.
225. Kraft, 176.
226. Green, "Identity Choices."
227. This figure is taken from Green, 53.

exactly in one circle or the other. Rather, they say they are somewhere in between (position C). Also, MBBs might switch their behaviors and socioreligious identity depending on their surroundings, where they are and who they are with.[228] They might, for example, celebrate Eids or Christmas and Easter with their two different groups of religious friends. This may be done openly or secretly.[229]

Due to the social and religious complexity of MBBs' identity in a context like Bangladesh, Green suggests the use of categories focused on "social identity." He provides the following description of the four different groups of MBBs in Bangladesh, as explained to him by an indigenous MBB leader Abu Taher Chowdhury when they met in Dhaka in 2008:[230]

> Christian – The first group is made up of the ones we call "Christian." They are completely assimilated in the traditional church with its festivals, language, and social relationships. They no longer have any contact with their Muslim relatives.

> Isai – In the second group are the ones called *Isai*. They mostly live in the Christian community but preserve a little contact with their Muslim relatives, visit them at *Eid*, and so on. They switch between Christian and Muslim terminology according to the group they are with. The Christians tend to understand the need of *Isais* to compromise in this way; their Muslim relatives view them as heretical but not beyond the bounds of social contact.

> *Isai* Muslim – Next we have what I call "*Isai* Muslim." They are mostly in the Muslim community but they preserve a little contact with Christians. They use Muslim terminology. Many in the Christian community view them as "fake Christians." Muslims view them as an odd kind of Muslim, but acceptable within the range of Muslim sects.

---

228. In his dissertation, John Cheong uses the term socioreligious identity considering the complex condition of Malay Christian identity. Cheong, "Socio-Religious Identity."

229. Green, "Identity Choices," 54.

230. Green, 59.

Muslim – Finally we have those who follow Jesus but are called "Muslims." They remain within the Muslim community, follow Muslim customs, celebrate Muslim festivals, and use only Muslim terminology. They have no contact with Christians [as described in the first category above]. They are considered as Muslim by the Muslim community and also by the Christian community. Within this last group there are two kinds of people: one kind say they are Muslim but do not attend the mosque or carry out the *Eid* sacrifice. They keep full contact with their Muslim relatives, who would regard them as religiously slack but nevertheless Muslim. Believers in this group meet for fellowship with each other. The other kind observe religious Muslim practices, including prayer at the mosque and the sacrifice at *Eid*. Others around them do not know they are followers of Jesus. And they do not meet up with other Jesus-followers either.[231]

Members of the "Christian" group are excluded by their Muslim relatives but incorporated within the traditional Christian community and religious activities. "*Isai*" and "*Isai* Muslims" have varying amounts of contact with Christians and Muslims, with *Isai* Muslims more accommodating than *Isai* Muslims to the majority Muslim community than *Isai*. Members of the "Muslim" group identify themselves as Muslims, and other Muslims and Christians recognize them as Muslims, regardless of their attendance of mosque and *Eid* sacrifice.

Using the circles of identity in Figure 7, Green provides a diagram (Figure 8) that can advance discussions of social identity categorization. It is slightly different from the Christ-centered community spectrum (C-spectrum) because he uses practical terminology used by actual MBBs to discuss each social identity. Also, as Green explains, Bangladesh has a more mature MBB community than Pakistan due to the two countries' different historical and social situations.[232] The diagram below reflects the "multi-dimensional realities of the situation" and reflects the presence of a mature community that makes the situation in Bangladesh different from those of other Muslim-majority countries such as Pakistan or the Middle Eastern countries. Using

---

231. Green, 59.
232. Green, 62.

Paul Hiebert's concept of "bounded sets" and "fuzzy sets," Green describes the Bangladeshi MBB community as having "more ambiguous social identities and more permeable boundaries" than a "long-established religious community."[233] All four "fuzzy" groups of MBBs in Bangladesh sometimes "merge and overlap with each other and with the traditional communities."[234]

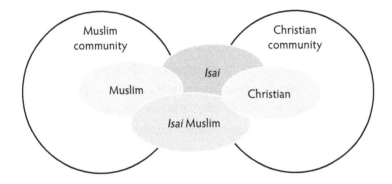

Figure 8. Groups of Believers from a Muslim Background in Bangladesh[235]

From my point of view, it is possible to compare Travis's C-Spectrum with Green's alternative categorization, even though the two cannot be directly matched: C1 and 2 – Christian; C2–C3 – *Isai*; C4 – *Isai* Muslim; C5 – Muslim. These two scales are similar, but Green's view, which was developed in consultation with an indigenous leader, moves one step forward by reflecting contextual details, using local terminology, and providing a visual representation of four groups.

Coping Strategies and Integration

Most of the MBBs interviewed by Tim Green expressed the perplexity of belonging to two communities simultaneously. Green analyzes their social identity in their inevitable dilemma of dual belonging by interacting with all three layers of identity, including core and collective identity. Using the illustration of a person who has two passports and can choose the more convenient one depending on the circumstances, Green introduces three coping

---

233. Green, 60.
234. Green, 61–62.
235. This figure is taken from Green, 60.

strategies for the dual identity holder: switching, suppression, and synthesis. First, the "switching" strategy involves changing their identity depending on their immediate situation and preference. Switching is expressed as changing behaviors and/or terminology. Second, a person employing the "suppression" strategy "gravitates to one group and lifestyle, suppressing the other side of [his]/her social identity and pretending this makes no difference at the core level." Third, the "synthesis" strategy tries to pursue a third, alternative culture, creating a position between the border zone of the two social identities.[236]

In her dissertation, Kathryn Ann Kraft[237] adapted Yang's theory[238] regarding immigrant converts' identity to discuss MBBs' identity. She introduces three options for integrating their two social belongings: fragmentary integration, fusive integration, and adhesive integration. Fragmentary integration occurs when one identity is dominant, even while a person adopts some behaviors and values of a second. Fusive integration involves blending the two different styles, but not completely fitting into one or the other. Adhesive integration, which Yang considers the best identity for immigrants, "can be a functional way to interact with people in a variety of different social settings" without losing either identity.[239] Kraft also agrees that "the same might apply to most of the participants" in her study of Arab MBB identity.[240] In this sense, Kraft maintains that MBBs, by naming themselves "followers of *Isa*" rather than "Christians," can redefine their identity, distinguishing their "religion from [their] ethnicity" and adhering to Christ without changing to become a Christian ethnically.[241] Complexity exists, however, when we apply adhesive identity integration to MBBs in diverse Muslim-majority contexts.

> Adhesive identity integration is much easier to achieve among Muslim-background followers of a Christian faith in contexts where there is not a pre-existing Christian community, and in places where nation identity is not tightly wrapped up in Islamic religious tradition. In North African countries, for example,

---

236. Green, 56–57.

237. Kraft, "Community and Identity."

238. Yang, *Chinese Christians in America*, 183–185.

239. Kraft, "Community and Identity," 172.

240. Kraft, 172.

241. Kraft, 175.

converts previously saw their Moroccan or Tunisian identities as including the Muslim religion but they also were aware that this was not always the case.

As MBBs, they argue that leaving Islam to follow Christianity does not negate their national identity. In the Middle East countries, including Lebanon and Egypt, there is a strong historical Christian community which functions as a distinct ethnicity. Adhering a Christian identity to a Muslim identity is complicated by the difficult relations between Christian and Muslim ethnic groups throughout many centuries.[242]

In Bangladesh, "Christians" are perceived to have a different ethnicity from Bengali Muslims, but the terms "Bengalis" or "Bangladeshis" have ethnic and national connotations, not religious ones. If we apply this adhesive identity integration to Bangladeshi MBBs, I think they could develop adhesive integration to Bengali ethnic or Bangladeshi national identity without emphasizing the changed characteristics of their MBB identity.

MBBs in Bangladesh Literature and Research Done in Bangladesh

There are a few Bangladeshi documents that provide helpful insight into the situation of Bangladeshi MBBs and their faith community (jama'at). These documents, originally written and published in Bangla, were translated by skillful local translators at my request. The document authors, such as Abu Taher and Chanchul Kashem, are considered MBB leaders in Bangladesh.

MBBs in Bangladeshi Literature

Abu Taher – who also interviewed with Tim Green and helped him to draw the diagram of four groups of MBBs in Bangladesh – wrote a very helpful article to understand the situation of the jama'at in Bangladesh.[243] In his article "Society of Bangladesh: The Obstacles to Build Up jama'at/somaj," he first describes the history of Bangladeshi MBB jama'ats since 1975 and

---

242. Kraft, 174–75.
243. Taher, "Society of Bangladesh."

influence of the publication of the *Kitab* for setting up *jama'ats* around the country. "In our country, the placing of *Jama'at* started from 1975 in larger populations . . . and after coming on hand of the translated version of the Bible of adapting fully national language, *Kitabul Mukaddash* (*Kitab*), around in [*sic*] 1977 to 1980, the work of establishing *Jama'at* had been started."[244] After observing that the *jama'ats* have not grown much in spite of relatively increasing numbers of *'Isa* believers, Abu Taher identifies seven obstacles to the establishment of *jama'ats* in Bangladesh and provides several suggestions to help solve these present difficult situations. The following is a translation of his discussion of the seven obstacles:

1. Substandard of the leaders: Most of the leaders do not read the Scripture, do not sit down for family worship, do not attend regular weekly worship, and do not do offering for God's activities. . . . The most lamentable thing is that most leaders of MBBs do not have membership of any *jama'at* and they don't have practical experience of pastoral work. So, even if someone came to *'Isa*, it is hard to find examples of being built up strongly in his faith.

2. Lack of Scripture's education and knowledge: Even though the *jama'at* was established, it is difficult to find established case of the *jama'at* in light of the *Kitab*. It is because of the lack of teaching of the *Kitab*, lack of experience, lack or real examples, and lack of courageous persons in faith.

3. Crisis of self-identification (identity): The most difficult things among our obstacles is the crisis of our self-identification. Until now, a follower of *'Isa* is not sure what kinds of identity they have. Someone lives on with Christian identity, or *Isai* identity, or *Isai* Muslim identity, or directly Muslim identity. For the issue of which identity is required, most *Isais* have had conflicts among them. As a result, the *Isai* society have not stood strong. Instead of respecting the other identity groups, they are busy criticizing each other about their minor mistakes.

---

244. Taher, 1.

4. Fear of fanatic fundamentalism: The increasing Islamic fundamentalism creates their fear. Additionally, the fear of being dishonored, being ostracized, being minority, and losing their jobs also create barriers to build up strong *jama'ats*.

5. Lack of fixed worship place. They are uncertain about gathering every week. They have inferiority complex due to lack of secured place to gather.

6. Vulnerable to move frequently for getting jobs and income.

7. Lack of cases of self-supporting *jama'at*: It is hard to find self-supporting *jama'ats* through members' offerings and tithes excluding foreign funds.[245]

Abu Taher also provides several suggestions about how to remove obstacles by setting up short and long-term goals. Short-term goals for speedy resolution of problems of *jama'ats* include (a) giving/delegating responsibilities, (b) fixing a specific place for worship, and (c) regulating the gathering and giving importance of *jama'at* gatherings.[246] Long-term goals for stabilizing the *jama'ats* are associated with "5–10–20–30 periodic yearly planning," and include (a) developing *Isai* leaders in various areas and jobs such as doctors, lawyers, engineers, businessmen, and theologians, and (b) building Scripture-based maturity and infrastructure. He concludes by describing his hope for a *jama'at* that is enlightened by Scripture and for leaders who are shaped by Christ's power and self-sacrificing. His narration of the obstacles currently facing *jama'ats* in Bangladesh corresponds closely with the results of my interviews. His encouragement of systematic change of *jama'ats* in Bangladesh through long-term and short-term plans is relevant.[247]

Chanchul Mahmud Kashem has written two insightful articles in Bangla about MBBs' society: "Actual *Isai Somaj* should have established" and "Needs of more concentration about preaching the gospel into the majority group."[248] These two articles provide background information on the relationship between traditional Christians and converted *Isa* followers' groups and prerequisite information for reaching out to the majority. Kashem deals with two

---

245. Taher, 1–3.
246. Taher, 3.
247. Taher, 3.
248. Kashem, "Actual *Isai Somaj*,"; Kashem, "Needs of More Concentration."

groups of MBBs: traditional *Isais* and converted *Isais*. These groups correspond to "Christians" and "*Isai*" in the vocabulary of social identity described by Abu Taher with Tim Green.[249]

In his first article, Kashem begins his argument by distinguishing between two groups of *Isais*: traditional and converted.[250] Kashem uses the term "*Isai*" as it is used in the *Kitab*, to mean "follower of Jesus." In his terminology, then, "traditional *Isai*" are Hindu- or traditional-background Christians, distinguishable from converted *Isai* (MBB) by differences in culture and background.

Kashem asks traditional *Isai* (Christians) – who usually do not trust converted *Isai* and do not let them go to their families during the *Eid* festival – not to discriminate against converted *Isai*. Traditional Christians, mostly converted from a Hindu or other non-Islamic religious background, have been influenced by foreign missions, especially from Western cultures. These traditional believers have sometimes introduced themselves as *Isai* by wearing cross on their necks or hangings photos of a film portrayal of Jesus on their walls. Kashem argues that being an *Isai* is not about wearing a cross on the neck, but about bearing a cross for 'Isa in everyday life. He continues by arguing that because traditional *Isai* [Christian] groups are still running organizations and denominations, they are discriminating against converted *Isai* by not allowing them to continue their family relationships with Muslims – by, for example, forbidding Eid visits – and by imposing traditional Christian cultural practices such as adopting names like Michael and Paul. Rather, he criticizes traditional groups' mindset of doing business with religion and argues for a harmonious society of real *Isai* believers:

> So, *Isai* society was put into confused situation by mixed culture. . . . I am not arguing to make new *Isai* society because it is also the work of dividing Christ. But, we need to discern the businessman. They don't know the feeling of leaving family. Why do they discriminate converted *Isai* and not trust them? They were born in *Isai* whether they actually follow 'Isa or not. If *Isais* were real *Isais*, the society would be changed. Actually, they have made 'Isa as their capital of their business. . . . We should avoid

---

249. Green, "Identity Choices," 59–60.
250. Kashem, "Actual *Isai Somaj*."

our egoism. We should try to establish fraternity. Our motive of our life should be an *Isai* by believing on [*sic*] *'Isa*. It is written in the *Kitab* that you all are the son[s] of God by believing on [*sic*] *'Isa*. . . . Therefore, the *Isai* should avoid all other distances [*sic*] each other and try to accept the ideal of *'Isa* so that they can build a real *Isai* society.[251]

Kashem's second article offers a good guideline for reaching out to the majority.[252] After mentioning the stagnation of the Christian population of Bangladesh below one percent of the total in spite of numerous missional investments, he suggests two important guidelines for more effective outreach: proper (Muslim-friendly) language and proper identity (without changing names) among evangelists.

Firstly, the language of the *Isais*: *Isais* need a clear concept about using the language where they are going to preach. If there is any mix-up, they would be failed. For sharing the Good News, language is vital, so, with whom it will share *Isais* need to know the language and culture before.

Secondly, the identity of *Isais*: It is a big issue when you share the Gospel to others. After conversion, many people are easily changing their name, like Michel, Hubert, Mary . . . etc. The Bible taught us to change our soul and mind, but not the name or the out looking [*sic*]. But some people try to understand that without changing name, dress and language, a man cannot be a good believer. . . . By using the weakness of the new believer, some leader is changing people's name in [*sic*] the baptism time. On the other hand, the traditionals are not changing their name at all. So, why this kind of discrimination is only for the majority background believers?[253]

After describing the importance of these two criteria for evangelism to the majority population, Kashem mentions two points of caution regarding the

---

251. Kashem, 7.

252. Kashem, "Needs of More Concentration."

253. Kashem, 8.

importance of evangelists' identity in Bangladeshi context and the need to avoid preaching Western culture:

> For sharing the Gospel in this country, the identity of the preacher is very important. The *Isai* are the people of this country. On the other side, some people are presenting the western culture before introducing about Jesus, which are opposites [*sic*] from Bengali culture too. That is why people avoid everything. If someone receives Jesus, they just hide themselves to save [themselves] from social violence. They cannot identify themselves as *Isai* [Christian] or as one of the majority [Muslim].[254]

He concludes by asking organizational leaders to send their evangelists for good training before they begin preaching to the majority.

> They are playing only a limited and very common word about salvation. Because of limited knowledge about the evangelism and organization's order, they are in wrong dimension by following only the organization's order. They don't mind about ethics and morality. By the way, this evangelist became a doll by rolling the role play. For working, they are choosing the minority peoples area rather than the majority.[255]

Two MBB Studies in Bangladesh

Jonas Adelin Jørgensen's doctoral dissertation, "Jesus Imandars and Christ Bhaktas: Report from Two Field Studies of Interreligious Hermeneutics and Identity in Globalized Christianity," is worth mentioning for its discussion of the Bangladeshi context and insider believers from a Muslim background. According to a summary version of his dissertation published in *International Bulletin of Missionary Research (IBMR)*, Jørgensen researched two cases of the insider movement among Muslims in Bangladesh and Hindus in India. In his field research in Dhaka, Bangladesh, he found a Bengali term being used to describe 'Isa followers: *Isa imandars*, which means "those faithful to Jesus."[256] Jørgensen found that they gathered together in groups called *jama'at*

---

254. Kashem, 8.
255. Kashem, 9.
256. Jørgensen, "Jesus Imandars," 171.

(fellowship) in their private homes, and also found that *jama'at* functioned for "worship, prayer, sermons, and social interaction."[257] He focused on conducting interviews and observing "their liturgy, religious ideal and identity." He provides a descriptive narration of their *jama'at* liturgy, noting, for example, the difference between their free style prayer and formal Islamic prayer.[258]

In terms of *imandars'* religious ideal and identity, Jørgensen explains their self-understanding of *iman* (faith). In their perspective, faith is "not abstract knowledge or belief but must be existential and relational, expressed first and foremost as faithfulness."[259] Therefore, being a Jesus *imandar* means "to fix one's *iman* on Jesus . . . who as a spiritual master will mediate the divine and transform the believer through his very presence."[260] Most importantly, Jørgensen raises two crucial questions: (a) To what degree this commitment to Jesus is compatible with the life of the wider Muslim community and (b) Whether the *imandar* was still a Muslim.[261] To these questions, *imandars* answer on two different sides, half identifying themselves as Muslims, and half not:

> Although most agreed that a newly baptized *imandar* could continue participating in the local mosque, roughly half the informants no longer identified themselves as Muslims, while the other half accepted Mehrab's line of argumentation that identifying oneself as Muslim is significant, even if it takes some historical and textual exegesis: specifically, a Muslim aims to submit to the will of God, and so does the *imandar*.[262]

Jørgensen explains the understanding of *imandars* who self-identify as Muslims by taking the example of Paul's explanation of the process of "inner transformation" in Romans 12:2. He says,

> When the *imandar* becomes faithful to Jesus, inner transformation is initiated, and the result is a regenerated Muslim who does the will of God from the heart by following Jesus' example,

---

257. Jørgensen, 171.
258. Jørgensen, 171.
259. Jørgensen, 172.
260. Jørgensen, 172.
261. Jørgensen, 172.
262. Jørgensen, 172.

and who transcends divisions between institutional Christian churches and Islamic mosques. According to some of the *imandars*, this understanding allows for participation in any mosque (or church) because mosque prayers are simply outward and hold only relative value.[263]

In his dissertation, Jørgensen adds his explanations of genuine personal prayer, especially mentioning someone who experiences two kinds of prayer: formal (outward) and personal (inward).

> The formal and regulated Islamic prayers are expanded or substituted by personal and inwardly prayers. Significantly, this is not seen as a *problem* but as a *solution* to the shifting claims of loyalty. To become faithful to God through following Jesus thus seems to imply a *personal* engagement also in the realm of prayer. The *imandar* is free to engage in the structured mosque prayers *because* the genuine prayer *is not* conditioned by outwardly space or external structures but *only* by the inwardly and personal commitment, it is reasoned.[264]

This kind of understanding of prayer allows some *imandars* to participate in *namaz* (formal) prayer in the mosque. In particular, Jørgensen mentions *imandars'* practice of *shahada* during *namaz* prayer. He says one *imandar* named Belim simply stops after the first half of the creed (affirming one sovereign God) and silently adds that "Jesus is the Spirit of God or . . . word of God" instead of saying "Muhammad is the Prophet of God."[265] Jørgensen asked the participant whether the other Muslim participants in the *namaz* accept his participation. Belim answered that a few people know about his unique way because he sometimes argues with them, and he was not sure whether other Muslims accept him or not: "they accept it but in their mind maybe they don't accept."[266] Jørgensen judges that Belim's participation in *namaz* prayer in the mosque was not welcomed, but rather tolerated. His detailed analysis of Belim's participation continues:

---

263. Jørgensen, 172.

264. Jørgensen, *Jesus Imandars*, 161; italics in the original.

265. Jørgensen, 235–36.

266. Jørgensen, 236.

Belim does admit that he is not sure whether the other members of the mosque accept his identity as a Muslim and compares his situation with other marginal and doctrinally deviant groups in Islam. The few persons with whom he has discussed his understanding seem to be critical; nevertheless, they have tolerated his continued participation in the *namaz* prayers. Belim's story shows that the imandars' interpretation of what it "really" means to be a Muslim is not always accepted by more ritually orthodox Muslims. In Belim's case it seems justified to say that participation in *namaz* prayers by *Isa imandars* is tolerated rather than welcomed by other Muslims.[267]

In conclusion, Jørgensen hesitates to clearly judge whether this practice of *shahada* is syncretistic or not because *imandars* are "at the same time exclusivists, inclusivists, and pluralists, but they are so on different levels and in relation to various elements. A typology of this process would make it clear that the result of the translation is not simply 'syncretistic' or 'authentic.'"[268] He concludes that while it has certain tendencies of a mixed process [he calls it translation process] among Islamic, Bengali, and Christian theology, *imandars*' understanding of Jesus is authentic "in the sense that the centrality and exclusivity of Jesus Christ is affirmed."[269] His dissertation provides a more detailed analysis of this translation process, which involves "significant recombination and reinterpretation of various elements in the interaction between Islamic and Christian theological universe."[270]

To conclude, the way in which faith in Jesus is experienced, expressed, and apprehended is in usual "Islamic" and "Bengali" concepts. The process, through which the contextual meaning emerges, is clearly a syncretistic one, that is, a translation of elements – concepts and symbols – from Islamic theology and popular Bengali culture into a Christian theological universe. This translation is accompanied by a no less significant recombination and reinterpretation of various elements in the

---

267. Jørgensen, 236.
268. Jørgensen, "Jesus Imandars," 176.
269. Jørgensen, 176.
270. Jørgensen, *Jesus Imandars*, 259.

interaction between Islamic and Christian theological universe in Christology and the imandars' understanding of Jesus as embodied sinless-ness and sacrifice.[271]

John Stephenson (a pseudonym) conducted research in Bangladesh for his dissertation, "The Messiah of Honour: The Christology and Atonement of Followers of *Isa Masih*." He examined Bangladeshi MBBs' view of *'Isa* in contrast with the dominant notion of Bangladeshis, among whom "the prophet Muhammad . . . is seen as a saviour figure able to intercede with Allah and able to take his people to heaven."[272] Stephenson asked his respondents one question about their spiritual journey, using SQUIN (Single Question aimed at Inducing Narrative) methodology.[273] He also explored diverse themes such as "hierarchy, collectivism, patronage, and shame" from anthropological and historical perspectives.[274] He found that these four themes from social life are closely mirrored in his respondents' thinking about their spiritual life and final destiny. His finding is that the hierarchical Bengali culture, which is rooted in the collective and patriarchal nature of broad family units, brings about dynamics of patronage and dependency.[275] The Bengali concept of the patron who has power to support and protect a beneficiary has naturally been connected to spiritual realms and influenced Bengali Muslims to seek a mediator's intercession (*suparis*) from sufi *pirs* or Muhammad, who is generally seen by Bengali Muslims as an ultimate mediator (*supariskari*) who can take them to heaven. Stephenson explains further that his findings reveal

> how people look to patron[s], particularly a patron with spiritual power, with hopes, expectations and aspirations in four main areas: eschatological salvation and intercession before Allah; protection from malevolent forces; blessing and prosperity; and guidance on the path into mystical experience. This relied on the personal power of the patron; his *borkot* (aura and personal force) and *doya* (grace and favour). For many in Bangladesh[,] Muhammad embodies these and he is seen to fulfill their hope

---

271. Jørgensen, 259.

272. Stephenson, "Messiah of Honor," 2.

273. Stephenson, 25.

274. Stephenson, 2.

275. Stephenson, 36–38.

to pass through to heaven on the Day of Judgement. Rather than the *mukti* as *fana* (annihilation through union)[,] this is *najat/ mukti* as eschatological salvation where the role of Muhammad (and to a lesser extent, the *pir*) is to act as a broker-patron who stands between his dependants and Allah, the benefactor patron. As the pinnacle of patronage he brings salvation, bestows blessing and *borkot*, and protects from harm.[276]

Among MBBs, however, "a significant change had occurred. There had been a change in allegiance and loyalty away from Muhammad and toward *Isa al Mosiho*."[277] Two steps are involved in this change: *attention*, gained by attraction toward *'Isa* and *intention* "to investigate who he is, usually looking first to the Qur'an."[278] Stephenson also examines the concept of shame and "how shame is an important part of how *imandars* of *Isa Masi* see salvation."[279] Even though the concept of shame is externally expressed by respondents' direct voice, the sense of movement from shame and impurity to honor and cleanness by the work (death and resurrection) of *Isa al-Masih* are implied in their responses.[280] My own assessment is that Stephenson's work provides insight into a new dimension of contextualization practice and analysis by examining a culture deeply rooted in the historical and social background and theological frameworks of MBBs in a particular context.

Four-Self Concept and Its Application to MBB Community

In his article on the fourth self, Paul Hiebert introduces the three-self concepts (self-propagating, supporting, and governing) as historically debated and "finally adopted by mission agencies as their guidelines for establishing autonomous churches."[281] He adds a fourth self (self-theologizing). This fourth concept relates to whether local churches "have the right to read and interpret the Scriptures for themselves,"[282] and was applied to various contexts,

---

276. Stephenson, 195.
277. Stephenson, 196.
278. Stephenson, 196.
279. Stephenson, 200.
280. Stephenson, 201.
281. Hiebert, *Anthropological Insights*, 194.
282. Hiebert, 196.

including African and Korean theologies. His explanation of the four-self movement is worth quoting at length:

> Self-propagating: The first principle, self-propagation, pointed to one of the weakness[es] of the early mission movement. The missionaries had planted churches, but often these churches had no vision for evangelizing their own people or sending missionaries to other cultures. Local leaders saw these tasks as the work of the original missionary. It became clear that young churches do not automatically become evangelically minded. That vision must be as consciously taught and modeled as the rest of Christian life.[283]

> Self-support: The second principle, self-support, raised more debate. Missionaries argued that young churches should learn to support themselves, that continued reliance on outside support created a dependency that hindered their maturation and growth. Missionaries also pointed out that the young churches would gain a sense of autonomy and equality only if they were self-supporting. In a sense[,] the missionaries were right.[284]

> Self-governing: The third principle, self-governance, raised the most disagreement. Ironically, here the tables were turned. Young churches wanted the power to make their own decisions, arguing that they would never mature until they had self-rule. The missionaries were reluctant to give up their power for fear that inexperience and local politics would ruin the church.[285]

> Self-theologizing: Do young churches have the right to read and interpret the Scriptures for themselves? . . . Most of the converts have simple theologies and accept with little question the theological teachings of the missionary. There are exceptions, of course, particularly among well-educated converts who were formerly leaders in other religions. After two or three generations, there emerge leaders who have been raised with

---

283. Hiebert, 194.
284. Hiebert, 194.
285. Hiebert, 195.

Christian teachings and trained in biblical exegesis. It is these leaders who often raise difficult theological questions. How does the gospel speak to their culture? What is the relationship of Christianity to the non-Christian religions in their land? And how does Christianity answer the basic questions being asked by the people?[286]

Researching the four-self dynamics of MBBs' community can be an examining tool of Bangladeshi MBBs' initiative for their own and communities' present and future development. Even though there have been debates regarding separate variables of each four criteria, Robert Priest's research has demonstrated the plausibility of "a single unitary construct," as the four factors show positive correlation with each other.[287]

Emphasizing the four-self characteristics of the apostolic movement's spreading and organic nature, Hirsch and Catchim in *Permanent Revolution* rename the four "selfs" as follows: self-generating (propagating), self-organizing (governing), self-sustaining (supporting), and self-reflecting (theologizing).[288] Researching MBBs' intention and know-how for self-generating in the Muslim majority society reveals the possibility of enhancing the gospel movement beyond the level of just managing their own lives. One may also wonder whether or not MBBs use similarities between Christian and Islamic beliefs when they share the gospel. The self-organizing and self-sustaining traits are related to continuity with the next generation of MBBs' community, minimizing the uncertain factor of missionary presence and maximizing local initiative. Self-reflecting refers to how they apply their understanding of Scripture to their own particular Muslim-majority society and culture.

In conclusion, researching these four-self dynamics in the context of Bangladeshi MBBs provides a good view into the present social dynamics and future prospects of MBBs and their development of their own faith community. It also helps us understand how they are interacting with the majority society for themselves, both with and without foreigners' cooperation and intervention.

---

286. Hiebert, 196.

287. Priest, "Researching Contextualization," 311–16.

288. Hirsch and Catchim, *Permanent Revolution*, Kindle.

Chapter Summary

This chapter has reviewed relevant precedent literature regarding the topic of the social identity of MBBs. The first section dealt primarily with the insider movement, the subject of one of the most popular debates about current missions toward Muslim. The relevant issue of religious dual belonging was introduced as well. The second section examined the social identity of MBBs using Tim Green's recent research and other relevant literature, especially works written by Bangladeshi authors and research conducted in Bangladesh.

The first part of this literature review began with the possibility of religious dual belonging, especially in a Muslim-majority context. Authors such as Geffre and Tan agree that this does exist, and Tan believes dual religious belonging is permissible within the insider movement as a legitimate paradigm in the Asian religious context, though he rejects syncretistic multiple religious belonging that embraces pluralistic theology. The second part of literature review examined key issues – such as C4/C5 identity and C5 believers' participation in Islamic religious activities – from both theological/biblical and missiological/anthropological perspectives. After discussing the diverse issues regarding the insider movement, I introduced Asad's suggestions regarding an appropriate C5 paradigm, and provided my own multidisciplinary assessments. In the third part, I used Tim Green's precedent research to focus on my research problems regarding Bangladeshi MBBs' social identity. In the last part, I introduced discussions of Bangladeshi MBBs' identity issues produced either by Bangladeshis or based on research in Bangladesh. In addition, I looked at Bangladeshi MBB *jama'ats'* from a four-self perspective, which may assist in both examination and prediction related to MBB society in Bangladesh.

CHAPTER 4

Research Findings

The primary purpose of this research is to explore the social identity of MBBs in Bangladesh by answering three research questions concerning (1) new social identity formation; (2) social integration of MBBs with the majority people; and (3) social identity of MBBs on a collective level regarding perceptions and four-self issue. This study is based on observation and individual interviews of MBBs, as well as two focus group interviews and interviews with foreign workers.

Restatement of Research Questions

The research was directed by three research questions:

1. What factors were involved in MBBs coming to identify themselves as followers of 'Isa? Have the ways in which MBBs identify themselves religiously changed since their conversion?
2. To what extent and in what ways are MBBs integrated into the social and cultural fabric of the broader Muslim community life?
3. To what extent and in what ways do MBBs think there is continuity and discontinuity between their own beliefs and practices and those of Muslims around them? Do their views affect whether, or how, they share the gospel with Muslims? Do they also pursue a self-standing (four-self) faith community in the long run?

There are several sub-questions associated with each research question; these are dealt with through the rearrangement, coding, and analysis of the data for each research question.

New Social Identity Formation and Identity Change (RQ1)

The first research question seeks to identify factors involved in MBBs' identity change following their conversion. Four themes emerged during the coding of the data relevant to this question: (1) family and society background; (2) background of faith in 'Isa and factors of their belief; (3) others' responses and changes (inner/outer); and (4) social identity and identity change.

Family and Society Background before Believing in 'Isa

All respondents were from a Muslim background, but they belonged to a diverse range of Islamic practices and family and village backgrounds. Nineteen respondents (39.5%) were from families that strictly observed most Islamic regulations. They kept regular *namaz* prayers at the mosque and served at their local mosques following their fathers' examples. Four respondents were the sons or grandsons of local imams, and two of them were imams themselves. The other twenty-nine respondents had experienced various levels of participation at their local mosques, from irregular participation in Islamic prayer at the mosque, to almost no participation in Islamic activities in their families. F03 commented that his friends "who came to faith in Jesus were not very religious Muslims." U07, however, commented that "there are no specific *mulla* (strict or strong in Bangla) Muslims, but Muslims are Muslims." This means that even though some Muslims do not participate in Islamic activities in the mosques, they also have to follow certain rules and regulations to live in a Muslim society.

I01 grew up in a wealthy and highly respected Muslim family which is open to people of other religions. The people in the village loved his father, a successful businessman who helped the poor in the village.

> The Hindu population in my village was big and many leadership positions were held by Hindus. Our family was a cultural family and open. My family had good relationships with Hindus.

Union members came to my house freely. Sitting and eating together with followers of other religions was not restricted in my house.

U10 said, "My father was a normal Muslim who worked hard and was respected by village members. His word was guaranteed at the court without proof, but he did not pray at the mosque."

In contrast, E04 was from an imam's family, and E04 and S02 were imams themselves before their conversion. E04 said, "My grandfather was *hazi* [someone who has gone on a pilgrimage to Mecca], and my father was an imam, and I also did imam's work for about five years in the village mosque. My uncle and younger brother are doing imam's work in the local mosque." S02 said, "I was born in a strict Muslim family and was imam of a big mosque. When I taught at the mosque, I got paid around ten thousand taka ($150) for two hours." Some respondents, such as I02, respected Muhammad very much in spite of their low level of practice of Islamic regulations. I02 said, "Before I believed in 'Isa, I respected our *nabi* ["prophet," referring to Muhammad] and I celebrated his birthday even though I did not follow the five time regular prayers at the mosque, and I also hated Christians."

Background of Faith in 'Isa and Factors of MBBs' Faith

The forty-eight Bangladeshi MBB respondents came to faith in 'Isa in diverse ways. Though most MBBs have multiple reasons to believe in 'Isa, four categories can be identified: (1) cognitive; (2) affective/relational; (3) experiential; and (4) other factors, including occupational influences, negative feelings toward Islam, and mixed reasons.

Cognitive Factors

Twenty-seven MBBs (56%) mentioned that small booklets and the Bible – the most mentioned are the *Injil Sharif* (the New Testament) and the *Kitab* (*Mussolmani* Bangla version of the Bible) – helped them to have faith in 'Isa. Most started with small booklets or the Qur'an before reading the Bible or the *Injil Sharif*. Their intellectual curiosity about another religion or way of salvation led them to read these books. They were surprised and inspired by the stories and character of 'Isa (Jesus).

From small booklets or the Qur'an to *Injil Sharif*

Several respondents (H01, N01, E04, U11) mentioned that small booklets raised their curiosity about *'Isa* and *Injil Sharif*. When H01 returned home from his work, he bought small booklets at a very cheap price in the market. At that time he did not fully understand what it meant because it was "traditional Bible language" (the Bible version using Hindu religious language). N01 and U11 mentioned similar books called "Certainly Go to the Heaven" (N01) and "The Way to Go to Heaven from the Light of the Qur'an" (U11). These books contained qur'anic *ayat* (verses) talking about the necessity to read the *Kitab* (the Holy Book) and stories about *'Isa Mosiho* (Messiah). U11 said, "After I read the small booklet, I was clear. Then, I started to read the *Kitab* and *Injil*, especially the book of John. And I certainly came to believe in *'Isa*." N01 tried to find the author of the small booklet and finally met him.

> I found a book named "Certainly Go to the Heaven" and I wanted to know the author's identity. I found him because he lived in the same district with me. Then he said he was an *Isai* Muslim. He was very afraid to see me. I checked his bag, but found only some books. Then, I started to read the book and there were some *ayats* [verses] from the Qur'an. And the book gave me hundred percent certainty to go to heaven.

E04 and H04 joined a week-long training course about God's way in the Qur'an. That training talked about *'Isa* and the way of salvation by *'Isa* using only the Qur'an. The training was organized by Al-Sunni (pseudonym) using Western funding; it was taught by both Western and local teachers. During the training, teachers did not use any biblical references, but only verses from the Qur'an and Bangla Qur'an.[1] E04 and H04 were baptized when they finished

---

1. This organization had a central headquarter and several training places around Bangladesh. During my interview with H04, he explained his work with this organization. They taught initial seminar/training attendees using only the Qur'an during a week-long residential seminar/training, but they offered follow-up courses that employed the Qur'an and the Bible together. H04 worked for Al-Sunni for eight years as an evangelist away from his hometown. "That time, I was working like an *Isai* Muslim. We taught five times *namaz* prayer and introduced *'Isa* in qur'anic way. For example, I preached that there was one *suparishkari* [mediator to bring them to heaven] using Qur'an verses such as *Al-Imran*." In this way, he preached about *'Isa* as a Muslim or an *Isai* Muslim. There were verses about baptism, *pak-koshol* [holy bath] in the Qur'an. They asked the attendees, about whether they want to get *pak-koshol* or not on the last day of the six-day seminar. Foreigners also came to teach and provided funds for training. Soon after he joined there, H04 realized all the situations and strategies in this organization. He asked

the one-week seminar. They said the concept of baptism also can be found in the Qur'an as the meaning of the holy bath. H08 said that after reading the Bangla Qur'an and the *Kitab* (Holy Book referring to *Mussolmani* Bible), he was enlightened and said that the *Kitab* is "ours" (Muslims').

> Now I read the *Kitab* because my eyes are opened. I think this is our *Kitab*, our Islamic *Kitab*. I read a lot and studied. When I was reading the Arabic Qur'an, nothing came to my mind, but after reading the Bangla Qur'an I realized the meaning little by little. Through help of the leader of this *jama'at*, I can fully read Bangla and read the *Kitab*. I realized that the idea of faith in Muhammad was wrong.

Intellectual curiosity about the Bible from their early years
Some MBBs had contact with small booklets or the Bible in their early years (S01, S05, U02, U12, E04). E04 bought "a sixteen-page book for one taka in class seven [around 13 years old]." S01 had become curious during his study at the madrassa.

> From my early years, I have had curiosity about who Christians are and what they believe. What are the holy books for Christians? What is in the *Injil Sharif*? When I was studying in early years in a high school level madrassa, I barely got *Injil Sharif* outside of the madrassa. There were similar verses like the Qur'an. It was written that "*Isa* is the Savior."

Correspondence courses also played a vital role in the early years of several MBBs' faith journeys (H04, L01, I01, I02, I04). I01 started to respond to the Bible correspondence course when he was thirteen years old, and L01 joined the course when he was eighteen. I02 found a flyer on the street about a Bible correspondence course by an Assemblies of God church and he contacted

---

the local director of the organization saying, "I am sure you are a [converted] Christian, and why are you pretending to be a Muslim and a Muslim organization?" The director answered that "this is not the time to open. Later." I asked H04 about why they did not teach the Bible. He said that they did it gradually. Later, they taught the *Kitabs (Taurat, Zabur,* and *Injil)* too. He said, "During this process, I was slowly revealed as an *Isai*." But the organization was closed after persecution by Islamic groups around ten years ago. After the organization [Al-Sunni] closed, the director became sick and H04 also came back home. From that time, the people in the mosque forbade him from entering his hometown mosque.

them. He came to believe in 'Isa after he finished a two-year course, searched for Christians and found that Christians are not bad persons.

> In 1983, I joined *Khodar Pot* [God's Way] course by "International Correspondence Institute" run by AG. During the two years course, I came to know 'Isa and was changed. I got a certificate and searched for Christians. I heard from mosque imams that Christians drink alcohol and eat pork. After I met Christians, I realized that it was wrong.

Contents of the Bible and feelings on first reading it

When MBBs read the Bible and *Injil*, they were surprised and inspired by the characteristics and life of 'Isa. When U12 read the *Injil*, he found that "'Isa gave his own life for others' salvation. He is the person who gives us the salvation, freedom, and rest that no prophet has brought." N01 confessed that he had never read the *Injil* before and was "astonished," saying,

> I had never read the *Injil*. After I read the small booklet, I was motivated to read the *Injil* and became astonished that this book bears testimony of the Qur'an, *Taurat*, and *Jabur*. And the person 'Isa, no one created him and one day he will come to this world again and he is the person who gives salvation to people. Then, my mind changed automatically and thought that this person can be followed. When I read the history of different *nabis* and *rasuls* [prophets], I found that every one of them was guilty, but 'Isa is pure and innocent.

I found it interesting that there were no reports of negative responses toward the gospel of 'Isa or to the Bible when these respondents received it. I can suggest two reasons for this. First, small booklets might have played a role in nullifying their negative responses. My respondents had read small booklets that contained nothing negative about 'Isa but suggested a true way using qur'anic verses and Islamic terminology. Second, these respondents experienced long spiritual quests. They might have sometimes responded negatively to tbeir Muslim family members and neighbors when questioned during their long journeys. They took a long time – five to ten years from the first time they touched the gospel of 'Isa to their final decision to follow him. Also, they may not have mentioned any negative responses to the Bible because I did not specifically ask about their previous negative responses to the gospel of 'Isa, and I had only asked them how they came to believe in 'Isa.

Affective/Relational Factors

People of Bangladesh are very relational in comparison with people living in an individualistic culture. They love to have chats in tea shops on the streets in their localities, and they are very friendly to their guests, including unfamiliar people as well as close relatives and friends. For MBBs, the pattern is not much different. They have new friendships with MBBs, foreign cross-cultural workers, and Christian families and organizations. Twenty-six respondents (54%) mentioned this affective/relational factor in their coming to faith in 'Isa. According to F02, "there are various motives for Bangladeshi Muslims coming to faith in 'Isa, but the motive is mostly relationship-based." Though they decided to have faith after reading the Bible, there were some friends or relatives who motivated them to read the Bible.

Friendship and helping heart

Bangladeshi friendship is radically emotional. Bangladeshis make friends easily and try to be on their friend's side. Also, they are interested in making new or foreign friends and try to help them. This relational factor helps them to have faith in 'Isa. U10, for example, accidently met an MBB evangelist and became his friend when he was waiting for a delayed train. He clearly remembered that night when he was drawn to faith in 'Isa and decided to be baptized:

> I was listening to the conversation between him and an Islamic student. He seemed to have a good knowledge of the Qur'an because he knew the exact place of the qur'anic *ayats* [verses]. I found that we were from the same village. I loved his speech about 'Isa. I sat right next to him on the train and talked with him all night. One week later, we met again with two or three other persons. At that time, he gave me a Bangla Qur'an and showed me important *ayats* about 'Isa as a Savior. I responded that I wanted to be baptized right then. He said that daytime is not good for being baptized. Finally, I was baptized at night one month after our first meeting.

U05 and U06 were school friends. U06 believed in *'Isa* when he was sixteen years old. When U06 was quarrelling with another Muslim friend about the issue of *namaz* (Muslims' formal prayers, said five times a day), U05 took U06's side:

> While I was defending my friend [U06], I talked to another Muslim friend: "What is the purpose of religion?" He did not answer that. "Is the purpose of religion to raise people and serve them? Isn't it?" After seeing that his friend is on his side, [U06] brought me to an office. His teacher was there and told me, through qur'anic verses, about *Injil* and *'Isa*. I thought Muhammad could lead us to go to heaven, but I found that he does not have that power. Also, I realized that all *Kitabs* are from the creator, and I accepted it. Then, I was baptized the next week.

Several respondents had good fellowship with foreigners and were led to believe in *'Isa* through meeting and helping them. L03 has had good relationships with a Roman Catholic Christian family and a foreign missionary:

> There were many Roman Catholic families in my hometown. We have had very good relationship with one family. I became a *dormo putro* [religious son] of his family. His other families are living in USA. In my town, Christians have a good reputation of helping the poor and not fighting against each other. I have also had good friendship with an Australian missionary. He said to me, "You do one thing. You read the Bible with all your heart." After reading it by myself for one month, everything that I didn't understand started to disappear.

S03 came to faith when he tried to help a foreign organization set up their work.

> In 1980, some people of a foreign organization were moving around in our village. That time I noticed a person walking on the road where I was sitting. He asked me why people of my region did not invite him to drink a glass of water. Responding to his demand, I brought him to my house and tried to show him as much hospitality as possible. After he listened to my past history of failing Union Parishad election, he suggested that I

form a *somitee* [committee] with ten members. Following his advice, I constituted a five-member *somitee*. After that time, they came to see the members of the *somitee* and taught them about 'Isa from the Qur'an and the *Kitab*.

I01 also helped foreigners when he was a student. This helping relationship led to a natural introduction to Christianity.

Local people came and questioned them [foreigners], and I answered for them instead of them. I was a helper for them at that time. Sometimes they invited me when they were meeting with MBBs at night, and I got the opportunity to be introduced to Christianity. One day, these foreigners asked me to translate books, and I became more interested in Christianity. When translating the first book, I did not convert yet, but after finishing the translation of the last of six books, I decided to follow Christ and got baptized.

Experiential Factors

Several MBBs had certain supernatural experiences such as dreams and visions (S02, H07, and U08) and miraculous happenings (L03) through which they experienced the power of God. U08, one of the female respondents, dreamed about 'Isa one night. Her father actually used to read the *Injil Sharif* and tell her stories about it. Her father's brothers and sisters did *namaz* prayer and read the Qur'an, but her father did so differently. U08 also had several brothers and sisters, but she was the only one who listened to her father's talks about 'Isa. Her other brothers and sisters did not understand that. Her father shared the truth about 'Isa healing the sick, and he himself read the *Injil*. U08 shared the story of her dream and how her husband came to faith in 'Isa during our interview:

I dreamed one night. Someone told me to bring some books to another Muslim's house and I followed the order. There was a jungle near a rice field. I saw one man standing on the field saying, "I am 'Isa." I said, "Please leave me." I was afraid. I told this dream to my family. They teased me, saying, "Oh, good! Then, you follow him." After that, my father also kept quiet, but

> I was encouraged by my father. I sometimes cried why 'Isa was persecuted and crucified, but my mother and brothers forbade me to do more things. I married a Muslim husband and I said to my husband, "I love 'Isa." Then, my husband [U07] used to be angry, saying, "Why do we have to do so?" Later, he sought the truth in his mind and met a friend who shared the gospel of 'Isa. Then, my husband told me, "I also received your dream."

H07 had a good discussion and received lessons about 'Isa in the Qur'an when he tried to convince an MBB of the credibility of Islam. His grandfather was an imam at a local mosque and he tried to follow all the regulations of Islam. H07 recalled that an MBB he met said that "'People who are not following the previous *Kitabs* before the Qur'an will not be counted as real religious persons.' He added that 'Isa had no father and that if a human wanted to get salvation, he or she should follow his way." After returning home, H07 read the Qur'an to check the MBB's words and that night he dreamed of 'Isa, who "invited me to become his follower."

S02 was the imam of a big local mosque. He heard the gospel from a Christian organization leader who lived in the same village after building a good relationship with him. S02 had been interested in 'Isa in the Qur'an, but he worried about believing in 'Isa for a financial reason: he got a good income from the mosque for his weekly teaching. When he read the *Kitab* secretly, he was especially curious about the identity of the Holy Spirit. When he asked God who and what the Holy Spirit is during several days of prayer and fasting, he dreamed of the Holy Spirit.

> I fell asleep one day after several days of praying and fasting for God to answer my prayer about knowing the Holy Spirit. I had one dream. I was in a place with dark shadows, after losing my way in the middle of a jungle. Suddenly, a bright light shone in the darkness and I heard a voice saying, "This is the straight path. This is the Holy Spirit." Isn't 'Isa the straight path? That time I was convinced that 'Isa is the Savior and the straight path.

N03 had a big burden in his mind due to difficult circumstances in his life. After listening to the advice of a foreign missionary to read the Bible carefully, he said, "Difficult things and burdens in my mind started to disappear during my self-study of the Bible for one month." He also experienced a miracle when he taught the *Kitab* to college students. One of the madrassa teachers called for a meeting against him and spoke badly about him because he was teaching the *Kitab* to college students, but he said, "Just before the meeting against me started, a large amount of rain began to pour in that place, so the meeting had to be cancelled."

F08 is a foreign supporter of the insider movement who is currently living outside of Bangladesh but visits the country several times a year. He shared the following observation about his insider friends. "According to my experience, most Muslims in Bangladesh came to faith [in *'Isa*] through miraculous events such as dreams or healings, and also when the gospel was explained using Muslim vocabulary [not Christian Bangla)] and reference made to the Qur'an."

Negative Feeling (Discontentment) about Islam

Ten of forty-eight respondents (21%) expressed negative feelings about Islam for reasons such as the uncertainty of salvation and Islam's acceptance of multiple marriages. Four of the ten foreign respondents (40%) also confessed that discontentment with Islam is one of the major reasons of leaning toward the gospel of *'Isa*. H01 said, "I tried to follow all of the Islamic regulations, but one day I started to doubt that I could get salvation in this way." He did *namaz* (five daily prayers) regularly and did *zakat* (almsgiving), but he did not find peace in his heart. U01 was also afraid of the teaching of a *hujur* (Islamic teacher) that "if you miss one *namaz*, you will be judged for eighty years." When he converted, he said, "I got eternal peace and light from the fear of being condemned." U012 said something similar: "I don't want to look down upon the religion of Muslims, but I could not find the salvation and freedom in that."

L01 began his journey to faith in *'Isa* by interacting with both Christians and an imam. He heard from the imam that "if you bring one person from another religious background to Islam, you will get a ticket to go directly to heaven." At that time he was teaching three Christian students as a private tutor and thought that if he could bring these three Christians to Islam, he would get three tickets. He started to communicate openly with these Christian students. During the conversation, they asked him several questions on subjects such as Muhammad's power to bring them to heaven. When he asked the imam these questions, however, the imam became angry:

I had such a conviction to convince them that Islam is the only true way because I heard from the imam that Christians are worshiping three Gods, eating without regulations, and doing ethically bad things. So, I tried to rescue them from the bad religion and started to communicate with them openly. I also tried to convince them, saying, "Islam is the only true religion." But they asked me, "How do you say that? If Islam is true, how can you believe it? You said Muhammad can bring you to heaven, where is that word written?" That night, I went to the mosque and asked the imam about it. The imam replied angrily, "How dare you doubt our *rasul* [Muhammad]? Are you being a Christian?" That time I bought a Bangla Qur'an Sharif and tried to find the answers, but I couldn't. I started to doubt whether Islam is the religion of the truth and way to heaven. After that, I got the Bible and during my reading of it, one verse came to my mind: "There is no other name under heaven given to mankind by which we must be saved." From that time, I started to read the Bible and the Qur'an comparatively.

As outside observers, foreign workers' views are helpful for an understanding of MBBs' background of faith. F04 answered the question about the reason for Bangladeshi MBBs' belief in *'Isa* in terms of "lack of assurance of salvation."

There are very few answers in Islam about the assurance of salvation and the solution for our sins. Through relationships or small booklets, they start the journey of finding answers about salvation such as a comparative study of the faith of Islam and *'Isa*. Also, another reason is that it is not easy for us to get the way of salvation that Islam provides, and it is too legalistic.

F01 provided two reasons for Bangladeshi Muslims to come to faith in *'Isa*: "future security such as avoiding hell or judgment after death, and hunger for relationship of union with God regardless of Sufi or law-keeper background."[2]

---

2. F01 explained that there are two types of Muslims in Bangladesh. One type is *Shorioti*, who believe that someone can get salvation by keeping the Islamic law. The other type is *Morioti*, who were influenced by Sufism who value direct experience of God such as secret knowledge, presence, healing, and power, and focus on pursuing closeness to God.

F02 added to this point: "Law is not going to save them. They need to get God's mercy and grace coming through '*Isa*. Not through their works and not through keeping the law, but through coming to understand that Jesus is the one who brings God's grace." F07 answered that Bangladeshi MBBs' come to faith in '*Isa* due to "discontentment with Islam and through finally hearing the truth."

Moreover, U12 expressed his discontentment about the possibility of multiple marriages within Islam. He said, "I disliked Muslims' multiple marriages." When I visited U12's home for fellowship, a neighbor who is the second wife of her husband, was also visiting and we had a chat. She was feeding rice to her child without her husband. She said that her husband used to come and go from time to time. She asked the researcher, "Don't your people have a second wife?" I said, "No."

Occupational and Multiple Factors

Several respondents have had chances to work for foreign Christian development NGOs. During their regular morning devotions at the office and *jama'at* meetings with other MBBs, they were naturally introduced to the gospel and faith community (M01, M04, I03, and I04). M01 worked on a foreign NGO's adult education program for seven years, first as a volunteer and then as a supervisor. During the period, he said, "I first attended many *jama'at* meetings or read books such as the *Kitab* and other books related to '*Isa*, and then I grew interested in believing in him." M04 also followed two MBBs who worked in a foreign NGO. "I wanted a job from them. They gave me an address. Next day, they came to our village and looked for me. I worked with them and came to believe in '*Isa* several years later."

When we see the occupational factors that drew some of the respondents to faith in '*Isa*, we can see the effects of other factors, such as cognitive and relational, at the same time. For example, after I04 started to work in an international Christian NGO, he started to read the *Kitab* and the Qur'an together for his own comparative study. He also had a good friendship with a foreign project director. He was baptized in the river by his director. I03 experienced a similar process, but was influenced and baptized by local colleagues.

> When I worked in this organization, my fellow worker tried to evangelize me. But, I responded negatively. One day, I started

to read the *Kitab* and the Qur'an by myself and I was slowly changed. During this personal study, my other colleagues invited me to come to their *jama'at* and I joined the course of the *Kitab* and Qur'an study. After that, I decided to follow *'Isa* and take baptism.

The faith of several other respondents has benefited from various trainings funded by foreign missions. H06 recently attended two four-day annual national conferences of IFB (Isai Fellowship in Bangladesh) near Dhaka. This is a nationwide invitation-based gathering. He was recently brought to faith by his father, and he received encouragement by attending this meeting with other MBBs. In my personal observation, the meeting gave MBBs an opportunity to meet three dimensions of needs – cognitive, affective/relational, and experiential – to help and encourage their faith in *'Isa*.[3] First, their time of hearing and meditating on the word of God helped their cognitive dimension of faith. Second, the meeting of national MBBs around the country provided them with affective/relational encouragement as they encountered new and old friends who have experienced similar kinds of social hindrances. Third, they might have spiritual experiences during communal prayer time, because they prayed out loudly and wholeheartedly. Overall, many revealed MBBs – such as self-identified Christian/*Isai* – interact with and are influenced by devotional moments or developments at this kind of meeting.

These conferences and trainings certainly benefit the faith of MBBs in cognitive (discussion with the Bible), affective/relational (fellowship with other believers), and experiential (prayer together) ways. On the other hand, several Muslims were invited to one-week training sessions on finding *'Isa*, the way of salvation, only through the Qur'an (E04, H04), while some others (M03, N03, U11, U12) have participated in one-year resident programs for

---

3. My personal experience of a National MBB Fellowship in Bangladesh by Isai Fellowship in Bangladesh, involved spending four days and three nights meeting with around five hundred national MBBs. After obtaining permission from a general secretary to participate in the meeting, I went to the venue alone. MBBs from almost all parts of the country came and started the first session. The speaker at the first session identified each group of MBB congregations by denomination or organization and asked them to stand up to greet each other. Basically, the gathering consisted of preaching and sermons by MBB pastors of IFB and foreign presenters from donating organizations, prayer meetings, regional gatherings for discussing the issue of persecution, and legal consultation from a Christian lawyer. Aside from some chaotic moments spent getting a book on government law, the three days of meetings were finished successfully.

discipleship training. These participants professed that these trainings were crucial moments in their faith journey.

Thus, most of the respondents have been influenced by a variety of factors. Some Muslims have read the *Kitab*, comparing it with the Qur'an with the help of MBB friends (cognitive and relational factors together), while some other Muslims, like S02, dreamed of 'Isa while talking about the *Kitab* with colleagues (miraculous, cognitive, relational, and occupational factors together).

Others' Responses and Changes

Most of the revealed MBBs – as distinct from the secret believers – interviewed for this study have suffered various degrees of negative response from their unbelieving families and their Muslim-majority religious communities (*somaj*). Several MBBs received direct damage to their property and business (U11, N01, U12) and had to defend themselves against social judgment (U02, U04, E04). We can, however, find some other cases in which Muslims' responses to MBBs changed from resistance to normal acceptance as time went by (H07, I02, U10, N02).

Negative Responses from Families and Communities

The various negative responses to MBBs include social isolation, economic disadvantages, and social judgment from their families and societies. Some MBBs have been expelled from their family and society and had to move from their hometown. (S01, N01, H01, H02, M01, U01).[4] S01 recalled that moment of expulsion painfully:

> After I got baptized, I was returning home, but the news about me had already spread to my whole village. My parents got angry and my elder brother especially gave a warning to me through another person, saying, "I will kill you because you brought disgrace on our family." So, I decided not to go home and came

---

4. This is a result of the power of *somaj*. Once a religious community hears the news that someone has recently believed in 'Isa (the time when they can easily identify that one has become a Christian), a mosque imam or Islamic religious leader orders or persuades young Muslims to try to bring the male convert back to Islam, warning the family members of the new believer of family disgrace or Allah's eternal judgment on him, his family, and community unless they bring him back to Islam. Thus, this kind of persecution means an effort for bringing back people to Islam and strengthening their *somaj*.

to Dhaka right away. It has been sixteen years. Now my father has died and sometimes I see my mother, but I still can't see my brothers. There is no land for me, nor do I have a relationship with the home town community. I did not expect these things when I got baptized. I might have done it differently if I knew this would happen.

Even though he did not express his regret of having faith in '*Isa* because he realized the gospel of '*Isa* was the truth, he regretted his baptism was revealed unexpectedly and so quickly. So, he has great concern for his disciples' timing in revealing their faith only gradually to their Muslim family and community. L01 suffered from the fact that his baptism was known to his family and village society.

Since that day [baptism], my relationship with family and community has been broken for ten years. Village people and religious community talked badly to my parents saying that "You did not do anything when your child became a Christian." And then, my parents said to me, "If you are still here, the *somaj* [religious community] thinks that we still have relationship with you so they will give us more social pressure." So, I had to leave my home and family.

In a similar way, M01 and U09 had to leave their family for five to six years. They have since returned to their house and restarted to repair the broken relationships, but they have not fully recovered. On the other hand, H01 prepared for social isolation in advance, saying "When I decided to believe in '*Isa*, I thought that my *somaj* would expel me. I thought that I did not need this society either. So, I bought land not far from my hometown and built a house in preparation for a new life. After building my house, I became a Christian and was baptized." Despite this precaution, persecution in the form of economic disadvantage continued to disturb the normal life of his family.

I was running a workshop for motorbikes. After word spread of my conversion, people of my area started to attack my shop and my family. They spoke badly about us and took out my stuff from the shop without my permission. They even broke and stole things from my shop at night and did not pay back their repair charges (H01).

Other respondents (U09, U12) also had to endure the pain of not receiving family inheritance. After U12 honestly confessed his belief in 'Isa and his calling to preach 'Isa to others, his father told him to "leave my family now, and you will not receive any of my inheritance." In contrast, some respondents (U11, N01) did receive small portions of inheritance from their fathers. N01 received a portion of land. After being separated from his parents, he built his house for his family and built a church for gathering 'Isa followers.

Several respondents noted that their families moved from rejection to acceptance of them over time (H07, U10, N02). After hearing of his new belief in 'Isa, the parents of H07 were at first against him. But, he kept speaking of his wish for his parents to believe in 'Isa, and he worried them by saying, "If you keep talking against me, I can't stay in this house and I might leave you." H07 explained that "because at that time I was the main earning person of our family, they forgave me and followed my faith soon." Similarly, when U10 first shared his new faith with his family, his wife and children responded angrily against him, saying, "You became a Christian." But, he says "now it is fine. I showed them the *Kitab*, proved it is truth, and it is the way of God [Allah]." N02 was also rejected by his family at first, but now his wife and his daughter-in-law have come to faith, though his son has not.

Social judgment was revealed as another issue by several respondents (U02, E04, H07). Even though their families accept their new faith to some extent, the *somaj* (religious community/society) is much stronger than one family. E04 had experienced social judgment because he attended the training of the qur'anic seminar about 'Isa. After returning to his home, when he invited his community people to his house for the festival (ceremony) of the satisfaction of his father's soul, social judgment occurred against him for his participation in the training and his baptism.

Someone dissented to my arrangement of the festival that it was not good to attend my festival. Many arguments had been continued about my participation in the training and my qualification of opening an Islamic festival in my house. They said that it is necessary to punish me. Then I prayed that "Hey Allah, you save me. I have none without you." At that time, an imam who was a friend of my father said, "He is a student and he can go to any place to know more." So, I needed to do "*touba*" [to repent publicly; confession of false (mistake)] and asked Allah to forgive my faults in front of other people.

H07 had enjoyed a good reputation among his friends as a leader, but after word spread of his family's religious change, persecution started. Various incidents happened and these caused him to return to Islam publicly. In response to the first social judgment against him, and a second, larger social judgment two years later, he was forced to become a Muslim on the outside and an *'Isa* follower inside.

> My friends were calling me a *guru* [leader or teacher]. But, after several days of the news being spread of my family's religious change, our village religious leaders called a social judgment meeting. They asked my family, "Did you become Christians?" I replied honestly "Yes." After listening to my answer, they decided to make us *ek ghore* [family which is banned]. They forbade us to get water for drinking and washing, communication with other neighbors, shopping at the local markets for foods. . . . After that, during the nights, they threw stones at my house and sometimes put excrement in my house. The son of a religious leader spit on my body. After suffering for one month, my father had brain stroke. And, my body became very skinny. People said that Allah gave his punishment to the betrayer, meaning me. I called my gospel introducer, a pastor of my *jama'at*. He said to me, "You have to endure these kinds of persecutions." With the help of one Hindu family, we could survive for one year.
>
> The next year, our village religious leaders called for another bigger meeting where they forced my family members to come back to Islam. They warned us, "Leave this village tonight if you want to keep Christians. Or you can *touba* [repent] your wrong and go back to being a Muslim." I thought that we don't have any land other than this house. We can't live outside of this place. That time, I called my pastor and he advised me to maintain Islam outside, but continue to have fellowship with our *jama'at* and keep faith as followers of *'Isa*. They brought me

to a field at night without my family and beat me. Through my
father's persuasion, we came back to being a Muslim family publicly. But, I do not attend any Muslim religious meetings. They
had another idea of keeping me a Muslim by marrying me to a
Muslim woman. Being forced by community pressure, I married
a Muslim woman without our family's willing agreement. But,
I still continued to be present at my *jama'at* from time to time
without informing my family members and kept my faith in *'Isa*.

S03 responded to the social judgment differently. He asked an influential
person to look at the *Kitab* and the Qur'an comparatively and then judge
him later.

Much pressure had been given by my neighbors socially; they
even tried to almost kill me. But the *Kitab* had saved me through
its comparative discussion with the Qur'an, when there was a
trial to throw me out from society by social judgment. At the
social judgment, there were two good persons from my large
family, and they were saying that "we will look into this matter." The people who opposed me also said "ok" and called me. I
replied that "I will show why I receive *'Isa,* and if I did anything
wrong, I must surely get punished. But before that, you [an
influential person of the village] read the *Kitab* [*Mussolmani*
Bible/the Holy Books] for two days first. If the *Kitab* is bad,
then judge me." After reading it for two days, he said it had no
harmful things, but rather it had good things. After that, there
has been no more judgment.

Change (Inner/Outer)

Diverse changes have happened in MBBs' lives after they came to faith in *'Isa*.
Inner changes have come from the assurance of salvation as a sinner, which
is related to inner peace and outer change of habits. Once they get assurance
of salvation, they don't need to worry about their future and their attachment
to earthly anxiety is reduced, and they instead think about and love others
more. The changes happen from their inner being to outer behavioral change.
Some respondents also reported outer and situational changes.

Inner change by the perception of being a saved sinner

For the MBBs, assurance of salvation is a main factor of their change. From feeling certain of their salvation, they began to feel peace from the fear of the uncertain future, to turn away from their sins, and to come to outer changes like being honest and controlling anger. U10 recognized that "the past way was not true" while he was reading the *Kitab* and he turned to a new way daily. In the past, I02 was not sure whether he could go to heaven. "After receiving *'Isa*, however, now I am sure that I am going to heaven. It became a starting point of my change." S01 said that "the biggest change is the confession that I am a sinner." After being a follower of *'Isa*, his life was changed from his inner being to his outer behavior.

> I came to realize that my life was contaminated. To be clear, I need to rely on and believe in *'Isa*, because God is holy. In this way, my inner change is connected to outer change such as not lying, not cheating, nor treating others badly. My language was changed too. When I speak, I naturally started sharing the gospel. In the past, my mind was bad and full of anger, but I realized that I don't have any right and authority to do like this, but rather he [God] is the only authority. During my reading of the Bible, I decided to lay down my sinful heart, and then my heart became softer.

U09 said, "I am clean now after believing in *'Isa*. I was changed and turned away from my sins." Most respondents shared similar kinds of statements. Several people pointed out that they got "new peace" (H08, U07, U08, U11, E01). Specifically, some respondents (U02, U04, U10, U12, N02) mentioned their change from speaking falsehood: "I lied much, but now I am changed" (U04). Some others confessed that they became able to control their anger toward others (H01, H03, H05, U02, U10, M03). In addition, U13 mentioned the change in her life that took place after reading a small gospel booklet from her husband:

> There was no peace and blessing in my mind. After my husband read the book of "The Straight Path," he passed on the book to me. After reading this, I was totally changed, for example, in terms of loving and treating others, in my speech, and feeling

of my belonging to the Lord. Now, I know *'Isa* saved me and my family and I have hope that he will finally save us too.

Inner change to outer change

Inner change is reflected in the practical outer changes that began to appear in respondents' daily lives. They started to love others with caring spirits and are gentler; they began to stop fighting, smoking, and get delivered from their drug addictions. Some respondents experienced situational change too. I01 spoke sincerely about the changes in his thinking and his transformed life of loving others by following the example of Jesus:

> I did not change my name. I tell others that I am a follower of Jesus. I was changed in my thought and action. Jesus told me to love people, not only Christians, but all people. Are you asking what changed in me before and after receiving Jesus? First, before coming to Jesus, I did not care, did not think I was a sinner. But now I know I am a sinner and I need Christ's help. Language and behavior were changed because these are related. Thinking and inner being were changed. Christ loves me, and I still enjoy his love. My thinking and worldviews are different. How loving he is! I am a sinner, but still he loves me.
>
> He did not begin to love me when I changed my attitude. When I was a sinner, he had loved me even before my birth. This kind of belief affected my love for others. That is my change. Yes. I am getting his love and his love motivated me to love others. If I don't do this, I am committing sins. I am still failing to transmit his love to others. I am enjoying his love, but I can't give others the same love he gave me. This is my failure.[5]

Several other respondents agreed that previously, they were only thinking of themselves and did not love others. They made comments such as, "Now I love and care for others" (U01, U12, N02, S04), and "now I am thinking about the welfare of the people and trying to take many people of my area to heaven with me" (N01). Fighting and quarrelling have been minimized for several respondents (N02, M02, M03, H06, E04). Some respondents became softer

---

5. My interview with I01 was carried out in English.

than before (N03, I02, M01), and M02 said, "People were afraid of coming to me, but after I started believing in *'Isa* they are coming to me." Habits of prayer and meditation on the *Kitab* were formulated for H01 and U02 after believing in *'Isa*. Some respondents quit smoking and taking drugs following their conversion (U02, U04, L03).

Some respondents found that their situation also changed after they came to believe in *'Isa* (L03, E02, U03). U03 was delivered from the threats of neighbors. "They were talking of breaking into my house and harassing my family. But, rather than bothering us, they fell into danger instead. After they decided to disturb us, they started to quarrel with each other and they could not break into my house. I thought that the Lord was helping us." E02 confessed, "When I did wrong things before baptism, my family members would fall sick and fight frequently. I thought that it was because of my sins. Now the situation has changed: the children have become healthy and we fight less."

U12 received a special spiritual gift of healing:

> People were healed when I prayed for them in the name of *'Isa*. In the past, I did not have this kind of gift of healing. I believe that the Holy Spirit works among us and praying in the name of *'Isa* has the power to heal people. Also, I used to be very concerned about what people would say about me, but now I don't worry anymore about people's opinion of me. I lack nothing.

I participated in one Sunday service led by U12. After sharing some verses from the *Kitab* with around ten believers, he prayed that more than forty visitors from diverse religious backgrounds would come to them one by one, especially people from Muslim backgrounds.

Social Identity and Identity Change

The issue of the social identity of Bangladeshi MBBs is complex in terms of the variety of reactions to and interactions with the social context of Muslims and Christians and their communities. This section is based on Tim Green's research (discussed in chapter 3) on four different types of social identity among Bangladeshi MBBs – Christian, *Isai*, *Isai* Muslim, and Muslim – and it examines why these MBBs move around rather than stay in one social identity. I actually showed the respondents Tim Green's visual diagram of two religious circles and four fuzzy groups of social identity. Most agreed that the diagram was consistent with their understanding of the situation and were able to point out their positions in the chart.

Before looking into each of the four social identities, it will be helpful to discuss three general characteristics of MBBs' social identity. Local MBBs' views about their own social identity are vital, but foreigners' views are also important for acquiring validity of the data through a comparison of outsiders' views with insiders' opinions of local MBBs. Two foreigners and an indigenous leader provided a good introduction to the three characteristics of Bangladeshi MBBs' social identity. The first characteristic is the problem of "exposure" as a convert, which produces three problems: lack of respect, persecution, and inaccessibility. According to L06,

> If MBBs are revealed as Christians or *Isai*, they fall into three problems. First, they do not get respect from the Muslim community or the traditional Christian community. So, it is hard for them to find spouses for their children because there are very few *Isais* in contrast to majority Muslims. Second, they can face various kinds of persecution. Third, it is hard to access Muslim neighbors for genuine relationship and gospel sharing. The majority community does not want to listen to the opinion of the converts. MBBs struggle with inaccessibility to others in terms of their relationship or gospel introduction to Muslim neighbors.

The second characteristic is that MBBs' social identity depends on their "introducer" to *'Isa* or the gospel.

> If traditional Christians or denominations introduce the gospel to someone, they shape his/her social identity. If introduced by Muslim insiders, they start from the earliest stage. As time goes by, however, in the process of experiencing diverse interactions with family and neighbors or persecutions, they used to change their identity. Someone feels like "I can't leave my Muslim community." If the groups of "*Isai*" or "*Isai* Muslim" become stronger, they continue to stay in that identity. Also, theological confusion can be a reason for identity change. (F04)

Connected to this point, the third characteristic is the "flexibility" of social identity in response to the society and social interaction. F05 described the reality well:

> All believers work out their identity, and that is continually changing. It is a process, not a point, so where they are today is not where they may be in the future. Most of the people are aiming toward *Isai* Muslim or *Isai*. However, their identity is not always the same in every area. For example, a believer's identity in his work area and his identity in his home village may differ. A student in university may have a different identity there than he has in his home. This is not encouraged and rather schizophrenic but a present reality.

Due to these three characteristics of Bangladeshi MBBs' social identity, it is difficult to draw clear boundaries between each of the four social identity possibilities. However, it is also true that this reality of four groups actually does exist, even though the boundaries are fuzzier than the distinctions portrayed by Tim Green (in Figure 8).

Four Groups of Bangladeshi MBBs

A revised visualization of the four groups of Bangladeshi MBBs may facilitate our understanding. Figure 9 shows my version of this classification system, which is a simplified version of Tim Green's description (summarized in chapter 3).

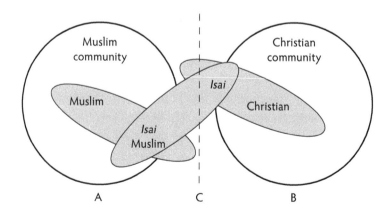

Figure 9. Four Groups of Bangladeshi MBBs

When I showed the respondents Tim Green's demonstration similar to Figure 9 above and asked them whether this figure accurately represents their understanding of their own or their MBB colleagues' identity, fifty-eight respondents – including the foreign respondents – generally agreed that this is a true reality of Bangladeshi MBBs. Compared to Tim Green's four categories, however, the responses I received seemed to coalesce into three categories: Christian/*Isai* (area B in Figure 9), *Isai/Isai* Muslim (*uboi* [both] identity, area C in Figure 9), and *Isai* Muslim/Muslim (area A in Figure 9).

The social identities associated with each participant in this study were primarily chosen by the respondents themselves, though supplemented by my analysis of their words and behaviors. The social identities of the forty-eight respondents are listed below (Table 7). C/I signifies Christian/*Isai*; I/IM indicates *Isai/Isai* Muslim; and IM/M means *Isai* Muslim/Muslim. F.N. is an abbreviation for file name and S.I. stands for social identity.[6]

Table 7. Various Social Identities among 48 Bangladeshi MBB Respondents

F.N.	S. I.	F.N.	S.I.	F.N.	S.I.	F.N.	S. I.	F.N.	S. I.	F.N.	S.I.
H01	C/I	U01	C/I	U09	C/I	I01	C/I	M01	IM/M	S04	C/I
H02	C/I	U02	I/IM	U10	I/IM	I02	C/I	M02	IM/M	S05	C/I
H03	C/I	U03	C/I	U11	C/I	I03	C/I	M03	IM/M	L01	C/I
H04	I/IM	U04	C/I	U12	C/I	I04	IM/M	M04	I/IM	L02	C/I
H05	I/IM	U05	C/I	U13	C/I	E01	I/IM	M05	IM/M	L03	IM/M
H06	I/IM	U06	C/I	N01	C/I	E02	I/IM	S01	C/I	L04	C/I
H07	IM/M	U07	C/I	N02	C/I	E03	IM/M	S02	C/I	L05	C/I
H08	IM/M	U08	C/I	N03	I/IM	E04	IM/M	S03	C/I	L06	I/IM

Christian and *Isai*

Among the forty-eight respondents, twenty-eight (58%) were characterized by a Christian and *Isai* social identity, but it is hard to clearly distinguish between Christian and *Isai*. Approximately, eight to ten respondents (17%–20%) can be said to be Christian rather than *Isai*, but this research demonstrates that the Christian and *Isai* categories are largely interchangeable among the respondents. In Tim Green's definition, the Christian group is "completely assimilated in the traditional church with its festivals, language, and social

---

6. The first letter (such as H or U) refers to the *jama'at* name.

relationships," leaning toward the traditional Christian community rather than the *Isai* community. The respondents interviewed for this study, however, seem to have relationships with both communities, though slightly closer with the *Isai* side. Eighteen to twenty respondents (38%–42%) can be said to be *Isais* rather than Christians. *Isais* have "a little contact with their Muslim relatives, visit them at *Eid* . . . switch between Christian and Muslim terminology." In my judgment, however, these two groups of respondents are interchangeable in terms of their use of both Christian and Muslim language and their flexible degree of assimilation with existing Christians.

Another reason for the interchangeability of these two categories lies in the judgment they both provoke from Muslim neighbors. It is interesting that even though some MBBs introduce themselves as *Isai*, Muslims are directly responding to them: "Oh, Christians!" In their eyes, these two groups are hardly distinguishable. Nevertheless, H01 worried about introducing believers as *Isais* rather than Christians because it made it possible to move closer to Muslim side than would a clear Christian identity.

> There have been many *Isais* – around forty-seven – in my large hometown. They were baptized, have attended *jama'ats*, and have worked in development NGOs. But, in my judgment, they were cheating foreign missionaries for a while. After the NGO projects were closed down, they stopped attending *jama'ats*. Now, they are not even talking to me.

H01's witness suggests that these individuals seemed to be *'Isa* believers when they were working in a Christian organization, but after they stopped working for the NGOs, they went back to their Muslim-majority villages and rejoined their *somaj* (religious community).

One of the focus group respondents said, "*Isai* is fine because it is an Arabic word for Christian, but *'Isai* Muslim' is not fine. If someone is introduced like this, people will ask him or her what *'Isai* Muslim' means, and they will call them to *namaz* if the word 'Muslim' is added." U07 agreed: "If people ask me my social identity, I answer that I am an *'Isa anushari* [follower]. Why do I need to call myself an *Isai* Muslim? If people ask me if I'm a Christian, I say yes." U02 introduces himself as an *Isai* rather than a Christian as one way of being close to Muslims saying, "I answer that I am an *Isai* to my friends and teachers. Even if I call myself an *Isai*, they understand me as a Christian.

Socially, Muslims do not call us *Isais*, but we are trying to build relationships with Muslims as *Isais*." U10 answered that "I am an *Isai imandar* [believer]." U04 said, "When people call me a Christian, I answer that I am an *Isai ummot* [disciple]. If people refer to me as a Muslim, I can say I am a Muslim too, but I prefer to say that I am an *Isai ummot*. By looking at this diagram, I can say I am an *Isai*." U09 said,

> I am an *Isai* as someone who is reading the *Mussolmani* Bible [*Kitab*].
>
> I became a Christian from a Muslim background. Now, I have fellowship with *Isais* and some relationship with Muslims too. Socially, I was sometimes called as Christian, but I stay as an *Isai*. I read the *Kitab* because the Carey version Bible [William Carey's traditional translation of the Bible, which adapts Hindu terminology] is hard to understand.

Isai and *Isai* Muslim (*Uboi* [both] identity)

Many MBBs who are working among Muslims or intend to live among the majority are concerned about proper identity and social introduction to Muslims. This section discusses the *uboi* ("both") identity and the meaning of "Muslim." Abu Taher, who actually defined the four groups of MBBs discussed in Tim Green's article, mentioned this *uboi* [both] *Isai* and *Isai* Muslim identity when I interviewed him. After explaining the context of the term of *Isai*, he shared the following exchange with me.

> Abu Taher (AT): After *Injil Sharif*'s birth in Bangla, diverse social identity issues and terms had also appeared, such as *Isai*.
>
> Researcher (R): Then, if they were asked about what *Isai* is, what were the answers?
>
> AT: When we say "*Isai*," many question about it, but Muslims understand it. Some people understand *Isai* as Christian. Some others understand that *Isai* is a part of Muslim, but a follower of '*Isa*. If so, two things are displayed. First, spiritual identity is shown as *Isai* or Christian, and second, cultural intimacy with Muslims is shown.
>
> R: It means *Isai* or *Isai* Muslim?

AT.: Yes, these two. If someone moves radically toward Muslim, then he can say "I am not an *Isai*, but a Muslim."

R: This is for helping others to think that "we are not the same as traditional Christians." If we divide two parts in this picture above [Figure 9], they might be not the side of B, rather A. Am I right? If they stay the other side, would it also be fine for believing in and following *'Isa*?

AT: I could say so. But, I could say we can add another circle in the middle of the picture [C]. We can say *uboi* [both] identity. They are calling themselves as *Isai*, or sometimes *Isai* Muslim.

R: Two identities depending on the situation?

AT: Yes.

R: When they use *Isai*, are they linking to Christians, and when they call *Isai* Muslims, are they linking to Muslims culturally?

AT: Yes. Imagine someone who has a mother church, a traditional Christian church near his hometown. When he goes to that church, he is a Christian or an *Isai*. But, when he comes to the field of the evangelizing work, then he can be an *Isai* or *Isai* Muslim. We can find many cases like this.

R: When someone is involved in evangelizing work to majority Muslims, you are saying that there are many cases of *uboi* identity. Isn't it?

AT: Yes.

In my interviews, eleven out of forty-eight respondents (23%) fit into this *uboi* [both] category, between *Isai* and *Isai* Muslim. H04 had worked as an *Isai* Muslim and sometimes a Muslim in the past, but now he is called a Christian, *Isai*, or *Isai* Muslim:

> I could say *'Isa* is a prophet, but He is Allah's *manonito jon* [someone who is near to God]. He is ours, not only for Christians. Now, I am calling myself an *Isai* Muslim. I am a follower of *'Isa*, but if I say that I am a Christian, I cannot preach *'Isa* to them. I am getting revealed more and more as an *Isai*, but I do not fear this.

H05 agreed with H04 and talked about the issue of changing religious identity in court:

> People refer to me as "Christian," not *Isai*, but I reply to them differently. If I call myself as a Christian, I need to go to the court for change. Someday, I am thinking to make this change too. If someone asks me my religion, I answer that I am an *Isai* Muslim who follows *'Isa* or is an *Isai imandar* [believer]. People talk behind my back that I am a Christian, but do not say this in front of me.

M04, who is sharing the gospel in various villages, spoke about the difficulty of revealing an *Isai* identity at first. "Because this is a Muslim *somaj* [religious community], we cannot say we are a Christian or *Isai* for the first time. I need to introduce myself first as a Muslim and as time goes by, my identity can be slowly and naturally revealed as an *Isai* identity."

Two foreign workers added their opinions of being introduced as *Isai* or *Isai* Muslim. F05 described the real difficulty of being part of the community when they call themselves only "*Isai*" in the village:

> There are pros and cons of both *Isai* and *Isai* Muslim. The concept of being an "*Isai*" is a textbook idea that has no meaning for the local people. If it is described in villages then automatically the local people refer to them as Christians. It is hard to see how the social identity of "*Isai*" will ever be part of the local understanding.

F02 also agreed that self-introduction as *Isai* Muslim is permissible unless it involves participation in religious activities in the mosque. When I asked him what position he wanted MBBs to nurture, he suggested that it does not matter whether MBBs are called *Isai* or *Isai* Muslim, as long as they have a clear identity of "who they are in Christ."

> There is no one definite position. But, I want to nurture people that understand clearly who they are in Christ and called to have relationship with him. I ask them to not go to the mosque but actively participate in *jama'at* whether they call themselves *Isai* or *Isai* Muslim. Probably, I would not encourage them to call themselves Christian. It wouldn't be a problem. I wouldn't

try to stop them from saying "*Isai* Muslims," meaning someone who surrenders to God. A follower of '*Isa* can be called as an *Isai* Muslim too. (F02)

Meaning of "Muslims"

MBB respondents who introduce themselves as *Isai* or *Isai* Muslims use diverse definitions of the word "Muslim," associating the term with one "who submits to God," or relating it to "peace" or just identity at birth. S01 commented that "it is not good to remain in Muslim identity for a long time," but he said, "I sometimes introduce myself as an *Isai* Muslim. It is not only because of my ministry among Muslims, but Muslim also means one 'who submits to God [Allah].'"

> If I say that I am a [convert] Christian, they do not listen to my words. Muslims only hear what Muslims say to Muslims. Thus, I try to slowly reveal myself to them. When they ask about my religious identity, I answer that "my religion is the biggest." I am a person who is an *ummot* [disciple] of '*Isa*. I add to them, "Do you believe in Muhammad? We believe a lot of prophets, but following [being disciples] is more important." When I say that I am a Muslim, it means, "I submit to God in '*Isa*." In this way, I belong to both sides socially, depending on the situation. (S01)

L06 agreed with S01 and gave the example of Jesus, who followed the Jewish culture in the Bible.

> Someone may introduce himself as a Muslim, but he can actually be *Isai*. Muslims have different languages from Christians. Those *Isais* use Muslims' language. While they use the same language, eat and dress similar to Muslims because they were Muslims before, they are Christians inside. Like Jesus, he did everything as a Jew, he was born in a Jewish family, and he followed Jewish culture and worshipped the Lord in their way. He attended all of their religious activities. People say that he was a Jew, but his faith was different. Muslim means someone who submits to God, like we are. So, we can say that we are Muslims. This is not because we follow Islamic activities such as *namaz* [formal prayer], *roza* [formal fasting for a month], and *qurbani*

[sacrifice] – actually, we do not follow these – but because we follow his words as someone who submits to God, the literal meaning of a Muslim.

E03 showed himself as an *Isai* Muslim "because *'Isa* did not say he is a Christian. He was a Muslim according to what the Qur'an said. *'Isa* only said that you believe in Allah and follow me." H05 and N03 said they could introduce themselves as *Isai* Muslims in relation to their forefathers and Muslim blood. According to H05, "My forefathers and families were Muslims. So, I can say I am a Muslim, but my faith is in *'Isa*. In this Muslim-majority society, I believe I can be a disciple of *'Isa* and his follower." U10 connected the word "Muslim" to peace: "General Muslims are called this because they follow Islamic regulations or go to mosque, but I am a Muslim who follows *'Isa*. Actually, the meaning of 'Muslim' includes peace, but I could not find this peace in them. But, I have peace, so I can say I am a real Muslim." U02 responded similarly: "I don't like to call myself a Muslim, but I can say I am an *Isai* or *Isai* Muslim. The meaning of 'Muslim' when I call myself *Isai* Muslim is that I am a Muslim socially, and it also means someone who goes to the straight path." N02 said the meaning of "Muslim" for him is "someone who submits to God through and by *'Isa Mosiho*." So, even though this group of MBBs sometimes express themselves as Muslims, they reinterpret the term "Muslim" in relation to *'Isa*, using it to mean something different from what it means to other Muslims.

Isai Muslim/Muslim

One of the foreign workers interviewed for this study, F04, introduced two reasons for MBBs staying in the *Isai* Muslim/Muslim group: connecting more to the majority Muslims, and building up a Jesus-believing movement inside Islam. He introduced the cases of his two local friends:

> First, I communicated with a familiar *Isai* Muslim/Muslim friend several times about identity issue. My friend said "I am from an Islamic religious society and was an imam before. Also, because the majority of society is still Muslim, if I am introduced in different ways, like as a Christian, my connecting link will disappear. For winning my families, relatives, and friends, this identity is needed. Also, if I use the Qur'an as the tool of

evangelism to Muslims but introduce myself as a Christian, I think it also does not make sense. Using qur'anic bridge is effective for earning their respect."

Second, I know someone who had tried to do Jesus movement without getting benefits from foreigners. The trial was not effective, so it did not last long. The term *Isai* Muslim is somewhat vague, but I understand their feeling of two tensions. Once they believe in *'Isa*, they feel some extent of their former way as false. So, some belong to existing Christian groups. But, if they look at the Christian side, they think Christians also do not have all of the biblical values, and Christianity in Bangladesh is also minimal, powerless, and unstable in terms of social status. *Isai* Muslims normally do not go to mosques, but Muslims [insiders] sometimes participate in Islamic religious activities.

One Muslim insider, M03, explained his calling from God in two ways:

> I had been trained for two years by traditional Christians, but after that, I had the feeling of being called to share the gospel among Muslims, living among them as a Muslim. I believe there are two decisions of God for me.
>
> One, it is God's decision for me to be born in a Muslim family and to live as a Muslim.
>
> Two, by living with the majority group, I was called to lead them to follow *'Isa*. I don't need to change my religion to follow *'Isa*, neither do other Muslims. It is better to stay in their religion at birth because it is God's decision, but they need to follow *'Isa* for their own salvation. It does not matter in what religion they remain, like Islam or Hindu, but everyone should believe in one God, and follow the word of God, and obey it. Sometimes, if someone asks me my identity, I answer that I am a full Muslim. Some Muslims, who do not believe in *'Isa*, can be called half Muslims because they do not obey *'Isa*, the closest one of Allah. Because they do not obey *'Isa* nor the word of *'Isa*, they cannot get saved. *'Isa* said in the *Kitab* that "my father and I are one." That's why we can say that we are true Muslims who submit to Allah by following *'Isa*.

M02 also said, "I am a Muslim who follows *'Isa*. And I can call myself a full Muslim." He shared this story about his identity:

> I had believed in *'Isa* as a Muslim for twenty years. It is not formulated by one or two years' decision or identity. Wouldn't it be difficult for a Korean to eat Bangla food, or for a Bengali to eat Korean food? It does not fit well. Now we are living in this society, we like to live together as Muslims with belief in *'Isa* all the days of my life. My son has the same identity, like me. The reputation of the Christian identity is too bad here. I will lose all things from all kinds of pressure. My family had experienced persecution from majority Muslims because we were following *'Isa*. But now almost all persecutions disappeared because we have more believers and our power has been increased. We were weak in the initial period, but now we have hundreds of believers and they don't attack us anymore.

E04 was born in a Muslim imam family, and he was also called to preach salvation through *'Isa* among Muslims. That is why he maintains an *Isai* Muslim/Muslim identity:

> I believed in *'Isa* when I was trained in a one-week qur'anic seminar about *'Isa* and the way of salvation. From that time, I had a calling to preach among Muslims. Also, as we live in a Muslim-majority country, if I have no Muslim identity, it is not possible to do any work among them successfully. This is my main purpose to stay here. Also, from time to time I have been preaching to traditional tribal people, and they know me as a Christian or an *Isai*.

F08 shared the experience of his friend, one of the leaders of the insider movement in Bangladesh:

> One movement began when a Bengal Muslim background believer said to several believers, "Keep your faith in *'Isa*, but don't become Christians . . . go back to your villages and tell your elders what you believe. . . ." He baptized them, and they came back several weeks later along with their elders, who also wanted to know more about faith in *'Isa* and they became believers.

Reasons for Identity Change

Fifteen of forty-eight respondents (31%) specifically mentioned that they don't want to change their Christian/*Isai* identity anymore. S02 confessed, "I don't want to come back to being a Muslim. Neither do I want to stay as an *Isai* Muslim. I became a Christian and became holy. Why would I want to remain in darkness?" While some believers, like S02, had their faith revealed accidentally, sometimes hiding or changing MBBs' social identity happens intentionally. Foreign respondents such as F03 and F05 commented that MBBs' identity changes have happened a great deal. These are "different in every case" and "gradual and ongoing." F03 helped explain the "difficult and struggling" reality of the issue of identity and the "pragmatic" characteristic of identity change:

> Their identity is difficult and they struggle with it. Someone that I know became a Christian a long time ago and changed his Christian name, but he is still struggling being a part of Christian community, so he can change from a Christian to an *Isai*. I know several self-identified Muslim followers of *'Isa*. When they go to a village, they call themselves Muslim instead of Christian because Muslims are much more than Christians. But it depends on whom they introduce their identity. The people of Bangladesh are very pragmatic. In the Christian community, they introduce themselves as Christians, but in the Muslim com-munity they introduce themselves as Muslims.

F05 explained more about the reality and sensitivity of the social identity of MBBs and change to this identity:

> When they come to faith, they don't reveal it as they slowly be-gin to acknowledge their faith in the community. This gradual change is due to sensitivity and not wanting to be misunderstood and cause a "knee-jerk" reaction. . . . They gain increasing self-confidence regarding who they are as believers and increasing courage as they see other believers also go through the change process. Remember, in some areas it is not just one single be-liever who is making this change. There are a number of situa-tions where people from one village came to faith in Christ out

of the village context and then together they slowly changed their identity.

In some sense, revealed MBBs such as Christian/*Isai* tend to retain and secure their social identity, but they experience several problems until the issues have cleared. S01 introduced some of the possible outcomes of two different approaches to revealing faith in *'Isa* too early or too late:

> One problem is here. Someone listened to the gospel, received it, was saved, and baptized. But, he cannot reveal himself as an *'Isa* believer because it will become very hard to live with his family. I also told him, "I can't support you because there are no organization or missions anymore in Bangladesh to fully support someone because of faith in *'Isa*." So, I could not guide him to reveal his faith to others in haste.
>
> One other case is here. He was my disciple studying at a college. He did not reveal his faith because he was worried about the consequence of revealing, like expulsion from family. However, he finished his study one day, married, got a job, and his faith diminished gradually and eventually disappeared. He is not an *Isai* believer anymore. Our relationship is also gone now . . .
>
> After receiving *'Isa*, if someone lives with family and society, it is better that he or she stays as a Muslim for some period of time. If someone introduces himself as an *Isai* Muslim, police and others will begin to doubt. But, if someone becomes a good believer, he or she will be revealed automatically.

H08, one of the self-identified *Isai* Muslims, confessed that "it takes time" to be secure, to support his family, and to lead family members to *'Isa*.

> When I was a Muslim, I was blind. But, now I have found the way. Nevertheless, it takes time to move from an *Isai* Muslim to an *Isai*. The reason why I do not move to an *Isai* instantly is that people do not read the *Kitab*, and will not understand me. They only react by hearing from persons [Islamic leaders]. If I come directly to Christian/*Isai*, I might face many uncomfortable pressures. I think I can come here [a Christian/*Isai* identity] when I can stand well economically and become a self-sufficient

person. My family and my security is important. For the security of my children and family and to avoid facing much difficulty for having faith in *'Isa*, I think it would be better for us to stay here for a moment and then move gradually. Also, if I do not stay in this place for some period of time, it would be very hard to find opportunities to lead my other family members and neighbors to *'Isa* later.

One national MBB leader, L02, analyzed three reasons for social identity change among Bangladeshi MBBs: "First, it is for securing social status (family and work) or avoiding persecution. Second, it is for following work field's or [mission] organization's policy and strategy. And third, it is for sharing the gospel with other family members or neighbors." Sometimes these three reasons are interconnected, but they also exist separately from time to time. E02 explained the first reason saying, "Normally, we have many extended family members. Sometimes, they fell into danger because of my *Isai* faith and identity. Also, I am working in a neutral Christian NGO serving Muslims. If I reveal my identity as a Christian, it can be a problem to work with Muslims and work among them."

In an example of the second reason for change, M03 actually changed his social identity from a Christian/*Isai* to an *Isai* Muslim/Muslim identity after participating in a Christian training center for several years. Following his organization's policy, he decided to voluntarily reach out to Muslims as a Muslim, thus becoming an *Isai* Muslim/Muslim insider. F03 gave the following critical comments about the influence of missionaries on local MBBs' social identity changes:

> I think missionaries and mission organizations' policy have had an influence. Bengalis are very pragmatic. Many MBBs are changing groups to get jobs and to get finances, opportunities, or advantages. I know some MBBs who get three jobs based on different social identities. This kind of effort comes from the intention of creating links to get some resources and income. Their theology also comes from the foreign founders.

Finally, several MBBs changed their social identity for the purpose of winning others, demonstrating the third reason for change. H01 changed his version of the Bible from the traditional Hindu-oriented Bible to the

Mussolmani Bible (*Kitab*) and his working community from Christian to *Isai* and Muslim. "Because Muslims are 90 percent," he said, "for reaching them, I need to change my language." It can be said his identity changed from Christian to *Isai*. L06 revealed that some Christians from Hindu backgrounds sometimes introduce themselves as *Isais*, following the organization's policy for evangelism. S01 also mentioned the difficulty for evangelistic activity with a revealed Christian identity saying, "if I introduce myself as a Christian, they don't listen to me. That's why I sometimes use an *Isai* Muslim identity for my first outreach period of self-introduction to Muslims. And, I only gradually reveal myself and they come to understand me in a real sense [of Christian spiritual identity]." Additionally, F08 shared his experience of social identity changes among *Isai* Muslim/Muslim self-identified believers who responded with mixed motives, such as conflicts with colleagues or getting new job opportunities: "I have seen someone who left the [insider] movement to become either the first [Christian] or second [*Isai*] type [in the diagram]. Sometimes this is due to conflict inside the movement. Sometimes it was because they were offered jobs by other organizations."

One of the interesting things about L03 is that he has a Christian legal identity even though he identifies himself as an *Isai* Muslim/Muslim to his urban neighbors in his work field. This may differ from the situation in his hometown as a more revealed *'Isa* follower. The reason is that he sometimes needs to go abroad to participate in Christian training, and he is required to have Christian legal identity to get a visa. He does have his own reasons for staying as a Muslim in his society, such as getting social benefits and pursuing Muslim identity publicly, but he also thinks it is necessary to have a Christian legal identity. This chameleon-style identity change often happens in Bangladeshi MBBs' society.

During my time of general interactions with Muslims on the bus or on streets, I sometimes asked them about their knowledge of the existence of MBBs in Bangladesh and their feelings toward MBBs. Their responses were varied and depended, I believe, in large part on their personal characteristics. One person said that Bangladesh has freedom of choice in religion and there is no problem with changing religions from Islam to Christianity. Some Muslims believe conversion from Islam to Christianity happens only because converts receive financial help from Christian missionaries. Others often exaggerate Muslims' dominance in Bangladesh beyond the 90 percent cited in national statistics, saying "99 percent are Muslims in Bangladesh," so other religious people are relatively very few. During my visit in the village, local Muslims' impressions also varied when they noticed that I am a friend of an MBB. While someone invited me to come and eat their food as a foreign guest because of their hospitable nature, some others did not want to even greet me because they thought that I was a Christian and I could possibly influence them to become Christian. Overall, I could sense some tensions between Muslims and MBBs in a village setting, especially under the influence of local mosques and religious leaders.

Social Integration of Activities and Participation of MBBs with the Majority (RQ 2)

The second research question addressed the degree of social integration experienced by MBBs of different social identity groups, and attempted to assess the strengths and weaknesses of each position. Some MBBs are living with Muslim family members, friends, and neighbors in their hometowns. Others live outside of their hometowns for various reasons, ranging from their own work-related choice to expulsion by family and society. Wherever Bangladeshi MBBs live, however, the majority of the Bangladeshi population is Muslims. Wherever they stay, MBBs exist in a *somaj* (religious community or society) as a social/religious minority. The following discussion of RQ 2 findings considers three aspects of the issue of social integration: (1) social integration of MBBs in matters of marriage, funerals, child education, and finance; (2) MBBs' social participation in Muslims' religious activities; and (3) the advantages and disadvantages of each social identity.

To better understand MBBs' participation in Islamic activities, it is necessary to know the meanings of several activities. First, Muslims have two big festivals: *Roza Eid* (*Eid al-Fitr*) and *Qurbani Eid* (*Eid al-Adha*).[7] *Roza* refers to a thirty-day period of fasting in the day time, after which Muslims celebrate with family and neighbors for several days, an event called *Roza Eid*. *Qurbani* marks the remembrance of Abraham's sacrifice of his son and his obedience to the Almighty. Early in the morning of the *Qurbani Eid* day, Muslims gather, perform *namaz*, and sacrifice prepared animals such as cows

---

7. The word *Eid* refers to a solemn festival.

and goats. *Namaz (salat)* is a formal prayer of Muslims. They usually perform *namaz* in the mosque, but during the days of these two *Eids*, there are special places for performing *namaz* in a field. *Jummah namaz* refers to Friday *namaz*, which takes place from 12:30 in the afternoon. Unlike daily *namaz*, it includes the imam's preaching and more attendees. MBBs differ in the extent of their participation in these Muslim religious activities, ranging from no participation to full participation. Several *Isai/Isai* Muslim self-identified MBBs sometimes join *Eid namaz* because they consider it a social *namaz* since it is performed in a field not in the mosque.

Social Integration in Marriage, Funerals, Education, and Finance

Marriage

Many respondents answered that if a believer was not married, "Marriage is a huge problem" among the four types of social integration (marriage, funeral, child education, and finance) covered in this study (F01, F03, F05). This is because it is "hard to find the same faith spouse" and Muslim culture makes it easy for unbelieving parents to overrule their believing children's intentions for marriage (F01). All foreign respondents said they encouraged believers to marry a believing spouse. Unlike dominant Muslim cultural pattern of marriages arranged by parents, all MBB respondents showed their intention to try to marry off their children to persons with the same beliefs, and also to respect children's intention. Only three respondents (H07, U10, E02) currently have a social identity different from that of their spouse. Two of them married Muslim women even after believing in *'Isa* due to social and family pressure, and one married before coming to faith in *'Isa*, and his wife is still in the process of knowing and believing in *'Isa*. Their spouses remain in their Muslim social identity because they have not decided to follow *'Isa* yet.

All of the male respondents interviewed for this study came to faith in *'Isa* earlier than their wives. Male respondents' earlier response than females to the gospel reflect the important role of men for family belief. On the other hand, in one case, S01 needed to divorce his wife after his faith and baptism were revealed.

> After getting to know about my belief and baptism, my wife
> left me. We were married three or four years before I believed

in *'Isa*. I had to get married to serve as an imam in a madrassa. My wife testified against me in the court, so we divorced legally and I took my son. I married again with a [traditional Hindu background] Christian woman. We could not get a new baby, but my new wife still takes good care of my son.

The cultural differences exist between traditional Christians and MBBs and between Muslim family and MBB family. One of the single male respondents, I03, mentioned that he would like to marry only an *Isai* woman, because cultural differences exist in both Muslim and traditional Christian communities. H01 expressed his unpleasant feeling caused by his children's marriage into different religious families. His son has a Christian identity from a Christian/*Isai* family, but his daughter-in-law's family are still Muslims, and they even did not agree with their daughter's marriage. H01 still regrets the absence of a good relationship with his daughter-in-law's family.

There are several differences between *Isai* and Muslim marriages. H01, for example, said "*Isais* ask their children's intention of preference." H02 compared a typical husband's view of his wife between two religions, saying, "A Muslim husband normally thinks lowly of his wife, considering that husband is a *malik* [owner or lord] and wife is lower than him." He also mentioned Muslims' allowance of multiple marriages. "They can marry more than twice, but *Isais* commit to each other and think equally because I learned through the Bible that God arranged this marriage, so we cannot divide it by our own will or interests" (H02). I02 mentioned Muslims' tendency toward male supremacy, saying, "Muslims bring someone's daughter to their family and demand work all the days of her life. Also, if they do not like her, they marry again. Christians/*Isais* work together and do not divorce their spouse all the days of their lives."

Funeral

Most of the Bangladeshi MBB respondents (83%) answered that they want to be buried somewhere other than Muslim graveyards. Three *Isai* Muslim/Muslims (I04, E04, M01) said they would be buried in Muslim graveyards: E04 and M01 stated that they prefer this because their family members are buried there. Five respondents said that wherever they are buried is fine for them, because they are uncertain at the moment (H08), there is no other place to be buried in (S01), or because it does not matter since all lands belong to God (U12, I01, I02). I02 added that it does not matter where they are buried, but he doubts "Muslims would allow *Isai*'s burial in Muslims' graveyard." S01 commented that "I don't know where I will be buried. There is little possibility to be buried in Muslim graveyards and I do not know the location of any Christian graveyard. My faith is in *'Isa Mosiho*. That is it. But, normal Muslims care much for their burial place." U12 agreed with that, saying, "For a Muslim, it is an important issue, but for an *Isai*, it is not important. Present faith is important and *'Isa Mosiho* will guide us." E03 said, " *'Isa* said that the fox has a hole and the bird has a nest, but I have no shelter to live. So, I am just like *'Isa*. I am not unlucky."

The majority of respondents (83%) who wish to be buried in a different place from Muslims either already have their own place to be buried in, or plan to buy land on their own or with a group of their *jama'ats*. As an outside observer, however, F02 had a different opinion of their reality. "They [MBBs] are buried in most cases in a Muslim cemetery because they have only one around them. It is surprising that they said they would not be buried there, but they finally do." U02 actually asked me for a solution to the problem of a lack of burial places for *Isais*:

> There is a Muslim graveyard in my hometown, but if they forbid us to be buried, I do not know how to put ours. I want to ask you about how we will do it. I wish there are some burial places for *Isais*, so that there will be no burial problems for us. It is necessary for *Isais* to be buried in a different tomb because Muslims do not allow us to be buried in their graveyard.

E02 mentioned his Muslim mother's worry about his burial because the majority of his family is Muslim, but he said that he did not care where he will be buried.

> My mother called me on the day after *Eid* festival. She worriedly asked me, "Where will you be buried?" I answered that "there will be various problems if I put my burial in a Christian graveyard. If it is difficult for me to be buried in a Christian graveyard because of social pressure, I do not have any problem about where I am buried. I am fine even in a Muslim graveyard."

As a concluding remark, one of the MBB leaders, L02, suggested having a clear identity first as an *Isai* and then preparing *jama'ats* or cooperating with other traditional Christian groups. He did not encourage Muslim funeral and burial.

> It is better for each *jama'at* or church to prepare for funeral ceremony. It is not right to have burial in a Muslim graveyard. There is no lack of place for *Isais*. If an *Isai* died in a Muslim society, Muslims have some tendency to do funeral ceremonies following their own ways. But this is not good. Socially, if someone is revealed as an *Isai*, Christians will also help in their burial.

Child Education

Most MBBs answered that they care for Christian/*Isai* education in their home even if Islam is studied as a subject in their children's school. None of them said that they were ignorant about the *Kitab*. Eight respondents commented on the benefits of a clear Christian identity and Christian education both at school and at home (S06, H01, H02, U01, U11, U05, U06, I02). According to H01,

> My children were known as Christians in their school. They study Christianity in their schools and read the Bible at home. During the last ten years, our family had gathered together every night for sharing the Bible at home. Now, we gather from time to time because everyone is busy with work. My children have attended our *jama'at* services every Friday and our annual seminars at our *jama'at*. I have sometimes sent them to Christian youth camps. I have always tried to advise something to them through the Bible.

In contrast to those whose children only received Christian education, several others informed that their children studied Islam at school and Christianity at home, but that this was not a problem (I01, N01). I01 said, "My daughter studied Islam and she needed to learn this too for passing. She read all kinds of Christian/*Isai* books and passed diverse Bible courses too. There have been some kinds of interactions in my house too. Also, there was little religious pressure in her school." U03 felt the insufficiency of both teaching on Islam at school and of the *Kitab* at home, so he is planning to send his children for two years of Bible school after they finish high school. On the other hand, N01 believed studying both Islam and Christianity has given some benefits of comparing the two with the help of parents' teaching of the Bible.

> My elder son is eleven years old. I gave him several books about *Isai* belief and in the school, he also read text books of Islam with other Muslim boys. In the house, I teach about *'Isa* and *Isai*. Other Muslim boys laugh at my son and tell him that "your father is a Christian," but I always convince him that the Qur'an also mentions the superiority of *'Isa Mosiho*, and *Isai imandars* also go to heaven in the end just as in the *Kitab*. I believe that it is essential for him to learn Islam for comparing two religions and he will get better understanding in the end. Also, this is 87 percent Muslim majority society. If we don't know about Islam, we can't preach the gospel to them.

Several *Isai* Muslim/Muslims mentioned that "in the past, we read the Qur'an more than the *Kitab*, but now we read the *Kitab* more" (E04). L03 said, "My children consider Islam as a subject, not a religion. I teach Christian terminology to my children too. So, they pray in Christian terms such as *Jisu* [Jesus] not *'Isa* sometimes." However, F04 pointed out the identity confusion experienced by *Isai* Muslims' children: "Because *Isai* Muslim is not a public identity such as school, they are introducing themselves as Muslims without [*Isai*] qualifier. So, their children often feel confused [between the two religions]."

F02 commented on the lack of passion for *Isais'* religious education in contrast to the passion for higher secular education. He urges them to have more passion about *Isai* religious education. "Most *Isais* are extremely concerned about the education of their children, but not much concerned about religious education. I sometimes encourage them to not just think of secular education but also think about the Scripture for our children."

Finance (Economic Activities)

All the respondents stated that they did not change their faith for the purpose of obtaining financial benefits. Many Muslims spread the rumor that Muslims convert to Christianity for the sake of money, so this is a finding that goes against the general perception held by Muslims. In fact, L02 observed that not only do *Isais* normally not receive financial benefits because of their faith, most *Isais* experienced their faith causing some kind of negative consequences in their economic life.

> People say that some Muslims became Christians after getting money. But they did not get financial benefits in exchange for their faith in *'Isa*. Actually, there may be several missions that gave the converts financial help or relief in the past. That is why some rumor spread before. But there are very few converts lured by financial benefits. Normally, *Isais* are poor and are struggling to get a job. There are some kinds of disadvantages of being *Isais*.

Fourteen respondents (29%) specifically mentioned that they "became worse off financially" after conversion and were discriminated against due to their faith in *'Isa*. S01 was expelled from his hometown, and S02 experienced much damage due to the loss of his job as an imam. U05 saw his business dwindle after his new faith was revealed: "Before that, my business was better. I preached the gospel to them, but they did not receive it, did not provide goods, and did not have intention to build up good relationship with me." Even though I02 is now facing some financial difficulty, he expressed his preference for earning the right way as an *Isai* over his previous wrong way of earning as a Muslim.

> In the past, as a Muslim who had a decent job, I was good financially, but after being an *Isai*, I got less income. However, in the past, I earned various kinds of benefits and income from different sources in a wrong way. Now, I get a salary only in the right way, so we are poor. Our shortage does not affect our faith and identity. Even though I have little money, I live in peace.

Six respondents (12.5%) mentioned that their financial situation has not changed with their new faith. N02 faced attacks on his shop by Muslims and needed to close it down, but he expressed his feeling that "I did not face any financial difficulty after believing in *'Isa*, God provided what I need." Five respondents (10%) confessed that they became "better" off financially after coming to faith (S03, H05, U03, U04, E04). U03 said, "I have a pond in my house, and the number of fish has increased. We don't go hungry."

For those who have a Muslim identity, it is true that it is easy to get a job in a Muslim company or an NGO. Conversely, it is possible for those who have a Christian identity to get a job in a Christian organization. While M01 mentioned that it was hard to get a job as a Christian but he got a government job with an *Isai* Muslim/Muslim identity, E02 confessed that he got a job in a Christian NGO because he proved that he was baptized and is a believer of *'Isa*. F03, a foreigner, partly agreed with these statements from MBBs. "If they get a job from a Christian community, they assume a Christian identity. If they get a job from Muslim community, then Muslims. Today this identity and tomorrow different identity. They don't mind changing. If they don't get a job from a Christian community, they do not associate with that community."[8]

However, two Bangladeshi MBB leaders (L01 and L02) revealed that educated people were not influenced by social and financial discrimination. According to L02, "Educated *Isais* can do various types of work in this society. I did not receive any information that 'I could not get a job because I became an *Isai*.' They can get a job in diverse areas and societies, and normally people in workplaces do not persecute any one because of their faith and religion."

Participation in Muslim Activities

All the Christian/*Isai* self-identified MBBs interviewed for this study refrained from participating in any kind of Muslim religious activities including *namaz* (formal prayer at the mosque), *roza* (thirty days of fasting), and *qurbani* (animal sacrifice). Six *Isai/Isai* Muslims mentioned that they participated in a very few social/religious activities, but only those that take place outside of the mosque. Six self-identified *Isai* Muslim/Muslims confessed that they have from time to time participated in religious activities in the mosque, such as *namaz*.

---

8. Actually, one respondent (I04) went back to the Muslim *somaj* because he felt denied by the Christian community after being forced out from his workplace at a Christian NGO. He currently has an *Isai* Muslim/Muslim identity due to conflicts with a foreign leader of a Christian NGO caused by the revelation that he had been pocketing the NGO's money. Although he did not completely deny his culpability, he feels that the leader's judgment that brought his withdrawal was wrong. After being forced out, he moved back to his village and to the Muslim *somaj* and began to participate in Islamic religious activities. He felt unaccepted by the MBB or Christian community.

No Participation in Muslims' Religious Activities

Thirty-two of forty-eight respondents (67%) answered that they do not participate at all in religious activities done by local Muslims. They did these activities before they believed in *'Isa*, but now they do not. Most of these have a Christian/*Isai* identity; several MBBs have an *uboi* (both) *Isai* and *Isai* Muslim identity. Some MBBs only participate in social activities when they are invited by familiar neighbors. U02 said,

> I do not participate in Muslims' religious activities among the community activities. I stopped going to *Eid namaz* from two years ago because we are now going in a different way. I did not do *qurbani* [animal sacrifice] and neither did *roza* [fasting]. For social assembly for important issues, I do not go anymore because they do not accept my opinion. I participate only in social invitation such as marriage of relatives and close friends – I go then. If I miss it, they feel sorry about it.

H01 said that Muslims didn't like his participation even in social festivals saying, "They do not invite me to their *cutna anusitan* [circumcision ceremony] or marriage. If they invite me, I have intention to go. However, some Muslims complain that they won't attend the ceremony since a Christian has been invited." U01 strongly rejected participation in Islamic activities of MBBs and also decided not to join Muslims' funeral ceremonies.

> I do not participate in any Islamic activities such as *namaz*, *roza,* and *qurbani*. If I start to participate in some, I might go to satanic direction. For social invitation, they invite me for money collection. I could go sometimes. If these are social activities, they do not forbid me to come. However, I do not go to Muslims' funeral ceremony. It might cause problems. One day, *Isais* participated in Muslims' funeral ceremony. Among the many, several Muslims demanded forcible repentance of the *Isais*, shouted badly, and beat them up. After hearing this happening, I decided not to go to Muslims' funeral.

Some Participation outside of the Mosque

There were several respondents who have participated in minimal social/ religious activities of Muslims such as *Eid namaz* and *qurbani*. Four respondents answered that they only participated in *Eid namaz* without joining the regular five daily prayers of *namaz*. I01 does not participate in *Eid namaz* regularly, but he did so once in the past with his American friends for the sake of social communion. He explained the social situation of *Eid* festivals, at which *Isais* come face to face with Muslim relatives and the difference of faith between Muslims and *Isai* believers.

> I eat *qurbani* meat. My family and sisters buy cow and I participated with them, but I did not join their cutting. I do not participate in *namaz*. Several years ago, I participated in *Eid namaz* with a foreign friend. He voluntarily joined *Eid namaz* and I did it with him. *Eid namaz* is very important for Muslims, but for me, it is just community union. They already know that I am not a Muslim anymore, and my faith and their faith are different. '*Isa* was a Jew at that time. The reason why I do not participate in *namaz* is that it is against my faith. *Namaz* means surrendering to God. Their way of *namaz* and my way of *namaz* are different. This is religion, a different way of believing. But, sometimes I pray for my Muslim friends, relatives, neighbors by laying hands on them when they are sick. I usually silently pray for them (without concluding in the name of '*Isa*). They become very happy. I give thanks in the name of '*Isa*.

M01, M03, E01, and L03 participated in only *Eid namaz* for retaining social status and social communion. All four of them expressed their social identity as *Isai* Muslims or Muslims, and I also categorized them as *Isai* Muslim/Muslims. E01 said the reason for participation is that "I had participated in it from my early years, and if I do not go, village people interrogate me." L03 participated in only the *Roza Eid* and its *namaz*, explaining this choice as follows:

> *Eid namaz* is a social *namaz* and not a religious one because it happens in a field outside of the mosque. I only participate in *Roza* festival and *namaz*. In *Qurbani Eid*, I do not even go to my hometown. The reason is that one man already did *qurbani*.

'Isa did *qurbani* for all of my sins. I sometimes do fasting. I will fast several days too around Easter Sunday.

Full Participation

The five respondents who participate in more than the *Eid namaz* have *Isai* Muslim/Muslims identities. Two of them only participate in Friday *jummah namaz* sometimes (H08, E03), and three of them (I04, M02, E04) participate in diverse Muslims' religious activities as well as *namaz*. H08 explained his situation:

> Now I am decreasing my participation in Muslims' religious activities. I used to go to mosque for *namaz*, but now I do not attend daily *namaz*. I pray in the morning and evening without performing *namaz*. On Friday, I go to *jummah* prayer in the mosque. If I go there, they do not block me. If I do not go there, they might think that I have gone to Christian religion. So, for making them understand that I am still on their side, I go there. Once a week, I remember the Creator with them and, I show them I am with them. But, I do it in my own way. They worship Muhammad, but I worship in the faith of *'Isa*. I did not say about this to them. I did *roza* last year, but I did not do it this year. If I do fasting that long, I can't do my job for living. I become weak. I did not do *qurbani* this year. For *namaz*, I don't need to perform it because I do my prayer. Regarding attending Friday *jummah*, there is a rule in this society. Other people sometimes say that I have received the Christian religion. So, I faced many social pressures. If people see me at the mosque, they think that I am still on their side. But, I am not going to say that I continuously go there. I am weak in terms of economic condition such as using electronics and water. I can't live without it. If I become free of these worries, I will be changed.

E03 and H08 are similar in terms of performing *jummah namaz* on Friday and in their *Isai* Muslim identity, but E03 used to have Christian/*Isai* identity. He shared his story and his reasons for changing his social identity from Christian/*Isai* to *Isai* Muslim/Muslim and participating in Muslims' religious activities. The two reasons are: (1) to remain in *somaj*; and (2) to bring people to *'Isa* through a good relationship.

> I was a normal Muslim like performing *namaz* regularly or sometimes. I believed in *'Isa* and was baptized by local MBB evangelists from a foreign organization who properly explained to us the *Kitab* from the Qur'an. That time, my father and grand-father agreed with the *'Isai* faith, so I did not get any pressure from my family. But, society blocked me from attending the mosque anymore even though I had intention to keep good relationship with them. I came to Dhaka and worked in foreign missions for evangelism several years. That time my identity was a Christian. . . . When I worked at an organization, I used to sell the New Testament [not *Injil Sharif* translation]. Many people asked me, "Who are you and what is your identity?" I answered that I am a Christian. But, many people shouted to me saying, "You look like a Muslim but why did you become a Christian?" I also replied that I believe in *Jisu* [Jesus] as my Lord and Savior in a traditional Christian language. We did not use *Isai* language in our training yet. If we use that, we might get fruit from it. People surrounded us and tortured us, but Allah and *'Isa Mosiho* [Messiah] helped me. Once I use the words from the Qur'an, people started to listen to my words like Allah, *nabi* [prophet]. *Nazatdata* [savior], not *trankorta* "savior" in traditional lan-guage. These Muslim-friendly languages had acceptance.

E03 went on to explain his reasons for changing his social identity from Christian/*Isai* to *Isai* Muslim/Muslim:

> After believing in *'Isa* for the first time, I had introduced myself as a Christian. But as time went by, I continued practicing di-verse Muslim cultures, and now I introduce myself as a Muslim. I believe in all the prophets and believe in *'Isa* as the Savior. I can call myself as an *Isai* Muslim too. In the Qur'an, *'Isa* is also a Muslim. *'Isa* did not say "I am a Christian nor a Muslim," but said that "believe in Allah and follow me." The reason I became an *Isai* Muslim/Muslim is that we have to work in a Muslim culture. It does not matter if we call God as Allah or *Issor* ["God"

in the traditional Bible], or the Creator. But, our main goal is to reveal *'Isa* as the Savior. When we work in this kind of culture, we can say and do like what Paul said and did. If you ask me my religion, I can answer that my religion is *Isai*. Islam is a "peace" religion. *'Isa Mosiho* preached a peaceful religion. So, I am at peace.

One local and one foreign teacher inspired me to think and do like this. I thought that we did not need to separate from the society. We need to work staying in society. Now, I perform *namaz* only on Friday in daytime and sometimes in the evening at a local mosque. It is irregular. *Namaz* means, if you don't mind saying from the Qur'an, calling Allah silently, not for showing people, but we call upon our Creator silently. I sometimes do fasting but do not continue it during *roza* for social participation. I did not do *qurbani*, but they gave me *qurbani* meat. If they give any social invitation, I participate. I have two reasons to participate in Muslims' activities: (1) to mingle and share with *somaj* (religious community); and (2) to find opportunity to lead people to *'Isa* by having good relationship with them.

M02 received *'Isa* as Savior through an *Isai* Muslim evangelist. After believing in *'Isa*, he preached the gospel of *'Isa* in many places near his hometown. People began to recognize him as a Muslim follower of *'Isa*. He said the *somaj* applied social pressure on him and his co-believers in various ways when they were few in number, but now they don't persecute them because they have increased numbers of believers like him. They can arrange marriages with other believers' family. M02 narrated his experience of conflict with other Muslims about burial: "When three of our co-believers died, we had some intention to bury them in a Muslim graveyard. However, they were denied permission because the Muslims recognized them as *'Isa* followers. So, we decided to bury them in our own places." M02 can participate in any kind of Muslim activities. For social invitation, he only responds to go to his co-believers' social invitation. In *namaz*, he practices a different confession from other Muslims:

> I sometimes go to a mosque for performing *namaz* around once a week. I do fasting. But I did not practice *qurbani* because of

lack of money to buy animal for sacrifice. I usually do not go to
Muslims' invitation, but I do go for our co-believers' invitation
like circumcision. Because Muslims don't invite us, we don't
invite them too. We confess in *namaz* "Allah is one and *'Isa* is
Messiah." They sometimes forbid our coming to their meetings
because we have different belief in *'Isa* as a Savior.

E04 gave a similar response. He participates in all kinds of Muslim religious activities including *namaz, roza,* and *qurbani,* but sometimes Muslims
have created problems. He was an imam in a local mosque before, but now
he is preaching around without staying in a local mosque.

I participated in everything such as performing *namaz* at the
mosque when I stayed in a village. I do fasting, attend marriage
ceremonies, and do *qurbani.* But, once or twice, Muslims created
some problems when I gave *qurbani.* That time, I faced social
judgment because of my faith in *'Isa* as an Islamic guest preacher.
So, I gave up doing *qurbani* from that time. Now, I attend all
festivals and get opportunity to do *milaat* which is the time when
five to twenty people gather to sing Arabic melody songs and
to preach something such as sharing stories. The main purpose
for me is to preach where I have been invited about diverse
topics like *zakat* (almsgiving) and *'Isa Mosiho* from the Qur'an
and Hadith, and creation stories from the book of Genesis in
the *Kitab.* These contents of teaching mostly come from and
start from the Qur'an and Hadith. *Zakat* is found in the Book
named *Malaki* (Malachi) and *Levio* (Leviticus). They listen to
my teaching, but they struggle to follow the principle of giving
one tenth (tithe) because it is a big amount for them.

E04 then said that his reason for participating in Islamic religious activities
is that they give him the opportunity to preach to Muslims about his own
understanding of religious activities.

Regarding my reasons to participate in religious activities, it is
because when I participate with or am invited by them, they give
me opportunity to preach among ten to twelve persons and they
invite me as an imam, I can talk on anything I want to preach

to them. During *namaz*, I speak about Ibrahim [Abraham] who is the father of a nation, and then pray Sūra *al-Fātiḥa* with another Sūra from the Qur'an. So, there is no dissimilarity with *'Isa Mosiho*, or there is no relation to Mohammad during *salat* [prayer]. Most of the languages in *namaz* are about Allah. In *namaz*, they have no Mohammad. So, I believe doing *namaz* is fine as a follower of *'Isa*. When I finish the *namaz*, I end it with only saying, "Allah is one."

In *qurbani*, there is Ibrahim [Abraham]. Ibrahim had sacrificed his son *Ismail* or *Isak* [Issac]. There is no debate whether he passed the test to sacrifice his son. It is a duty for us to remind them [of their passing God's test]. Regarding *qurbani*, I can get a good chance to teach about *qurbani* as a sacrifice. During the discussion of *qurbani* with Muslims, I can raise a question like how we can give big *qurbani*. Learning from the *qurbani*, I can extend my teaching from Adam's leather-wearing by spilling blood and Ibrahim's lamb. I ask them the meaning of the blood and lamb. I also ask them who did the last *qurbani* and lead them to know about *'Isa*, the lamb of Allah. During this discussion, I often ask them who Allah's lamb is. I tell them that the answer is *'Isa Mosiho*. Fasting is no problem too following *'Isa's* warning: "Do not fast to show others."

E04 reinterpreted the five pillars of Islam through his own understanding by faith in *'Isa*. His new journey began with joining Al-Sunni for one week of training, and continued with his own interpretation from his reading of the Qur'an and the *Kitab*.

Advantages and Disadvantages of Three Social Identities

MBBs have several advantages of staying in their present social identity, and they also face some difficulties and problems when they live in their social identity. This section deals with the struggles and advantages of three social identities: Christian/*Isai*, *Isai*/*Isai* Muslims (*uboi*; both), and *Isai* Muslim/Muslims.

Christian/Isai Identity: Advantages and Disadvantages

MBBs who have a Christian/*Isai* identity have certain advantages: (1) spiritual benefits like assurance of salvation and peace; (2) benefits of a clear identity, such as government protection and less possibility of coming back to Islam; (3) no requirement to participate in Muslims' religious activities such as *namaz, roza,* and *qurbani.* First, the Christian/*Isai* identity has spiritual benefits. U03 said, "This way has special benefits for eternal life." Similarly, H06 said, "This way is what I love. It leads me to salvation. I believe the gospel has the power of the truth." S05 pointed out the benefits of worshipping freely: "We can worship God in a right way and freely. We praise God with songs, preach the gospel, and are connected with our *jama'at*" (S05). U12, U02, U04, U05, U07, and N01 expressed feelings of spiritual joy, fellowship with God, and inner and eternal peace: "I live my life with spiritual joy and confidence because of walking in the truth" (U12); "I got eternal peace" (U02); "Now I have inner peace" (U07); "My benefit is to get to heaven and get happiness in the world" (N01); "God is with us and leads us" (U04); and "I am thankful for the Savior because he accepted me by grace" (U05).

Second, a Christian/*Isai* identity has the benefit of clarity. U01 emphasized on revealed identity, saying, "I can preach the gospel openly with my Christian/*Isai* identity, so they can ask me how I became a Christian from a Muslim background. Revealing myself as a Christian is the best way because if I call myself an *Isai* [or *Isai* Muslim], it has the possibility to hide or lie" (U01). H01 has the benefit of police protection because of his open identity. "I asked my pastor and made my certificate of baptism. If I didn't have this, local police might not believe me and would not protect me" (H01). Finally, MBBs with this identity do not need to follow Muslims' regulations. I02 said, "We don't need to participate in, nor follow *namaz, roza, qurbani,* or any other Muslims' regulations."

Nevertheless, a Christian/*Isai* identity has some disadvantages, including (1) receiving side glances and abusive words from Muslims, (2) lack of acceptance and social bans, and (3) lack of social relationships with other Muslims and Muslim family members. First, Muslims look down on them and speak bad words to them. U12 said, "Because our country is a Muslim majority society, Muslims have the tendency to look asquint at *Isais* and I sometimes feel inferiority complex. They do backbiting to me and spread wrong rumors about us and blame us." S01 was scolded by a Muslim who asked him, "Why did you change your religion? You are a really bad person. How much money did you get from Christians?"

A second disadvantage of Christian/*Isai* identity was shared by many respondents: lack of acceptance from Muslims – including unbelieving family members and neighbors – and social bans. I02 said, "Muslims talk to us badly, don't like us, nor accept us. I think they hate us because we converted to another faith and stopped being a Muslim." "They just listen (or pretend to listen) to our speech, but do not accept us" (U06). "We are not sure where we will be buried because we don't have a specific graveyard and they don't accept us" (U02). "My Muslim family doesn't accept me publicly and other children laugh at my children" (N01). Some kinds of discrimination and attacks were experienced by MBBs with Christian/*Isai* identity. H01 said, "There is a community decision committee. There are Muslims, Hindus, and Christians. But they said, 'We don't need a Muslim convert to Christianity in our committee.'" H01 thought that some kind of jealousy and ignorance is operational here. A local chairman said that they should "help only other persons," not Muslim converts to Christianity. N02's small shop was destroyed by Muslims.

Third, MBBs with this identity face a lack of social relationships with the majority. H02 said, "I don't have much relationship with my relatives." According to U09, "We have some social loneliness." I02 said, "Now they don't attack me, but I don't participate in their activities and have no fellowship with them. We do not have any relationship and feelings between us." U11 was sad about being sidelined by his Muslim family members. "My Muslim family members did not call me when my father died. They did not allow me to join the funeral ceremony and all other sons from my father got his inheritance except me" (U11). U03 confessed that a fundamentalist Muslim group called and threatened them saying, "We will punish you and beat you," but he did not care about their warnings and stated, "I was not afraid of this. Because I did not harm them, why should I be fearful? I am ready to talk with them. I studied the Qur'an and have the *Kitab* too. Because they cannot show me that I have taken the wrong path, I am not afraid."

Isai/Isai Muslim (Uboi; Both) Identity: Advantages and Disadvantages

The benefits of this *uboi* (both) identity are: (1) the ability to be flexible in response to the situation; and (2) it raises Muslims' curiosity about this (*Isai* Muslim) identity, which can create opportunities to share the gospel. First, the *uboi* identity is flexible depending on the situation. M04 is currently working in Muslim evangelism. He does not want his identity to be revealed too early. "Because this is Muslim *somaj*, we cannot easily say we are *Isai* for the first time. I need to introduce myself as a Muslim and slowly, my *Isai* identity will be revealed" (M04). E02 does not want to harm his work in a mission field by fully revealing his spiritual identity: "After having this *Isai* belief, I could get this job in a Christian organization and got benefit from it. When I work in a field, I need to be a Muslim socially even though I have spiritual identity as a Christian/*Isai*. It is because it might be harmful if my Christian/*Isai* identity is revealed to my work field at this moment."

Second, the *uboi* identity uses Muslims' curiosity about this identity as an opportunity for evangelism. S01 said, "If I introduce myself as an *Isai* Muslim, I don't lie to them because Muslim means 'someone who submits to God.' Sometimes they ask me what an *Isai* Muslim is and I use this question as an opportunity for sharing the gospel of '*Isa*" (S01). Similarly, E01 explained that

> when people heard about *Isai* Muslim, they ask me what it is. Then, I have had the chance to answer by using the Qur'an. I show them good verses such as Sūra *al-Mā'ida* to understand '*Isa*: The son of *Marium* [Mary] '*Isa* who came as Daud [David]'s descendant. You tell me I am a Christian, but the Qur'an also talks about '*Isa*. I use verses from the Qur'an. I am a Muslim. If they ask me who '*Isa* is, then I answer it by using the Qur'an first.

The disadvantages of the *uboi* identity are that: (1) Muslims might doubt the unknown identity; (2) Those with *uboi* identity sometimes feel guilty about deceiving others regarding their Christian identity; and (3) Muslims continually try to draw them back to Islam. First, Muslims have doubts about the unknown identity. S01 said, "Some doubts might spring up in Muslims' mind that it is a new religion if they hear the word '*Isai* Muslim.' So, one might fall into trouble in the process of trying to make them understand, and if they notice that I am a Christian, they might get angrier." E02 confessed that he felt guilty when he introduced himself in two ways as socially Muslim and spiritually Christian/*Isai*. "Because I do not introduce myself as a single identity, I sometimes feel that I am lying morally and even that I betray the Lord. It hurts my heart when I introduce myself as a Muslim in spite of my Christian/*Isai* [spiritual] identity." H08 said, "I am troubled in my mind that I should have moved more toward *Isai* direction." Third, Muslims continually try to draw them back to Islam. H04 and H05 made almost the same comment: "Muslims sometimes tell me to come back to Islam." I believe this occurs because their introduction to their identity includes the term "Muslim," which may cause others to feel that it is possible to make them turn back to Islam.

Isai Muslim/Muslim Identity: Advantages and Disadvantages

The advantages of the *Isai* Muslim/Muslim identity are: (1) no social obstacles and no harm for family; (2) living with the majority; (3) no diminishing faith, rather getting preaching opportunities; and (4) less persecution while there's a growing number of believers. First, the people who have *Isai* Muslim/Muslim identity expressed that they have not experienced any social obstacles. "There are no obstacles to do anything in my society" (M01). "They do not speak badly about me" (L03). Second, this identity makes it possible to live with the majority and avoid harm to one's family. M03 said, "I can freely visit my neighbors, stay with them, and have deep relationship with them. My family members can also do that" (M03). "They do not harm my family too" (L03). H08 compared the social benefits between two communities. "It has social benefits. If I am sick, it is more possible to get help from my Muslim neighbors staying near me. If my house is on fire, won't it be my neighbors who would help in putting it out? My *Isai jama'at* is a little far from my house and socially, I am getting less benefits from my *Isai jama'at*" (H08). M02 and E03 similarly said that advantages of this identity include "living with society people together and finding the way to share '*Isa* interconnectedly."

Third, respondents said people who have an *Isai* Muslim/Muslim identity do not have diminishing faith – rather, they get preaching opportunities. E04 said, "There are more advantages than weaknesses in this social identity such as getting more preaching opportunities." M03 said, "Muslims are not angry when they know that I am a follower of '*Isa*. It is because I can preach the gospel through the Qur'an and I can introduce the necessity of salvation even though they remain Muslims by telling them that if they accept *torika* [repentance], they can become a follower of '*Isa*." Finally, those with *Isai* Muslim/Muslim identity experienced that persecution became less as time went by and as the number of believers increased. M02 said, "There were more persecutions and problems when our number of believers was small. But, after the growth in believers' numbers, social pressures have slowly decreased."

The disadvantages of the *Isai* Muslim/Muslim identity are: (1) some Christians' criticism and exposure that they are actually Christians; (2) fewer opportunities to work in Christian organizations; (3) some persecution; and (4) the ease with which faith can disappear due to lack of sacrifice. First, some Christians criticize them for lying to Muslims. M03 said, "It is hard to fully reveal all of my inner identity and belief, but in some places, I have been exposed as an *Isai.*" E04 said, "In some places, people have criticized me, saying that I am lying." Second, they have fewer opportunities to work in Christian organizations. L03 supported his own decision to stay in a Muslim identity, avoiding financial benefits from being hired in a Christian organization. "I can be a director or a leader of a Christian mission organization if I become a revealed Christian. But I did not choose my identity because of position or money, but due to my faith and conviction." In my judgment, however, L03's statements do not quite match his current position. He is now head of a Christian school run by a Christian mission organization, and although he presents himself as a Muslim to parents at the school and his neighbors, his current position does not support his comment.

Third, people who have an *Isai* Muslim/Muslim identity have to endure persecution from time to time. "I have been beaten four times because I preached 'Isa with a Muslim identity," M03 reported. "I have been subjected to *somaj* judgment five times because of my baptism and evangelistic activities about 'Isa" (E04). One can surmise from their statements that their persecutions or social judgments came not just in response to their faith in 'Isa, but also in response to the contradictions between their faith in 'Isa and their Muslim social identity, because general Muslims do not think this way. Finally, it is relatively easy for people with this identity to lose their faith in 'Isa due to the lack of sacrifice involved in remaining faithful. S01 spoke about his difficulty finding real believers ready to pay the price for faith without hiding their faith and unconcerned with material benefits. According to S01, "Many Muslims oftentimes have been baptized secretly and sometimes openly when they could get blankets and towels, but now we find it really hard to see where they are and whether they still believe or not."

F01 mentioned the weaknesses of each identity group, explaining that each group's weakness is a herald of strength on the other side. He also noted, however, that each social identity group needs a certain number of members to make up a strong faith community.

> We can't avoid weakness because weakness is a herald of
> strength. Two things go together. You've got to build community,

maturity, and numbers. Community can only be strong in this country when it has sufficient numbers. When you have small numbers, a minority community could be squashed anytime whenever the majority chooses to do so. Fifty or a hundred people do not get too much pressure. A Muslim community tolerates because there are enough people there. Nobody can do anything against it.

Social Identity according to MBBs' Perceptions and Four-Self Faith Communities (RQ 3)

The third research question tried to investigate two things: MBBs' perceptions about key issues such as Allah, 'Isa, Muhammad, and the Qur'an, and also about the features of a four-self faith community (self-propagating, self-supporting, self-governing, and self-theologizing). With regard to MBBs' perception of key issues and figures and the comparison of their views with those of Muslims, most MBBs answered that their concepts of 'Isa, Muhammad, and the Qur'an are different from general Muslims, but that their concept of Allah is similar to that of other Muslims. With regard to the four-self characteristics of MBBs' community, MBBs and foreign respondents mostly agreed with the concept and its directionality, but most respondents said that fully embracing the four-self methodology in the faith community is difficult at this moment and more time is needed to actualize it in Bangladesh. In sum, this third research question and its answers fall into two parts of data coding and findings: (1) comparison and contrast of MBB and Muslim concepts of four issues and figures; and (2) social identity in view of the four-self faith community. In addition, MBBs' diverse views of contextualization in Bangladesh are introduced at the end of the chapter.

Comparison and Contrast of MBBs and General Muslim Views of Allah, 'Isa, Muhammad, and the Qur'an

All of the forty-eight Bangladeshi MBBs confessed that their understanding of Allah, 'Isa, Muhammad, and the Qur'an differs from those of general Muslims. Because the research does not primarily focus on theological issues or metaphysical concepts of God such as Trinity, I will simply narrate what

MBBs think about these four subjects and how their thinking differs from the concepts of general Muslims.

Allah and 'Isa

All forty-eight respondents agreed that they used the term Allah to refer to the almighty God of the Bible. I think it is because the MBBs that I interviewed read the *Injil Sharif* (New Testament) and *Kitab* (*Mussolmani* Bible), which use the Arabic term "Allah" for God. Generally, MBBs think and agree that Allah is one, a creator, invisible, and almighty. This concept of Allah is not different from the beliefs of general Muslims. One of the findings about MBBs' use of the term Allah is that they add the word "*Mabud*," which means the Lord. They frequently refer to God as *Mabud* Allah (Lord God) more often than general Muslims. On the other side, there was one respondent (H05) who expressed a difference in his view of the character of the *Mabud* Allah (Lord God) compared to the views of other Muslims. He contrasted Muslims' feeling that *Mabud* Allah is a long distance away with MBBs' feeling that he is near. H05 responded that "their concept of Allah is different from us." He continued:

> I start the day with prayer to *Mabud* Allah. I entrust this day to him. I feel peace when I read and hear his word. When I go to my neighbors at night, I pray to him saying, "Lord, please keep near me." Because general Muslims don't know about it, they feel God is far away or above them and they lack relationship with him.

Even though the MBBs and general Muslims' understandings of Allah are similar in several senses, there are major differences in their views of his relationship with 'Isa. Muslims' concept of 'Isa is very different from that of MBBs. MBBs discussed three characteristics of 'Isa: (1) 'Isa is Allah (and a [spiritual] son of God); (2) 'Isa is Savior; and (3) 'Isa will not return to this world as a disciple of Muhammad.

'Isa is Allah

Twelve respondents (25%) stated that "*'Isa* is Allah itself." This draws on the same expression found in the verse John 1:1 in Bangla *Injil Sharif* that "*Tini* [He, referring to the Word, 'Isa] *Nijei* [itself] *Allah*" ("He is Allah itself"). S03 said, "*'Isa* is Allah himself. Allah is the father of 'Isa Mosiho spiritually, not physically." Other respondents made similar comments.

Actually, I think Allah and ['Isa] *Mosiho* [Messiah] are the same. When *Mosiho* came to the world, he was separated from Allah. He did all the rituals like us and finally he gave his life for us. But Muslims don't think so. We think *Mosiho* is the son of Allah. But Muslims don't think the same. (I03)

My belief is very different from Muslims. Allah himself is 'Isa *Mosiho*. Allah himself is the Word. The Word is 'Isa *Mosiho*. 'Isa *Mosiho* is Allah, and Allah is 'Isa *Mosiho*. Two persons are actually one. 'Isa is Allah's precious son. There is no difference of 'Isa from Allah. Father and Son are one. I cannot understand this fully. This special relationship is very deep. (E01)

'Isa *Mosiho* is him. Muslims think that Allah and 'Isa *Mosiho* are different. They know that Allah is the creator and 'Isa is a prophet. But, 'Isa *Mosiho* and Allah-the creator are not two, but one. . . . 'Isa is the creator, Savior, someone who is worth following. Allah-the creator and 'Isa *Mosiho* exist differently, but are one. This is like doing a photocopy of the front side and back side. We cannot see God, but 'Isa said that "If you see me, then you see God." (S01)

I01 explained the relationship between Allah and 'Isa *Mosiho* deeply. He also agreed that Allah and 'Isa *Mosiho* are one. He gave the interview in English.

I think God and Jesus are the same. His human form is Jesus. Normal Muslims don't believe like this. They believe Jesus is just a prophet sent by God. To me, God and Jesus is [*sic*] the same. Regarding the Trinity, God, the Son, the Holy Spirit, I think Trinity is tri-unity. Not three men, but three persons. Person and man are different. Muslim people and even some Christians think person and man are the same thing. [There are] three entities or three identities from my body such as blood, flesh, and bone, with these three together, [compose the] human body. If I separate from my bones, it will not be a man. So, unity of these three is God. Three identity and three persons, this way I believe. In terms of the concept of God, Allah, it is similar to

Muslims. Similarity is that God is omnipresent and almighty . . .
etc. But, many differences are here. Difference is that they think
that they are slaves of God, not children of God. I believe that
Father and Son relationship is human understanding. I need to
understand this way. I can't understand spiritual things totally.
You are a foreigner. I don't know all your country's culture. I also
don't know all heavenly things. This is window. Through this, I
can only see the eternity.

Muslims think that Jesus is a prophet, but my understanding
[is] that he is God. He came to save me, and he jumped into the
water to save me. So, I don't need any religious book than he
himself. He is the most important for me. Many things I can understand and explain, if I fix my eyes on him, it become[s] easier
to understand. [Interviewer asks: Are God and Jesus different?]
Same. I told you this is a spiritual thing. I have worldly understanding. I can't understand completely the spiritual things. To
give this spiritual thing in my limited understanding and this
worldly understanding, he told the religious term as son. But he
is not the son in the sense that I am the son of my father. Only
to bring into my understanding, he named this a son. Muslims
take this term "son" literally. That is the difference of us from
[*sic*] Muslims.

Other respondents emphasized the relationship between Allah and *'Isa*
as a father and his spiritual son. U03 confessed that " *'Isa* is a spiritual son
of Allah," saying,

Muslims commonly say that "Allah *shorik nai.*" It means that
there is no sharer of Allah. Therefore, they say that *'Isa* is not
the son of Allah, but they do not read the *Kitab*, and neither the
Qur'an. *'Isa Mosiho* is the son of Allah and we are also children
of Allah. The Word became flesh and dwelled among us. He was
conceived by the Holy Spirit and a spiritual son of Allah. It is
written in the book of John.

U05 explained Muslims' questions about Allah's son. He said that distorted
teaching in the mosques about the term "son of God" made Muslims dislike
the gospel and *'Isa*.

Muslims say "Allah is one, but how is it possible to have a son?" Generally, the term "son of God" is the most troublesome word for Muslims. This word makes it difficult for them to receive the gospel and make them dislike the gospel in the society. This is because of the teaching in the mosque. I explain to them like this. "Look at the sun. This is one, but we receive many things from it such as heat, light, and power. In this way, I explain Allah's oneness and the word of Allah. He is the Word, the living word in the gospel of John. In the Qur'an, we can also find this kind of expression of Allah's word, *'Isa*.

'Isa the Savior

All three groups of MBBs agree that *'Isa* is the *nazatdata* (savior) who has the power to give salvation. Several self-identified *Isai* Muslim/Muslims also confessed that *'Isa* is Savior (L03, M02) and the Word of Allah (E03). L03, a self-identified *Isai* Muslim/Muslim, said that he believes *'Isa* is a spiritual son of Allah and Allah himself. "I believe that *'Isa Mosiho* is the Savior. He is a spiritual son of Allah. He died, resurrected, and will come again. My Allah is *'Isa Mosiho*. The Creator is the father of *'Isa*."

M02 mentioned that "Muslims consider *'Isa* as a prophet,[9] but we believe in *'Isa* as *nazatdata* [savior]. When I do *shahada* [Islamic creed at *namaz*], I confess that Allah is one and *'Isa* is *Mosiho* (Messiah)." E03, a self-identified *Isai* Muslim/Muslim, expressed his view, which was based on the Qur'an saying, " *'Isa, Ruhullula* [Spirit of Allah] and *'Isa, Kalema* [the Word]. Hey, *Marium* [Mary]! I am giving you the good words [news]." The *Kitab*, he continued, also said, " *'Isa* is the Word of Allah himself. Allah created all things by the Word. And, the Word was with Allah. In this way, I believe in *'Isa*." S04, a self-identified Christian/*Isai*, also identified *'Isa* as the Savior:

> *'Isa* is the Savior. Muslims acknowledge only Allah, the Creator. But, I believe in the Father, Son, and the Holy Spirit and also

---

9. In the Muslim view, a prophet (*nabi* in Bangla) is a messenger who delivers messages from Allah. Twenty-five (some say near around) of the prophets mentioned in the Qur'an also appear in the Old Testament or New Testament. Muslims' prophets include Ibrahim (Abraham), *Daud* (David), *Musa* (Moses), *'Isa* (Jesus), *Yahya* (John the Baptist), and, of course, Muhammad. General Muslims in Bangladesh do not think *'Isa* is a high and important prophet as much as other prophets, but in contrast consider Muhammad as the highest and closest one to Allah.

believe that these three are one. I know that the Word became flesh and dwelt among us. I believe that '*Isa* suffered, died for us, and will come again. I know that if I believe this, I am saved.

H04, a self-identified *Isai/Isai* Muslim, introduced the concept of a *super-ishkari* (the one who leads people to Allah and heaven, the mediator). He believes that '*Isa* is a real *superishkari*:

I believe in this way and I preach it in this Muslim majority context. There is a *superishkari*. He will lead people to heaven. I don't have a ticket now. One man will lead us. There is a prophet to lead us to heaven. Muslims think that he is Muhammad. But, I introduce the idea that '*Isa Mosiho* is a real *superishkari*. I introduce '*Isa* to them through the Qur'an.

'*Isa* will not return to the world as a disciple of Muhammad

Three self-identified Christian/*Isai* (H01, U04, U09) mentioned a Muslim rumor about '*Isa's* second coming as a follower of Muhammad. This rumor is widespread in Bangladesh, and comes from the teaching of imams at mosques. H01 said, "Muslims say that '*Isa* will come again as a follower of Muhammad, but I believe in '*Isa* as Allah's spiritual son." U04 introduced Muslims' understanding of '*Isa* as a regular man. "Muslims say like this: ''*Isa* is a man. '*Isa* will come back here as a disciple of Muhammad.' General Muslims do not read the Qur'an, nor the *Injil*, but they say something only by listening from imams. So, they do not want to hear the truth, nor believe in it." U09 also said, "Many Islamic teachers say that when '*Isa Mosiho* comes again, he will come as a disciple of Muhammad. I reply to them that '*Isa* is in heaven now, so how can he come again as a disciple of Muhammad? Then they tell me, 'You are a Christian,' and the conversation is finished."

Muhammad and the Qur'an

A quarter of my MBB respondents (25%) who mostly self-identified themselves as *Isai* Muslim/Muslims except for two Christian/*Isais* stated that Muhammad is a general prophet who brought the Qur'an, but that he does not have power to lead them to heaven. This belief differs from the thinking of general Bengali Muslims. Muslims believe that Muhammad is the *superishkari* (the one who leads people to Allah and heaven, the mediator), but *Isai imandars* (believers) generally believe that they can go to heaven by believing in *'Isa*, while Muhammad is just a *shutorkokari* (warner) and a *shungbatdata* (introducer of the way). In this sense, he is called a prophet who warned them to worship one God and introduced the direction to the *Kitab* (Bible or Holy Books). Regarding the Qur'an, while most self-identified Christian/*Isais* consider it to be a general book of guiding toward the *Kitab*, some *Isai* Muslim/Muslims believe that the Qur'an came from Allah as well as the *Kitab*, but they value and read the *Kitab* much.

Muhammad

The self-identified Christian/*Isais* generally consider that Muhammad is a man or a warner not different from other persons (U01, U04, U11, N02). The self-identified *Isai* Muslim/Muslims consider Muhammad as a prophet not different from other prophets like *Musa* (Moses) and *Daud* (David), who brought Allah's words and revelations in the line of *Taurat, Zabur,* and the Qur'an. They do not consider him to be someone who has power to give salvation, as salvation comes only through *'Isa* (M02, E03, E04).

One of the self-identified Christian/*Isai* MBBs, U11, quoted Muhammad's own words in the Qur'an. "I don't know the future of mine, so how can I lead other people to heaven?" According to U11, "Muhammad is a general man. He can't do any special things for us." N02 agreed: "Muhammad is a man like us and just a warner. He was sent for telling the true way of the gospel of *'Isa*, but he did not fully accomplish it. I receive only some part of the Qur'an which accords with the *Injil*." Other respondents made similar comments. "Muhammad is a prophet and a *shungbatdata* [introducer of good news] (S02) and "a postman" (H02). H02 continued: "He came for telling people that *'Isa Mosiho* is the Savior. Muhammad is not a savior, but I know that *'Isa* is the only Savior and Muhammad cannot save people by his own power." S04 said that Muhammad is not in the *Kitab,* "so, he is not very important for us. He is a man like us. The Qur'an is also their [Muslims'] ideal, but it does not matter with me."

M02, a self-identified *Isai* Muslim/Muslim, said, "I consider Muhammad as a prophet and *'Isa* as the Savior. Muhammad doesn't have the power to give us salvation, but *'Isa* has." M01 agrees that "Muslims think about going to heaven by good works and the help of Muhammad, but I think of going to heaven directly by following *'Isa Mosiho.*" M03 said, "Muhammad is a prophet.

Salvation comes only through 'Isa. Allah sent many prophets to the world, but the Savior is only one. Prophets are much lower than the Savior. 'Isa is the Savior and *Komakari* [one who has power]." E04 views "Muhammad as a prophet not different from other prophets like *Musa* (Moses) and *Daud* (David), but 'Isa is the Savior." E02, one of the *uboi* identity MBBs, said "I consider Muhammad as a prophet." He continued,

> I thought he [Muhammad] could save me. During the time of becoming a believer of 'Isa through reading the *Kitab* and the Qur'an, I realized that 'Isa was the Savior, and Muhammad was a prophet and a warner sent by Allah. Muhammad was sent for warning people to follow the *Kitab* and turn from their sins. General Muslims believe that they can go to heaven through Muhammad.

While Christian/*Isai* self-identified MBBs consider Muhammad as a general man or at least a warner to direct to the true way – previous *Kitabs* and *Injil*, the gospel of 'Isa – several respondents from self-identified *Isai*/*Isai* Muslim/Muslim commented that Muhammad is a prophet. If they say Muhammad is a prophet, in what sense do they confess this? In my observation of their statements, I found two things. First, many MBB respondents expressed that the Qur'an is one kind of guide to know and believe in 'Isa, the way of salvation. The qur'anic verses that support 'Isa as the Savior give them a good image of Muhammad as someone giving direction to the true way. MBBs generally admit that the Qur'an came from Muhammad whether it is revealed by God like the other three *Kitabs* (self-identified *Isai* Muslim/Muslim's view) or not revealed (Christian/*Isai* view). The self-identified Christian/*Isai* group does not consider Muhammad as a prophet, but just a warner, (Islamic) religion introducer, or at best gospel (truth) introducer in terms of having verses that introduce 'Isa in the Qur'an. Second, self-identified MBBs who are living in a Muslim *somaj* and are trying to engage other Muslims about 'Isa do not want to look down on the Qur'an and Muhammad (M03, H01). They are also using many qur'anic references to introduce 'Isa.

The other interesting finding is that, unlike Western Christian believers, Bangladeshi MBBs held very few negative views of Muhammad. To supplement the contents of my first interviews, I met a second time with three *jama'at* leaders (H01, U01, N01) who have Christian/*Isai* identities, and asked a question about their honest views of Muhammad. N01 mentioned several of Muhammad's negative influences in areas such as early [child] marriage,[10] multiple marriages, and *jihad* [war]. U01 mentioned the falsity of his prophethood. H01, however, does not want to look down on the Qur'an and Muhammad. He said,

> If there exists no Qur'an, I could not have known the Old Testament and the New Testament. After I believe in *'Isa* after reading the Bible, I needed to compare the Bible (and *Kitab*) with the Qur'an. The Qur'an does not enable us to grow in faith in *'Isa*, but I believe that MBBs do not grow in faith firmly without this kind of comparing process. Also, studying the Qur'an is necessary for sharing the gospel of *'Isa* to Muslims. I also believe that Muhammad is also a follower of *'Isa* in some sense in view of many references in the Qur'an regarding *'Isa* and direction to *Kitabs*.

The Qur'an compared to the *Kitab*

The Bangladeshi school textbook on Islam for class (year or grade) three states that Muslims have four *asmani* [revealed from heaven, heavenly] *Kitabs*: *Taurat* by *Musa* [Moses], *Zabur* by *Daud* [David], *Injil* by *'Isa* [Jesus], and the Qur'an by Muhammad. Even though the religious textbook of Islam from the Bangladeshi government does not say that the first three *Kitabs* are modified or corrupted, general Muslims in Bangladesh have heard that these three *Kitabs* are not necessary because the final revelation, the Qur'an, fulfilled all the previous revelations, leaving no need for previous *Kitabs*. They also hear that these three *Kitabs* are modified by Christians. These perceptions are generally acquired and propagated by imams in the mosques in Bangladesh.

Bangladeshi MBBs had these perceptions before they came to faith in *'Isa* due to teaching and practices in the mosque and in the school at the time of religious teaching. After MBBs read the *Kitabs*, especially *Injil* – the New Testament – their previous perceptions changed. Most of the MBBs are still in the process of changing from their previous perceptions, acquired from

---

10. Despite laws against early marriage, Bangladesh still has some problems with girls in villages being married off when they are around thirteen to fifteen years old.

the mosque, to new perceptions of the Bible, the only revelation of God.[11] However, the Qur'an is an important book in the faith journey of MBBs. It was important as the most precious revelation before, but during the faith journey, it generally serves as an important (or sometimes the first) account of 'Isa for them. A time of comparing the Qur'an and the Bible is an essential step in their faith journey of accepting 'Isa and being developed in the knowledge of him.

Christian/*Isais* have some tendency to see the Qur'an as a general book or a book that directs people to go to the *Kitab*. U03 introduced Muslims' view of the Qur'an and the *Kitab* as follows: "Muslims say that the previous *Kitabs* are changed [modified], so the previous *Kitabs* are not to be followed. But, in my point of view, the Qur'an tells us Muhammad is a general man like me, and tells us to go to the straight path and pray. The Qur'an has a role to guide and direct to the previous *Kitabs*." H01 said, "The Qur'an is the word which leads to the previous *Kitabs*. I don't believe it is revealed from heaven and by Allah. The Qur'an is a book of collections from the previous three *Kitabs*." N01 agreed that "the Qur'an is written based on the teachings of the previous three *Kitabs – Torah, Zabur*, and *Injil*. So, I do not value it much." S01 uses the Qur'an only for sharing 'Isa with Muslim neighbors: "I use the Qur'an for evangelism, but I don't believe it is one of the *asmani* [heavenly revealed] *Kitabs*." H01 described the role of the Qur'an this way: "The Qur'an has only one role of giving direction, directing toward the previous *Kitabs*. By doing this, the role of the Qur'an is finished." H02 and H03 agreed with the view of the Qur'an as a collection of the previous books and not revealed from heaven.

> The Qur'an is written based on the Old Testament and *Injil*, and came from Muhammad. I am not sure whether the Qur'an is revealed from heaven or not. I thought the Qur'an was also true, but after comparing with the previous *Kitabs*, I believe it includes human thoughts (H02). I don't think it is fully revealed by Allah and from heaven. I believe the Qur'an is written by Muhammad's own research and his disciples' thought. *Torah* has the proof that it is written by *Musa* (Moses), but the Qur'an does

---

11. MBBs call the Bible "*Kitab*," short for *Kitabul Mokaddos*, the "Holy Books."

not have any. I believe in the Bible as the truth, but I receive the
only common points between the Qur'an and the Bible. (H03)

E02, who has an *uboi* (both) *Isai/Isai* Muslim identity, said he believed
that the Qur'an was revealed by Allah like previous *Kitabs*, but he focused
only on its common points with the *Kitabs*.

> For example, if I go to some place, I go by a bus. When Allah
> reveals the books like the Qur'an and *Injil*, it comes through
> angels or men, and it was supposed to be written by disciples
> of Muhammad and *'Isa*. I only focus on the common points
> and do not focus on the different points. The purpose of our
> faith is to be delivered from our sins, to receive his mercy and
> grace, and to show others the true and right way. I got lessons
> like this from the *Injil* and now all of the *Kitabs*. I acknowledge
> that all four *Kitabs* are *asmani* [heavenly] *Kitabs* which came
> from Allah. I know there are wrong teachings in the Qur'an. If
> I did not read the Qur'an, I might not know these things. For
> getting teachings like salvation, grace, and right way of life, I also
> follow the Qur'an as well as the other *Kitabs*. I use and read the
> Qur'an for teaching other Muslims and MBBs and letting them
> know that they need to look at and follow the previous *Kitabs*.

Isai Muslim/Muslims tend to see the Qur'an as one of the four major heavenly books (*Torah, Zabur, Injil*, and Qur'an), but they place a higher value on
the *Kitab* and read it more. M01, a self-identified *Isai* Muslim/Muslim, said,
"These four heavenly books are the same to me. I read every book because the
Qur'an also talks about *'Isa Mosiho*, but the *Injil* provides a proper guidance
to lead one's life in the right way." M02 values the previous *Kitabs* more than
the Qur'an, saying that "the Qur'an also includes the story of *'Isa*. I do not
value the Qur'an more than the *Kitabs* because I think the previous books are
more valuable." I04, who changed his social identity from Christian/*Isai* to
Isai Muslim/Muslim, provided comparison between Muslims' and *Isais'* view:

> Muslims generally believe that *'Isa Mosiho* is a prophet and all
> four *Kitabs* came from heaven, but these *Kitabs* were modified
> except the Qur'an. They say they need to follow four proph-
> ets, and then they can go to heaven. But, on the other hand,

Muslims say that once the final revelation came down to the earth, the previous *Kitabs* are not needed any more. I follow what the Qur'an says because the Qur'an tells us to follow the previous *Kitabs*, and the Qur'an itself contains many contents from the previous *Kitabs*. There are also many stories about *'Isa* in the Qur'an. *'Isa* was named as the spirit of Allah [*Ruhulla*] and I believe *'Isa* is the spirit of God and the son of God born by the work of the Holy Spirit. *'Isa* is the *nazatdata* [savior] who died for my sins. That is why I was baptized.

M03, a self-identified *Isai* Muslim/Muslim, said that the portion about *'Isa* is the only part of the Qur'an that is revealed by God. He focuses only on common points between the Qur'an and *Injil*.

There are many stories about *'Isa* in the Qur'an. I believe that the portion of *'Isa* is only revealed from Allah. I do not agree with all the points of the Qur'an, especially the points of disagreement between the Qur'an and the *Kitab*. I value the *Injil* more than the Qur'an, but I am working among Muslims, so I don't want to devalue the Qur'an. I only follow the common points of the Qur'an and use it for preaching to Muslims.

In addition, several foreign workers' views are worth mentioning. Most of them agreed that MBBs need to come to an understanding that " *'Isa* is the Lord and the Savior" (F01, F02) and that "at some point in their spiritual walk they need to understand the Qur'an is not God's word and Muhammad was not a genuine prophet. Otherwise, they will never truly reach maturity in Christ" (F06). F07 added a point about using the Qur'an as a bridge, saying that it would be better to know "how they [MBBs] can use it [the Qur'an] as a bridge to get to a place where they can share the gospel with people." F04 made a comment about how to nurture MBBs to value the Bible more highly in terms of *Isai* Muslim/Muslim believers' view of the Qur'an and the Bible (*Kitab*). He stressed the need to provide the opportunity to read the *Kitab* more:

The matter of giving more value to the *Kitab* is connected to how much they read these four *Kitabs* including the Qur'an. If they read the *Kitabs* more, they raise the value of the *Kitab*

inevitably. In rural areas, most of the houses are open to neighbors, so it is hard to put the *Kitab* even in leaders' houses. It is
difficult for them to read the *Kitab*, but when they read it, we
hope they find the fact that it is worth reading more. There are
few smartphone users for Bangladeshi MBBs, but it is a good
idea for using general mobile because it is also possible to listen
to the *Kitab*. It would be better for them to use the Qur'an as a
helper to get closer to the *Kitab*.

Collective Level of Social Identity and Four-Self MBB Community

This section attempts to examine MBBs' community and discuss the present
reality and directionality of this community in terms of the popular "four-
self" formula: self-propagating, self-supporting, self-governing, and self-
theologizing. Most of the respondents generally agreed with the necessity
and directionality of the four-self dynamics. In this section, I will review
critical comments from national leaders of MBBs and foreigners about the
situation of Bangladeshi MBB community regarding self-direction and dependency, and then present my findings regarding each four-self issue in the
MBB community.

L01 commented on the present reality of the Bangladeshi MBBs' community and the urgent need to build a good model of actualized four-
self community:

> For developing MBBs' community in Bangladesh, we need to
> think differently and innovatively. There has been very little en-
> couragement and inspiration for building up *jama'ats* [house or
> local church of MBBs]. We have to think differently if we build
> up *Isai somaj* [*Isai* religious community]. Now, church planting
> is going on everywhere in Bangladesh, but most of the cases are
> dependent on foreign funds. In this way, we cannot build up
> self-supporting and self-governing believers' community. Even
> though it grows, it always exists in a dependent mentality. The
> attendants of the *jama'at* do not think that "I am a member of
> this *jama'at* and my *jama'at*." There is no sense of ownership in
> it. This is the urgent task to build a good model in Bangladesh.

The model, which builds up the *jamaʿat* through their own power and effort, is needed even though it is a small faith community. I just heard that there are several believers who are trying to do it, but I have never heard a model *jamaʿat* that is worth mentioning to others. Doing ministry and building up *jamaʿat* is different. We can do ministries, but this is not a *jamaʿat* or local church. I am seeking a model, but I am yet to come across the real church. I know many persons who are thinking in this way.

L05 mentioned the chronic problems of dependency in a majority world country like Bangladesh. He criticized the situation of Bangladeshi churches including MBB community; he also criticized foreigners who have worked with foreign money, and the lack of independence in the current Christian and MBB society. He spoke English in his interview.

In the third world country, they have nationwide problem, not just in a specific people group. The donor gives conditions. So, they should follow the direction and they are lack of [*sic*] own thinking, vision, and strategy. In traditional Christian communities in Bangladesh, it is the same as MBBs' community. I can say that it is "baseless community," like a doll. We have around one hundred denominations. Why did they become these many denominations? They are buying land and doing many other things, but whom they are preaching [to]? Denomination is growing in a lower level of people. I am not [the] right person to analyze this. No problem to reveal my name. We don't have any books about it. They did not mention any name. That is why I am telling "baseless community." It is also one kind of hiding thinking [*sic*]. Why bring money? Don't ask security reasons when bringing money from outside. I have several donors, but they are not influencing me, and neither changing my faith.

On the other hand, F03 described Bangladeshi society including MBBs as a self-oriented community. He said that Bangladeshi churches, including MBB churches, are thinking more about themselves than the community.

Churches are still very immature, like babies in Christ. Four areas of self-community are very little actualized. There are very few willing to become a community. They are very self-centered. They do what they want. The whole country and society is concerned about power, and they want to become more influential people. So, before they become a believer, they need to govern themselves. Governing themselves as a community is also very difficult.

I04 commented about local believers who have worked with foreigners. He criticized their "eye washing" (pretending and not genuinely believing):

The Bengalis who are working with foreigners are doing eye washing [pretending]. They are not receiving 'Isa wholeheartedly. They are trying to show like this way. Once the project is done, their faith is also done. When I was working here, there were many *jama'ats* here. We were gathering together every week or every month for believers' fellowship. We did teaching by comparing the Qur'an with the *Kitab* and nurtured them. But, once the project was finished, *jama'at* meetings disappeared. If they had received spiritual nourishment, they would have gathered continuously. There were believers here before, but there are no such believers now.

Self-Propagating

Most of the respondents (90%) confessed that they voluntarily shared the gospel with others to some extent. The five of forty-two[12] respondents who responded negatively to this question on sharing the gospel (H03, H07, U09, M01, I04) are currently surrounded by social pressure from the majority community and facing some degree of difficulty due to their faith. M01 confessed: "I preached before, but I did not get any positive results from them. Also, I am living in my hometown surrounded by the majority Muslims." Because U09 is also living with the majority pressure, he is not doing any preaching activity in his hometown. He does, however, sometimes share his faith when he visits another town in Bangladesh.

---

12. I did not ask this specific question to most of the N/L group, which is why the number of the respondents is forty-two rather than forty-eight.

All but four of the respondents who do share the gospel (89%) use commonalities with Islam when they share about *'Isa*. Four respondents do not use the Qur'an when they are sharing the gospel, but sometimes use common knowledge with their Muslim neighbors (S04, I01, L02, U12). U12 said, "I do not use the Qur'an for evangelism. I only use the *Kitab*. I do not feel that I need to remember the verses in the Qur'an and cite them to others. I mostly use *Injil*. It has most of the answers for all subjects. There is a purpose of life in it." L02 and I01 responded similarly, but added that they believe that the Bible itself has authenticity and the power to change people.

> I do not want to share the gospel by using the Qur'an. The Bible is the word of God, and it has the power to change. I go to people by teaching of the Bible. I speak to my people through my experience. There have been many troubles when I share the gospel by using the Qur'an. Why do I use a Muslims' religious book for sharing the gospel? (L02) It is silly and I don't want to prove the authenticity of the Bible with the help of the Qur'an. I can pick up some illustration from the Qur'an but not prove the Bible through the Qur'an. This is my strategy (I01).

S04 does not use the Qur'an, but he uses common points. He said, "I share the gospel out of my own will. I do not show the Qur'an to them, and neither do I use it. But, I pick up some knowledge of *'Isa* in the Qur'an and the Bible and share it. For example, he came to the earth, died, resurrected, and will come back. I say to them, "Come to my *jama'at* and listen to my words" (S04). I01 also started sharing the gospel from what others already know.

> In my life, I wanted to share the gospel. Sometimes, when I preached, I started from what they know. If I start from what they don't know, they don't agree with me, and are not interested in it. What they know – similar points like Joseph, twenty-seven prophets – they may hear about it from mosque teachers. I teach them from known things to unknown things.

Most of the respondents, however, answered that they use the Qur'an and Islamic commonalities in evangelism after building up good relationships. This pattern was discussed by several respondents (H01, N01, U01, U02, M03, S01). S01 showed the process of evangelism. "When I share the gospel,

I firstly build up good relationship, share about the issues of the Qur'an and religion, pick up an issue from them, and lead to *Injil* and the *Kitab*. If they want to know more, I share more. Unless I suggest the common points, they are not interested in our conversation." E02 gave a specific example of his use of Islamic commonalities:

> I use the Qur'an, the most Islamic commonality. From the beginning, I build up good relationship with them. They understand my words and behaviors. After several months, they ask me first whether I am a Muslim or a Christian. They ask me, "Why are you helping me?" If they are interested in me, I first introduce myself as a Muslim. They ask questions about me because general Muslims do not help others. Then, our conversation can go deeper. I can show the Qur'an to them and explain that the word of Allah does not change. Then I can show them the *Kitab* and *'Isa*. They invite me to go for *namaz* together. I say to them that I don't go for *namaz*. If they ask the reason, I reply with another question: "If you do *namaz*, do all your problems disappear? Don't we have to change our inner being first? Don't we have to know the truth and straight [right] path? Can we go to heaven with our sins?" I share the gospel in this way.

One example of the use of Islamic commonalities for evangelism is the concept of *superishkari* [someone who brings them to heaven]. Most Muslims believe that this *superishkari* is Muhammad. That is what mosque teachers are teaching. H04 gave us an example of it:

> I preach the gospel in a Muslim-majority environment. There is a *superishkari* [mediator] who brings us to heaven. We don't have tickets to go there, but one prophet can do that. People know that this is Muhammad. But, I show them the Qur'an Al-Imran saying *'Isa Mosiho* is a true *superishkari*. I introduce the gospel to them through the Qur'an. In this way, I share *'Isa* in Muslim society as one of the [*Isai*] Muslims. After sharing *'Isa* through the Qur'an, I continue to teach them through the *Torah, Zabur,* and *Injil*.

I02 identified two of the most used commonalities from the Qur'an as "God's unchanging word and concerning the need to follow *'Isa*."

In this way, there have been many evangelistic activities in a Muslim context, carried out by both diverse foreign organizations and local believers, but M01 said that "there have been very few established *stanio jama'at* [local church]" developed and being nurtured by local people and foreigners that take independent decisions and are self-funding. This statement leads to the subject of the next "self."

Self-Supporting

Unlike the general agreement of foreign and national believers that many MBBs try to share the gospel by their own initiative, the concept of self-supporting is hardly becoming actualized in Bangladeshi MBB society. According to F04,

> Because MBBs have families, relatives, and friends who want to reach out, I agree that they have a heart of evangelism and they are actually doing so in some sense. However, Christians and *Isais* lack the idea of becoming self-supporting because they are already getting support. I think it is important to have a mind of self-support. It looks like the historical tendency of traditional Christian culture of dependency is influencing the emerging MBBs' society. This is also one of the mistakes of missionaries and foreign organizations. It is necessary for foreign workers to come together and discuss the matter.

The dependent culture is already prevalent in MBBs' community, but F02 said this culture of dependency is not only found among traditional Christians and MBBs, but exists everywhere in Bangladesh.

> *Jama'ats* need to be operated without outside fund, from their own offering. In organizations and seminars, we can see the culture of no self-payment. They give food, housing . . . everything. So, common people start to expect that they could get everything without paying anything. It is hard to go against the flow to try to encourage a self-supporting fellowship because they don't have responsibility. It is like habit and culture. That is the way it is with so many things. For example, if the government gives training for English teachers, they pay them to come to the training center, for their travel, daily allowance, housing,

and food, etc. It is not just for Christian and MBBs community, but everywhere.

L02 mentioned the difficulty of self-support in MBB communities because of the lack of a habit of giving offering:

> It is still difficult because most *Isai* believers do not give one tenth offering [tithe]. If believers start to give tithe, *jamaʿats* will be self-supporting. They can do diverse ministries on their own. Pastors also build a church while they work in a field. If churches are habituated to getting support from outside, they are hard to sustain properly. To give an example, in one organization, the people were given a land, houses, a place to worship, pastors' salary for five years, but after five years, the pastor left and believers no longer gathered properly.

I02 also had critical views of *jamaʿats* getting funds from outside, but he thought that "it still needs time."

> Self-supporting church is a good idea, but it is not possible at this moment because *Isais* do not give tithe offering habitually and voluntarily. They couldn't give some money to pastors. We need to prepare for self-supporting churches in the future. If *jamaʿats* are operated by foreign funds, these *jamaʿats* become subject to foreigners' policy and thinking. It is necessary to operate *jamaʿats* based on our own culture.

L03 suggested an alternative process for self-support based on the case of his *jamaʿat*. It involves foreigners' voluntary cooperation and self-control of imprudent support.

> *Jamaʿats* in Bangladesh were started by the help of foreign funds. Now, we [traditional Christians and MBBs] are not free of this tendency. Our *jamaʿat* is challenging this current trend. We decided not to get foreign funds and are trying to give tithe. For making self-supporting *jamaʿats* in Bangladesh, it is necessary to first close the foreign offering and funds. Second, believers need to give tithe after receiving teaching about the obligation to collect offering. A rural mosque is also not operated by foreign funds. In rural areas, there is no need to pay rent fee and it

does not require much operating expenses for *jamaʿats*. Offering tithe in rural areas can give opportunities for believers to have a meal together when they meet. They need to plan for decent operating system for a *jamaʿat*. Also, unless they become better economically, it will not be still possible to operate a *jamaʿat* on their own.

Bangladeshi MBBs are actually trying to be self-supporting, however. Several respondents are already practicing to be self-supporting, but they feel that they still need money for sustaining *jamaʿats* at this moment and seed money for a business platform for the future. Several Christian/*Isai* respondents who are members of visible *Isai jamaʿats* said that they need money for sustaining local churches such as pastors' living expenses (U01 and S01) and ministry outreach funds (H01) because *jamaʿat* members' offering is not enough and there is no seed money for self-support. S01 said, "I want to be a self-supporting pastor, but I do not have power to do it now. I have plans to start a small business and to get profits from it, but I do not have seed money either." H01 operates his *jamaʿat* from members' offering, but the members who participate in ministries are getting salary from outside funds.

> My *jamaʿat* does not get outside funds. However, we are getting outside support for our ministry for paying our staff. They are members of *jamaʿat*. They are giving tithe like me. We are operating our *jamaʿat* in this way. We are always thinking about self-supporting. We hope to have some wealth in *jamaʿat* to manage to get long-term profits from it.

On the other hand, some *Isai* Muslim/Muslim respondents need money for training believers, not for the financial survival of each *jamaʿat* (M02, M03, E04). M02 described the situation of his *jamaʿat*. Even though he was invited to work with a denomination, he did not go because the policy of that denomination was different. E04 made a similar comment.

> We are gathering one or two times a month. Normally, we gather in a believers' house. Each *jamaʿat* has a leader. Rural *jamaʿats* are operated with believers' small offering. *Jamaʿats* do not get funds from outside. There is no need of money for gathering, but there is need for training them. We do not pay *jamaʿat* leaders. I

do not get any support either. Someone invited me to join their denomination and get paid, but I did not go [implied because of difference of ministry style and theology]. (M02)[13]

> Training program for believers needs a financial support to organize it. They do not maintain their livelihood well, but nevertheless we try to collect our offering for supporting poor and vulnerable (sick) people in our community.
>
> Major offering is from me. But, it is not possible for me to cover all these things. If some financial aids are provided with them, it would be apparently better for them. (E04)

F01 insisted that MBBs still need partnership because of their culture and low economic situation at this point of time.

> They have to have partnership. There is a culture of partnership here in organizations, football club, and youth club too. Place of partnership is in a comprehensive way. Of course, it [self-supporting] is the direction for the future. But, it is a long way down the line. True. It does depend very much on the economic situation in the country.

Self-Governing

Seven of the eight *jama'ats* researched for this study are doing some self-governing activities such as meeting with small group leaders each month (N01) and rotating the teaching opportunities of each member (I01). For the remaining *jama'at*, even though it has a local leadership group, they felt that foreigners' decisions were stronger than theirs. Many of the respondents also confessed that they lack experiences (H02) and opportunities (M01) to build up new leaders because although they have the intentions, they do not know how to build up new leaders (L02). One of the foreign respondents, F10,

---

13. MBBs or MBs (Muslim believers)' move to another organization (or denomination) is not new in Bangladesh. Because of lack of indigenous workers, they often move to different organizations or denomination/organizations who recruit workers from other groups for better opportunity and advantages such as salary, reputation, etc. This type of culture (moving frequently to another) is widespread in Bangladesh society too. It also brings about trust issues with one another.

said that "one of the reasons for lack of knowledge on how to build up new leaders is that there is no culture of building up new leaders." He continued:

> I think self-supporting and self-governing are deeply related to each other. Also, it is related to Bangladeshi culture. I believe that there exists biblical leadership like what Paul did for building up Timothy. However, there are differences in Bangladesh. Once one charismatic leader passed away, the next leader struggled to stand properly because of lack of building up successor. If someone is suddenly encouraged or built up for the same area, people might worry about possibility of loss of their current position. I asked a local faculty to respond to the need of filling up an additional professor. He resisted and said that if there are two local professors in this seminary, there could be trouble and he said, "Why do you want to do that?"

F03 agreed that the culture of pursuing more power is a problem. "The whole community and society is concerned about power and everyone wants to become a bigger person." L03 mentioned that "there are very few leaders." He continued: "Everybody is working for his or her survival, so we don't have enough time. There are very few authentic believers. There are very few skillful persons. If we have much money, nobody knows where we can invest it."

Leaders across the whole spectrum of social identity groups were seeking qualified potential leaders with characteristics such as being teachable to the *Kitab* (H01), being amendable to the teaching of the *Kitab* and *'Isa* including the qur'anic view (M02), and exhibiting steady attendance in their *jama'ats* (H01). One *jama'at* (*Jama'at* I) is not working under one leader, but everybody makes the decision together and takes turns to teach every week. "I do not lead the *jama'at*. Preachers take turns in our *jama'at*. Everybody is a leader of the *jama'at*. Everybody decides. If everybody has a chance to preach, it is an acknowledgment that everybody has God's potential and gifts. They are doing well" (I01). The reason why this *jama'at* rotates the preachers of every week is that all members know how to read and preach the word of God.

Normally, most MBBs send their potential *jama'at* leaders to Dhaka for training (S04, N02). N02 said that "There are good potential leader candidates in our *jama'at*. One is still studying at college. We are thinking to send him to Dhaka to get trained and prepared for being a good leader of our *jama'at*

or starting a new *jamaʿat.*" Finally, F01 commented on the necessity of two
kinds of balanced leadership and a model of partnership between [materi-
ally] influential and [spiritually] faithful persons, about the needlessness of
continual foreign money input, and about the need for time to get resources
on their own such as manpower and money:

> We need a new model of partnership. Who is a leader in this
> country? It can be said as powerful, influential, and rich per-
> sons. We try to establish a new model. But, all the time, it has
> to be a balance. You can't ignore rich persons who are part of
> the church. Sometimes a very poor person with deeply spiritual
> devotion may not be the best person to be a leader because
> others do not listen to him. Two models need to work together.
> This is not related to a foreign partnership. There is no differ-
> ence between a matured MBB who is related to a foreign or-
> ganization and a purely local MBB without relationship with
> foreigners. Rather, they can become bad input for them when
> they bring foreign funds. We need to get rid of this key struggle,
> corrupter, and trouble maker – money. Money creates problems
> wherever it comes from. We can pray that the money gets cut
> off completely.
>
> But, in Bangladesh's situation, it is not realistic. Think about
> Chinese underground churches! On the whole, money has nega-
> tive influence. You can't live with it and you can't live without it.
> We have to move forward working with some of the strengths and
> weaknesses and we must try to build when the churches grow in
> numbers and in maturity with the growth of the country's GDP.
> And then some of these problems get solved on their own. But,
> until that happens, we can do nothing. If the number of believ-
> ers grows from twenty to two hundred or two thousand, we can
> get manpower and some financial resources too. A completely
> different picture of the prevalent situation will then emerge.

Self-Theologizing

The concept of self-theologizing is not easy for local MBBs to fully understand. There are many theological schools and seminaries for traditional

Christians, but there are few for MBBs using *Mussolmani* Bangla and the *Kitab*. Some MBB leaders and *jamaàt* leaders participate in short-term training ranging from a week-long seminar of Isai Fellowship in Bangladesh to diploma or degree programs from Christian seminaries or Bible colleges for MBBs. Some places offer correspondence courses, like TEE (Theological Education by Extension), and others have residential programs supported by foreign funds. Although theology is not new for Bangladeshi MBBs because they were acquainted with Islamic theology, theology is generally considered as a religious teaching and perspective. In fact, it is difficult to define it and to ask MBBs about their understanding of self-theologizing. I therefore asked three styles of questions: (1) how to apply the word of God, (2) which teacher they prefer, foreigners or locals, and (3) how to impact the Muslim majority.

For the first question about application of the word, the respondents answered that they practice following the word of God in their daily life to get fruit (H02) and following the way of life of 'Isa as a model (U03). H02 said, "I am meditating on the word of God regularly and trying to apply it to my everyday life. It can be a good example for others as sharing my fruitful life." U03 said, "I am doing my TEE course. I want to learn from it and apply what I learned to my life. Before sharing the gospel to others, I think I need to build myself up first and follow the way of life of 'Isa. And then, I can share the gospel to them through my right and changed way of life." Several others responded that they prayed to be a good person so that they could influence others after showing a changed behavior (N02), and they also pray to share the gospel more with others (U11).

For the question on their preference of local or foreign teachers, respondents answered on both sides, but showed a preference for foreigners (foreign preference: 9; local preference: 4; both needed: 6). Some respondents answered that they preferred the teaching of their local teachers and leaders because of their communication skill and knowledge of their own culture (U01, E04, I02, I03). U01 said, "Even though foreigners have more knowledge than nationals, it is sometimes hard for us to understand what they are saying because of different pronunciation and expression from us." I02 said, "I don't like foreigners' teaching. I prefer local teachers' teaching. Among the persons who are prepared for the teaching of the Bible in our context, I prefer their teaching more than foreigners' degree and knowledge because they are well aware of our language and culture." E04 said, "There are many of us who can give a good teaching for two day-workshop and I am also an expert in giving training about *'Isa* through the Qur'an and Hadith."

Some respondents answered that the foreigners could share the story of how they developed Christianity in their country (U07), give deep and new teaching of the Bible (N01), and display good characteristics such as transparency (S01, I04) and a match between words and deeds (E01, E03). U07 said,

> My will is to learn from them how to develop Christianity and increase the number of Christians in their country. Now, we are building up *'Isai* religion in this country. Some people say this way, and the others say that way. I want to know how Christianity has grown in that country and also want to know how social dynamics happen and believers interact. If we can listen to their experience, we can know how to apply it in our context. (U07)

S01 said, "I prefer foreigners' teaching because I can't fully trust national leaders of MBBs in Bangladesh in terms of financial transparency and personal character." According to I04, "Foreigners have good character like honesty, good deeds, and less anger than local people." E01 observed that

> local teachers' teaching has pros and cons. They taught us well because they know much of our culture, but their words and deeds oftentimes did not match. They sometimes lie, so I have some doubts about their teaching. Local teachers say much, but their practices are little. But, foreigners do not say much, but they keep what they said. (E01; and E03 also expressed the same view.)

E03 made similar comments, and several other respondents expressed the necessity of both local and foreign teachings because there are strengths, such as those mentioned above, on both sides (S05, H01, U03, U05, I04).

For the question on how to impact and influence the majority Muslims, the respondents gave various insightful answers. Three categories of answers are narrated: more connection to the majority, more good works, and clear conversion and identity. The major answer to this question was to connect more with the majority society and engage the majority's religion (Islam) and its culture deeply. For this, the respondents suggested applications of both digging into *somaj* and Islam and connecting the Qur'an to the *Kitab*.

H04 said, "We can do various kinds of good works, but we need to connect to the *somaj* [religious community] and its needs and interests. Through this, we can broaden our relationship with them." U04 said, "By engaging with them, we can share our commonalities. We need to go among them."

For connecting the Qur'an and the *Kitab*, they said that starting from the Qur'an and moving to the *Kitab* would be better for engaging the majority (H05, H08, U10, S01). H05 said, "I inform qur'anic verses to them through commonalities between the Qur'an and the *Kitab*. The qur'anic mentions of 'straight path' and 'necessity of reading the previous *Kitabs*' might motivate them to look at the *Kitab* to find the 'straight path.'" According to H08,

> With showing the Qur'an, I can connect it to the *Injil* and *Taurat* to them. It can be a good bridge if we use it well because general Muslims think that there is no other *Kitab* except the Qur'an. But, as their beliefs on *'Isa* grow, they can think that the Qur'an is not enough for salvation but just a guide toward the *Kitab*. If we dig into the Qur'an more as a guide, we can lead them to the *Kitab* well for learning more about salvation.

Finally, S01 said, "They can start from the Qur'an, but they have to finish with the *Kitab*."

Two of the MBB leaders made two practical suggestions of self-theologizing work in this country: (1) learning and interacting more with Islam as a subject in the MBBs' or Christians' seminary or Bible college (L01); and (2) learning the unique style and tone or tune of what the majority Bengalis have acquired religiously (L03).

> I am a Bangladeshi and the majority of Bangladeshi are Muslims. So, we need to share the gospel in considering the context of Bangladesh. There are many problems when we go to preach to Muslims. First, we need to learn language, culture, and religion. Second, we need to have sound knowledge of the *Kitab* and *Injil*. But, there are very few who have this. For evangelizing the majority, we need to learn Islam properly. One of the solutions is to introduce Islamic studies as a subject in Bible schools or

seminaries. It is not for studying their negative parts, but for interacting with them. If we want to build up good evangelists, we need to learn this properly. If they only know about the Bible or *Kitab*, they can't share the gospel with them rightly. (L01)

Christians' traditional terminology is not good to the majority Muslims. This is an urgent issue. When foreigners teach, there are differences in word and pronunciation. Religion teaching has a unique tone or tune. Even between similar words, there are differences. Bangladeshis cannot eat [absorb] that when foreigners teach their own ways such as European style of preaching or translated teachings from English to Bangla. We have to learn the tunes and styles from Islamic preachers and teachers. After learning these, we need to learn how to preach and teach. When Muslims learn the Qur'an Sharif with their unique tunes and style, they are answering "Amin, Amin." Christians and MBBs have preached the gospel to them for fifty years, but there is almost no difference. If we think and preach in European ways, we cannot get any result. We need to contextualize the gospel. While we keep the deep inner value of the gospel, we need to find appropriate tunes and styles for sharing with the majority. (L03)

One of the respondents introduced his case of nurturing and sending out a diverse spectrum of believers depending on their situations and decisions (H01). In his *jama'at*, someone might have *Isai* Muslim identity during the time of winning their families and neighbors in *'Isa* as well as growing their faith in *'Isa* and influencing other neighbors.

While some members of *jama'at* are performing *namaz* sometimes, they are continuing relationship with me. I cannot go to their place, but they can come to me, discuss about various issues of the Qur'an and the *Kitab*, and get nurtured by me and the *jama'at*. Through them, we can share the gospel to anyone including Islamic teachers. I can let them stay in *Isai* Muslim a short period of time, we can build up new *Isai* society if their numbers grow to several dozens.

The second part of the answer of how to impact and influence the majority is to do more good work, such as helping the poor and responding to practical needs (H02, U01, U05, U09):

> We can share the gospel directly, but we can start and focus more on serving them indirectly such as through school, hospital, and economic development. If we do these good works and provide more opportunities to work, we can build up more believers too. (H02)

> Most of all in the situation of Bangladesh, we need more economic opportunities. There are many poor people around the country. If I have money as a Christian and help five persons in any way, they can listen to me and they like me. Normally Muslims' leaders and teachers do not give money and help others. Rather, they look down on the poor and hate them. But, Christians try to help them. (U09)

The third part of the respondents' answer is to have a clear Christian/ *Isai* identity (I02, H02, U07). I02 said that "clear identity is a big issue for impacting society and succession of faith to the next generation of *Isai*." He continued,

> If *Isais* learn Christianity correctly, the second and third generation of *Isais* do not need to endure hard times of adjusting their identity and society. If they have clear identity, they can successfully pass on their faith to the next generation. Even though it creates a bigger gap and break from the majority, clear identity is better. Alternatively, when they share the gospel to them, they can do it in accordance with their culture and language, not from the culture of Westerners or foreigners, such as by saying *'Isa* and Allah instead of *Jisu* or Jesus and *Issor* or God. When this happens, new *Isais* can be born.

H02 agreed with the idea of clear identity comparable to Hindu converts, saying, "*Isai* community grows slowly. There is no continuity and durability. After evangelizing them, it is necessary for them to change their heart deeply and their social identity clearly as new persons."

Foreign workers expressed two opinions about the development of thinking and partnership. First, self-theologizing still needs time to grow in Bangladesh because Bangladeshi people do not have a chance to develop their own thinking (F03):

> I cannot deny that they are reluctant to think. For developing their own theology to become a leader or elders of the body of Christ, they have to hear God speak to them directly. It is very few of them who are willing to do that. They are habituated to listening to their teachers and to just repeat what their teachers told them. So, self-theologizing is difficult at this moment, but I agree with the direction.

Second, F01 mentioned the need of partnership between foreigners and locals, but noted that platforms for good discussion between foreign and local workers have not yet been established.

> We still need a partnership. We have had no chance to meet and discuss both sides of thinking. We can have a meeting between local people who have experienced Western theology and Western people who learn local theology and culture and learn from them. I agree that importing theology is not enough nor desirable.

Diverse Understandings of Contextualization in Bangladesh

Given the diversity of partnership levels in Muslims' religious and social activities among MBBs, crucial questions can be raised about whether such participation is permissible as a follower of 'Isa and how far believers can go. Who can decide whether it is syncretistic or biblical? How can we do exegesis of the cultural and religious activities on the one hand and Scripture on the other, and interact with both?

How was the contextualization of the gospel initiated in Bangladesh? F09 commented on the initial motive of contextualizing activities in Bangladesh such as "the *Kitab* translation": "translation of the *Kitab* adapting the terms that Muslims are currently using implies allowance of many potential activities to preach the gospel and to identify their groups and themselves in this way. I believe it gives enormous power to do this way." In this section, we can hear diverse views of contextualization in Bangladesh from the respondents.

Since the middle of the 1970s, missionaries and local believers started to use the small Bible booklet adapting Muslim terminology. The *Injil Sharif*, translation of the four Gospels and the New Testament, was published in 1980. As F09 mentioned above, it can be said that the diverse range of contextualized ministries started in Bangladesh with the use of the small booklets about the *Injil Sharif* in the mid-1970s. Foreign missionaries and local preachers have sometimes formed teams for reaching out to the majority, and they have received fruitful result from their works.[14] At that time, one local MBB had a calling to reach out to his majority neighbors without changing religious identity from Muslim to Christian, saying to his disciples, "Keep your faith in *'Isa*, but don't become Christians . . . go back to your villages and tell your elders what you believe" (F08).

On the other hand, S01 analyzed that the beginning of contextualization work around 1975 was actually the beginning of the weakening of churches.

> Until 1974, the work of mission had been going well. But, after that time, missionaries came to Bangladesh with a different strategy. After changing the strategy like hiding their faith or not revealing their faith in *'Isa* to others, the ministries had not worked well. In the past, for believing in Jesus, they had to change fully themselves, participate in the church, and reveal themselves. From that time until now, missionaries might think that the number of Christians in Bangladesh has increased much, as if many mosques have changed to churches. Believers have only a basic knowledge in *'Isa*. They are not well rooted in *jama'ats*, so they do not stand in their faith firmly.

Two Bangladeshi MBB leaders who have a Christian/*Isai* identity, L04 and L05, also commented on the shortcomings of radical contextualization in Bangladesh. L04 commented on religious identity change as an essential part of growing in the knowledge of God:

> Muslims cannot live in a Christian society, and Christians cannot do that either. It means that we receive a communal faith. This is a distinctive social division. For that reason, the important point of religious change or faith change is which society

---

14. Johnson, "Training Materials," 25–27.

they are going to live in. Anyone who wants to be changed properly has to be separated, changed, and moved out of the previous religious society. The church [*jamaʿat*] and its membership, fellowship, communion, questions and answers of his or her baptism, children's education, obligations are all essential. Without membership of *jamaʿat*, we cannot get to the points of healthy spiritual growth. Bengalis are very emotional. If some teachings impact them, they are easily overwhelmed. But, it lasts for only a short while. Missionaries think that it can happen successfully. But it will be possible only if Bengalis could be built up to become independent.

L04 was also critical of the C5 contextualized movement in Bangladesh:

Their work has badly affected us. Such a concept itself, that even if someone believes in *ʿIsa*, he or she can stay in Muslim *somaj*, is one of the bad examples of their teaching. Who will they marry? Will they marry Muslims? It makes them deceptive if they do not reveal their faith and even if the marriage happens, the result is that they become Muslims. Children could be confused about their parents' faith. Muslim believers are saying that they are good Christians and they can do more if they receive more funds. Also, foreigners could think that they earned many believers, but what are the benefits for the body of Christ? They do not build up visible *jamaʿat* and are staying on as Muslims. They do not understand the Lord properly and do baptism in a secret place with taking pictures and do little fellowship. But, what are the benefits?

[I asked, "Could they reach out the majority more?"]

They were Muslims, are Muslims, and will be Muslims in the future. The only beneficial thing is the feeling of joy, as it seems like the work has been successful and many have become believers. But, they are not the body of Christ. If they are so, they would understand the Lord more and grow more, but they are not doing so. Foreigners have wasted money.

L05, who was interviewed in English, argued that missionaries divided groups with various kinds of teaching and efforts such as making another version of the *Kitab*.

> We have many people who divide the churches but very few people know and practice how to unite people. We need to pray that God sends us people who can work for unity not for division. Anyway, when someone destroys the foundation, it is very difficult to rebuild it. There exists only a special name for Muslim Background Believer (MBB). Who was making the wall? Whom are they using? You are not telling Christian Background Believer (CBB), Hindu BB (HBB), Tribe BB (TBB), but you are telling me MBB, why? You say this is for establishing identity, and categorized us. So, we can't remove it. Who taught us to call ourselves *Isai* Muslims? Missionaries! Who taught us to keep the faith in your heart and keep going to a mosque? Missionaries! In the world, is there any country who calls the Bible as the *Kitabul Mokkados* [*Kitab*]? What is the Christian religious book? The Bible. What is Muslim's religious book? The Qur'an. You are separating us from the world. What is the *Kitab*? Whose religious book? If my children read the *Kitab* and if they were asked what their religious book is and if they answer that it is the *Kitab*, then do they pass the exam? The elite traditional Christians have said to us, "You corrupted the Bible!"

L05 also expressed a negative viewpoint on radical contextualization without distinguishing religion from culture. He judged missionaries for importing the idea of this kind of contextualization saying,

> When we think about social contextualization, there are very technical problems here. While we are going to be socially contextualized, we feel that social contextualization hampers our spiritual context. Then I have to avoid that contextualization. Okay. For social contextualization, I have to go to mosque. Then, what does contextualization mean? Why do they do that? Is it about culture or religion? You are following one religion. Then, how could you contextualize another religion? Is it possible? Culture and religion are different. We are Christians, so our

religion is the same. But, our culture, nationality, food . . . what-
ever is different, but our religion is same.

[I asked then, "So, do you believe every believer from Muslim
background has the same kind of existing Christian culture?"]

You are still missing the point. Why are you mixing religion and
culture? That is my point. You and I, we have the same religion
but two cultures. Culture is like the way of eating, dressing,
etc. – non-religious neutral culture. That is my point. But, in
Bangladesh, isn't it different? *Punjabi* is a Bengali dress. It is not
Islamic dress. Everyone uses this. But, *tupi* [cap] is different.
Hindus use different *tupi*. You can take many kinds of examples
like this. You can go to the mosque. What is the intention? I
want to go to the mosque and I pray with them and preach the
gospel like Paul in the book of Acts? If you do like Paul, I will go
with you to the mosque. You did not do anything. Then, why are
you going to the mosque? Avoiding social pressure? How many
percent of Muslims go to the mosque for praying in Bangladesh?
In the village, does everyone go to the mosque? Check it. That
is the problem. Some missionaries put that poison. Now you
have to go to mosque and then people know you [that you are
still a Muslim]. So, Bengalis accepted it. Some missionaries are
saying like this, isn't it? This is not from the local people. That
is all imported. The result of this is almost zero percent growth
in Bangladesh.

On the other hand, E02 and L06, who have *uboi* (both; *Isai* and *Isai*
Muslim) identity expressed their flexibility about contextualized activities and
need for acceptance. E02 noted that different teachers teach different things:

A Christian can stay with the majority Muslims. I think he can
go to social ceremonies with them. This is a social fellowship for
having good relationship with them. There are different teachings depending on the teachers. They say, "You do not eat *qurbani* meat because '*Isa* did it for us." . . . The *Kitab* did not write
about whether I could eat or not. Leaders' teaching is different
too. Someone said we could it, but some others said you don't.

For the sake of social harmony and fellowship, I think they could do it. In spite of doing this, I believe they can stay on in their faith. Among the Muslims, there are several Muslims in my hometown church. They say they are followers of Muhammad. Then, if one *Isai* goes to *namaz* for saving himself from the society, I think it is permissible. His faith still exists. It could be possible to have social participation for saving themselves. I don't think it should be forbidden. But, most of the *Isai* teachers do not allow the practice.

When I asked about the danger of mixing two religions, E02 pointed out his (*Isai*) Muslim colleague (E04) who participates in Muslims' religious activities. He answered that spiritual identity and social identity can be different, and that changing mind and behavior is crucial.

There is no problem in mixing two religions once someone already became a believer. Rather, they can grow in understanding and teaching about their faith. If they can apply the word of God, they become changed. If they put on their faith in *'Isa*, their minds and behaviors are changed by the *Kitab* and the Qur'an. Even if someone goes to mosque and introduces himself as a Muslim, I do not think it is a problem. It does not matter wherever he is once he reads the *Kitabs* and his life is changing. He can be a good example among these kinds of persons. Religion on the outside is not very important, inner change and behavior is more important. There are many self-identified Christians/*Isais* who conduct their religious life like a business. If this happens, I think someone with (*Isai*) Muslim identity could be more accepted than one with Christian/*Isai* identity in God's eyes. Someone could reveal a Christian identity while working with Christians, but he is actually a Muslim. Also, someone who works with Muslims can be a Christian. I believe that spiritual identity and social identity can be different. But, through their work and behavior, their belief and real being are automatically revealed.

L06 also spoke in favor of self-identified *Isai* Muslim/Muslims:

I believe many people like them can become Christians some-day. After experiencing many things, they could make the at-tempt. Some people have the tendency to speak badly of them, referring to them as spies and speak against them without giving any chance to defend themselves. I hope that even though we are not doing ministry with them, we should not say anything against them. Actually, one day these self-identified *Isai* Muslim/ Muslims may come to me to know more about *'Isa*. They might want to know the reality and the truth. If I do not give them a chance and instead expel them, how could they know *'Isa* and the *Kitab* deeply? It would be better to build good relationships to teach them well. I hope the time would come shortly to wor-ship in Islamic surroundings using language, worship, and ter-minologies. General *Isais* do not like insider workers and there are conflicts too. The three identities like traditional Christians, *Isais*, and Muslim insider believers are natural. Traditional Christians also have their own culture because most of them came from Hindu background. Judging others sometimes hap-pens because of the differences. As time goes by, the time will come to understand one another, relationships will be better, and then we will understand one another. Actually, traditional Christians are also using the *Kitab* for reaching out to Muslims. More and more, there is growing understanding and tolerance.

In sum, there are diverse opinions about contextualization among Bangladeshis: One group of respondents believes that, among other negative consequences, contextualization has weakened the churches, there is no real growth and maturing in faith, and the investment of time and resources has been a waste. Another group of respondents believes that contextualization is necessary to maintain social harmony and establish good relationships with the majority Muslims so that they can be gradually brought into the faith, among other benefits.

CHAPTER 5

Research Analysis

This chapter brings together the findings in chapter 4 with the precedent theories and literature discussed in chapter 3. The major purpose of this chapter is to present the analysis of my research findings, and ask probing questions about certain patterns that emerge. I will summarize the findings of each research question before interacting with and analyzing the previous literature and my findings. In the analysis sections of this chapter, I interact not only with authors and theories discussed in chapter 3, but also with several other studies to see if these suggest alternative paradigms and can be related to my findings. The social identity of MBBs is still actively discussed and debated, with diverse viewpoints defended in various types of missiology literature.

Summary of Findings in RQ 1

Bangladeshi MBBs have come to faith for several reasons, and they have formed a new social identity in interaction with others' responses or changes. I found several factors of having faith in *'Isa* to be primarily cognitive or affective/relational. The other factors were experiential, negative (feelings toward Islam), and occupational. However, these factors were not found independently, but they were instead intersectional. Family and majority society members responded negatively to converts, but changes in MBBs were evident both internally and externally. The changes MBBs experience after coming to faith have generally come from the assurance of salvation and inner peace, which then extend to behavioral changes such as loving others and quitting bad habits. In terms of social identity, all MBB and foreign respondents generally agreed on the existence and reality of four groups of social identity in Bangladesh: Christian, *Isai, Isai* Muslim, and Muslim. The social identity of MBBs has three factors: MBBs' exposure to Muslims (security issue), their tendency to adopt the social identity of whoever introduced them to the gospel, and the flexibility of social identity depending on their situation and intention. An analysis of these factors and the present reality revealed through this research suggests that there are three major categories of MBBs, and that MBBs can move across categories or sometimes beyond categories for various reasons.

Analysis of RQ 1

Based on the findings related to RQ 1 above, I present my views by analyzing the findings alongside precedent literature. Research Question 1 asks:

> What factors were involved in MBBs coming to identify themselves as followers of 'Isa? Have the ways in which MBBs identify themselves religiously changed since their conversion?

To answer RQ 1, I compared my findings with previous literature and found that my findings were generally predictable in that they agreed with previous literature on the conversion and social identity categorization of MBBs. First, MBBs' conversions are caused by multiple factors, particularly cognitive and affective/relational factors, and proceed gradually through the process of awareness, decision, and incorporation. Second, the social identity of Bangladeshi MBBs can be similarly categorized using Travis's C-Spectrum[1] and Tim Green's research.[2]

Multiple Factors in MBBs' Conversions

A significant body of literature has developed in the area of conversion theory and practice. In particular, diverse studies have researched Muslims' conversion to 'Isa. The issue of Muslims' conversion and the factors involved was not introduced in chapter 3 because it is not the main purpose of the research. Even though the major focus of this research is not on the issue of Muslims' conversion to Christianity, however, it is necessary to bring my

---

1. Travis, "C1 to C6 Spectrum"; Travis, "Must All Muslims Leave?"
2. Green, "Beyond the C-Spectrum?"; "Indentity Choices."

research findings into interaction with previous literature. My finding is that the factors influencing MBBs' conversion are multiple, and include cognitive, affective/relational, experiential, negative (feeling of Islam), and occupational factors. The first two areas (cognitive and affective/relational) are dominant, and all factors are mixed and present in varying degrees.

From the Straight Path to the Narrow Way: Journeys of Faith focuses on reasons and factors involved in Muslims' conversion to Christianity (or *'Isa*).[3] In one of the essays in this book, Andreas Maurer categorizes the motives of Muslims' and Christians' conversion as religious (or cognitive), mystical, affectional, sociopolitical, and material. Maurer suggests five steps for helping new converts adjust to existing faith communities: (1) need for welcoming groups consisting of trained believers; (2) need for genuine care for converts to help develop their faith by themselves; (3) need for converts to be introduced to larger groups; (4) need for single converts "to be adapted into a family of the new faith community"; and (5) need for addressing the spiritual and social needs.[4]

Published in *Longing for Community*, Reinhold Straehler's research on East African MBBs shows results similar to mine in terms of two main factors (cognitive and affective) and their working together. According to Straehler, "In each conversion process, both dimensions play an important role," and the two factors work together.[5] To facilitate these two factors, I suggest following Straehler's advice: (1) communicate truth to get more opportunities for them to dedicate their life to *'Isa* by their own decision (cognitive factor); (2) build good relationships to show believers' lifestyle honestly, treat them in love, and share personal testimony with them (affective factor).[6] These ways have been applied and have borne fruits in Bangladesh too.

---

3. The case studies and research findings about Muslims' conversion to *'Isa* from different backgrounds were introduced by authors such as J. Dudley Woodberry, David Greenlee and Rick Love, Jean-Marie Gaudeul, Andreas Maurer, and Hasan Abdulahugli. Woodberry, "Global Perspective on Muslims"; Greenlee and Love, "Conversion through the Looking Glass"; Gaudeul, "Learning from God's Ways"; Maurer, "In Search of a New Life"; Abdulahugli, "Factors Leading to Conversion." One study about the conversion process of believers from Muslim backgrounds was introduced by Reinhold Straehler in a book about the identity issue, *Longing for Community*. Straehler, "Areas of Change."

4. Maurer, "In Search of a New Life," 108.

5. Straehler, "Areas of Change," 132.

6. Straehler, 134.

In terms of the timing of MBBs' faith in 'Isa, I found that the transition was not done by one-time decision making, but was a gradual process that took a certain amount of time. In the case of H05, eight years passed between his initial interest in 'Isa and the Bible (*Kitab*) and his decision to receive baptism. These years were spent developing friendship with an MBB pastor and conducting his own comparative study of the Qur'an and the Bible. Unlike the "one-step decisionism" style of conversion, Muslims' conversion takes more time due to self-struggle.[7] According to Conn, this is actually the biblical sense of conversion. Conn defines conversion as "the process of change of vesture (Eph 4:24, Col 3:9–10) . . . metamorphosis over a period of time (Rom 12:1–2)," and, most of all, "a life-long process of allegiance conformity to Christ, initiated by a confession of submission to the resurrected Lord (Rom 10:9)."[8]

In this sense, Alan Tippett's discussion of the three periods of the conversion process – which was also applied in Syrjanen's study of conversion among Pakistani Muslims (1984) – is worth mentioning.[9] Tippett identified periods of awareness, decision, and incorporation as parts of the conversion process.[10] Richard Hibbert slightly modified and upgraded Tippett's model of conversion process by adding a period of identity negotiation in the middle of the incorporation period. In this negotiation period, Hibbert said people can go one of two ways: a "suppression of Christian identity," or a "period of incorporation and maturity."[11] Hibbert's addition reflects MBBs' identity dilemma regarding whether they can easily receive Christian identity and rituals or they remain in their family and cultural background. Hibbert writes,

> These believers often feel unable to display their decision to identify with the Christian community through a visible demonstration such as baptism or responding to an altar call, because this would signify a rejection of their culture and their family. Instead, they enter a phase of identity negotiation in which they

---

7. Conn, "Muslim Convert," 102.

8. Conn, 102.

9. Tippett, "Conversion as a Dynamic Process," 218–20.

10. Tippett later added a period of "maturity" after incorporation, after seeing converts turn away from their new Christian communities. Tippet, 218–20.

11. Hibbert, "Negotiating Identity," 63.

work out how they can express being a follower of Christ in ways that are most meaningful to them and helpful in exposing their communities to the gospel.[12]

To summarize this analysis, Muslims take time to make a decision of dedication to *'Isa*, and they negotiate their identity depending on their own backgrounds both before and after their dedication to him.

Coping with Dual Belonging

As introduced in chapter 3, research works by Tim Green[13] and Kathryn Ann Kraft[14] about coping options and strategies for a dual Christian and Muslim identity are relevant to my findings. This is an application of the idea of negotiating identity. Even though these two authors' categorizations do not fit perfectly either with each other or with my own analysis, Table 8 is a helpful diagram for comparing these two with my research in terms of understanding MBBs' social identity negotiation. These theories and strategies are originally taken from the different context of ethnic identity, but they are also applicable to social identity of MBBs.[15]

Table 8. Models of Coping Strategies

Kraft (dual belonging integration)	Green (coping strategies)	Characteristics	Yun
Fragmentary integration	Suppression strategy	One dominant, but the other suppressive or fragmentary	Christian (H01)/Muslim (M01) social identity of MBBs; secret believers
Fusive integration	Switching strategy	Blending and melting, but one side stronger than the other; switching	*Uboi* (both) identity (E02)
Adhesive integration	Synthetic strategy	Not losing either one, a functional way to interact with two identities	*Isai/Isai* Muslim/ Muslim. Any identity which is managed comfortably (L03, E04)

----

12. Hibbert, 63.
13. Green, "Identity Choices."
14. Kraft, "Community and Identity."
15. Green, "Identity Choices," 56; Kraft, 172.

First, the fragmentary integration and suppression strategy signifies suppressing or ignoring one identity or another. For example, H01 and S01 radically converted to Christianity from their Muslim family and societal backgrounds. They still do not have contact with their close relatives and sometimes feel loneliness, and their children lack a feeling of family belonging and closeness compared to other Muslims. M01, on the other hand, has an *Isai* Muslim/Muslim identity. He continues to adopt Christian values in his life in a fragmentary way, but he spends most of his time with his Muslim parents and society, including his unbelieving wife. He suppresses his core identity as an *'Isa* follower and mingles harmoniously with his Muslim neighbors. M01 had actually tried to build up a local *jamaʿat* fellowship in his hometown, but members failed to gather continuously due to social pressure and he gave up with a sense of failure.

Second, although fusive integration and the switch strategy do not seem to take an identical shape, I believe there are some connections between them. I would redefine these two concepts to emphasize that MBBs can switch from one social identity to another, but feel that one identity has a deeper feeling of belonging at their core identity level. Most of the respondents with an *uboi* identity have a strong sense of belonging as an *Isai*. However, due to several reasons such as security, job, or evangelism, they switch their social identity from time to time. M04 explained his switching identities and revealing his major identity slowly, saying, "Because this is a Muslim *somaj* [religious community], we cannot say we are *Isai* at the first meeting. I need to introduce myself first as a Muslim, and as time goes by my identity is slowly and naturally revealed as an *Isai*. But, it is not being untruthful because I was born in the blood of Muslims."

Finally, adhesive integration and the synthetic strategy signify good assimilation of two identities, allowing an MBB to be a follower of *'Isa* spiritually and a Muslim culturally and socially without much struggle. E04 and L03, who identify as *Isai* Muslims/Muslim, are examples of this. Even though E04 participates in activities in the mosque, he does not feel much trouble or guilt because he understood the gospel of *'Isa* from the Qur'an first and the *Kitab* later. He has two identities as a Muslim and a follower of *'Isa*, without self-contradictions. L03 does not like the feeling of dishonor implied in the term "Christian" as used by general Muslims. Even though he changed his legal identity to Christian in order to respond to invitations to Christian trainings outside Bangladesh, he tries to preserve his Muslim identity in public. Two identities co-exist in his inner and outer life.

While scholars of ethnic identity recommend this adhesive integration and synthetic strategy, I do not believe that these two coping strategies represent the best option for MBBs. Even though these two identities are perfectly mixed or well harmonized outwardly, it could one day create conflict between them unless they solve the problems of their identity's biblical appropriation and ethical conscience. In the next section, I dig deeper into the social identity of Bangladeshi MBBs in interaction with the C-spectrum and Tim Green's categorization, as well as my findings.

Social Identity vis-à-vis Travis's C-Spectrum and Tim Green's Research

The C-spectrum introduced by John Travis is well-known in missiological discussions regarding MBB communities.[16] One of the MBB leaders interviewed for this study expressed unpleasant feelings about the introduction of these terms regarding contextualization and the C-scale in terms of dividing groups without proper alternatives. He believes that it has brought more problems and divided believers:

> What kinds of people do I need to work with? Christians made C1–C6. Who brought C formula? Missionaries! What are their suggestions and guidelines? Nothing! What is their vision? Nothing! They divide people instead of bringing work for unity, but expend their money, talent, and time on how to divide people. But Jesus died in order to bring people together. (L05)

It is worth listening to L05's critique of diverse missional approaches which have resulted in various groups and denominations. However, the C-spectrum itself did not harm local MBBs, but rather it helped observers understand the current reality of various MBB communities.

The C-spectrum has been criticized for various things, such as its one-dimensional character[17] and its creation of "illusion" for ministry among

---

16. Travis, "C1 to C6 Spectrum."
17. Green, "Identity Choices," 63.

Muslims.[18] First, Tim Green pursued a more developed model that would reflect the detailed realities of MBBs' three levels of identity: core, social, and collective. He said, "If identity is indeed the watershed issue (not cultural practices), then a one-dimensional spectrum, or a single-point 'great divide,' cannot possibly depict the multi-dimensional realities of the situation. I therefore believe that Abu Taher's categorization goes one step further than the 'C Spectrum' in depicting the realities of identity and community."[19] I generally agree with Green's argument, but I believe the C-spectrum still fits well and can be aptly applied to Bangladeshi MBBs' realities of identity. On the other hand, Roger Dixon argues that the C-spectrum "creates the illusion of offering insight to ministry while only giving a cursory view. Inexperienced workers are deluded into thinking the spectrum reveals special insights whereas it isn't [sic]. New workers are subject to being incorrectly indoctrinated by this tool."[20] It is true that new workers can face contradiction beyond their theological perceptual boundaries when they see an *Isai* Muslim/Muslim group, but I think knowing is better than ignorance or unawareness. Without understanding this reality of diverse groups, new workers might be inclined to do ministry only with traditional Christians with their traditional theological applications in a Muslim-majority context like Bangladesh, and not even try to have fellowship with MBBs. In this sense, I believe the C-spectrum is still helpful to understand the situation and reality of Bangladeshi MBBs.

Based on my research findings, the situation of Bangladeshi MBBs covers a range similar to that of the C-scale. Bangladeshi MBBs can be categorized into six groups following the C-scale's determinant factors of language, culture, religious forms, and identity. In my opinion, this scale is not overly one-dimensional, but rather it reflects important language and cultural differences between traditional Christians and MBBs. Three groups can be distinguished within the Bangladeshi Christian community, including MBBs: the traditional Christian community, moderate MBBs, and highly contextualized Muslim insiders. The C-spectrum addresses characteristics of these different groups.

The C-spectrum differs in two respects from Green's four groups and my three groups of Bangladeshi MBBs. The first difference is in the matter of

---

18. Dixon, "Moving on," 9.

19. Green, "Identity Choices," 62.

20. Dixon, "Moving on," 9.

language. There are two Bangla translations of the Bible, one for traditional Hindu-background Christians, which adapted Hindu terminology, and the other (*Kitab*) for converted believers from a Muslim background. Those who converted to Christianity from a Muslim background a few decades ago had to use the traditional Bangla Bible and its terminology. Since the publication of the *Injil* and *Kitab* around 1980, however, many MBBs have been comfortably using this *Mussolmani* Bangla Bible (*Kitab*). There is a categorical ambiguity here. Can MBBs consider the traditional Bible language as an outside (or different) language, and can those who use that traditional Bible be regarded as C1 believers? I think so. Then, someone who reads the *Kitab*, which uses Muslim terminology, can be defined as C2. However, it is still hard to clearly distinguish between C1 and C2 in the Bangladeshi context, because some MBBs begin using the *Kitab* at first and later use both translations interchangeably. While some MBBs who have a Christian identity can be described as C1 or C2 due to their use of a foreign or traditional Bible language, some who have an *Isai* identity can be regarded as C2 or C3 in terms of using *Kitab* language and adapting neutral cultural expressions such as clothing and diet. This is one of the ways in which the range of Bangladeshi MBB identities differs from the C-scale.

Another reason for the smaller range found among Bangladeshi MBBs than indicated in the C-scale arises from their cultural uniqueness and their own terminology for describing their social identity: Christian, *Isai, Isai* Muslim, and Muslim. The social identity of Bangladeshi MBBs has a tendency to move from one of these to another due to unique cultural factors such as Muslim dominance, poor economic conditions, and a culture of honor and shame. My use of three categories – Christian/*Isai*, *Isai*/*Isai* Muslim (*Uboi*), and *Isai* Muslim/Muslim – reflects this mobility of social identity. Motives for altering social identity include: (a) avoiding shame and social pressure (L06); (b) following the social identity of their gospel introducers (F04) or an organization's policy for sharing 'Isa more secretly or openly (M04, L02); and (c) being flexible in response to diverse situations (F05).

For more detailed illustration of this Bangladeshi MBB context, we can look at one respondent from each social identity category examined in this research (see Table 9). Their answers will be used in the following analyses of the three research questions.

Table 9. Three Representative Cases of Social Identity

(full answers to RQ1 in Appendix 4)

	E04	E02	H01
Social Identity	*Isai* Muslim/Muslim	*Isai/Isai* Muslim (*uboi*; both)	Christian/*Isai*

A Bangladeshi MBB who has a Christian/*Isai* identity has overcome the "hiding" issue, whether voluntarily or unintentionally. H01 is an example of this because he decided to adopt this identity even though it meant giving up his family inheritance and his relationship with them. *Isai/Isai* Muslims, on the other hand, were still able to introduce themselves to others in different ways depending on their context. E02, for example, has revealed his *Isai* identity in his hometown, but he introduced himself as a Muslim or an *Isai* Muslim when he needed to secure work for evangelism. Finally, *Isai* Muslim/ Muslims tend to shape their social identity to match that of their gospel introducer. E04, for example, received *'Isa* as Savior following a qur'anic seminar about *'Isa*, and has also worked with the same organization that organized the seminar. The person who introduced him to the gospel of *'Isa* encouraged him to keep an *Isai* Muslim/Muslim identity. This tendency to follow the social identity of gospel introducers is found not only in *Isai* Muslim/ Muslim identity, but all three social identities, and is an important finding of this study.

Anwarul Azad, himself a Bangladeshi MBB, recently concluded a study of MBBs in Bangladesh that showed results quite similar to those of my own research in terms of both observation and analysis.[21] Azad, too, identified three social identity groups among Bangladeshi MBBs; he also noted this tendency to follow the lead of one's gospel introducer in establishing a social identity. He described this tendency in a paper he presented as the keynote speaker at a conference in a Muslim-majority country:

---

21. I read Azad's paper when I was almost finished writing my own analysis, and was surprised because his work is very similar to my research issues/questions and findings. Azad also grouped three social identities of MBBs such as BMB (Believer from Muslim Background)1 (Christian), BMB2 (*Isai* and *Isai* Muslim), and BMB3 (Muslim). Because he himself is a Bangladeshi MBB, he has an emic (insider's) view of this topic. The similarity of his findings and analyses with mine gave me some sense of confidence and encouragement.

If the Preacher identifies them as Christian so the converted Believers also gave their identity as Christian. This tradition has been continuing up to date. In most of the case the Believer's identity are determined by the preacher. Thus the preacher identity would become the Believer's identity. If the preacher is Baptist or AG or Isai, even SDA then obviously the Believer's identity would change. The honeycomb they can get honey, so he always try to identify him or her selves according to the preacher desire.[22]

After reviewing my respondents' answers and interacting with the work of John Travis[23] and Tim Green,[24] I have compared my findings with the categorizations offered by these two authors and summarized the results in Table 10.

The difference between Tim Green's four groups and my three groups of MBBs is also crucial. Since most respondents agree with the reality of four groups of Bangladeshi MBBs, we can use these categories that are actually shown. However, my use of three categories, which allows for overlapping social identities, reflects mobility that is common in the identities of Bangladeshi MBBs. This movement is limited, however, in that an individual's identity generally shifts only within one of the three categories. For example, someone who has Christian/*Isai* identity tends to move from Christian to *Isai*, but does not express himself or herself in terms of a Muslim identity. Some others, who have an *Isai* Muslim/Muslim identity, usually do not easily jump to a revealed Christian identity.

Azad drew a small diagram to show the reality of social identity among Bangladeshi MBBs, reproduced in Figure 10. He identified three groups of BMBs (Believers from Muslim Background). BMB1 corresponds to Christian; BMB2 to *Isai* Muslim or *Isai*; and BMB3 to Muslim.[25]

---

22. Azad, "Discipling, Identity, and Belonging," 317. Grammar as in the original.
23. Travis, "Must All Muslims Leave?," 665.
24. Green, "Identity Choices."
25. Azad, "Discipling, Identity, and Belonging," 17.

Table 10. Comparison of the Research Findings with C-Spectrum and Tim Green's Research

(Travis, "Must All Muslims Leave?," 665.)

C-spectrum	C1	C2	C3	C4	C5	C6
Points (Citation is original;	Traditional church using a language different from the daily language of the surrounding Muslim community	Traditional church using the daily language of the surrounding Muslim community	Contextualized community using the daily language of the surrounding Muslim community and some non-Muslim local cultural forms	Contextualized community using the daily language and biblically acceptable socioreligious Islamic forms	Community of Muslims who follow Jesus yet remain culturally and officially Muslim	Secret or underground Muslim followers of Jesus with little or no visible community
Tim Green	*Christian*	*Christian/Isai*	*Isai*	*Isai Muslim*	*Muslim*	
My study		*Isai/Isai Muslim (uboi; both)*			*Isai Muslim/Muslim*	

Figure 10. Azad's Explanation of Three Social Identities of Bangladeshi MBBs

Azad's explanation of the three groupings is similar to mine, and compares the different opportunities available to the three social identities, such as the particularly open characteristic of the BMB2 (*Isai* or *Isai* Muslim) identity:

> We have two boxes and one is open: If we confined ourselves in one box, then the opportunity of preaching is decreasingly proportionate. This is applicable for BMB1 and BMB3. But, for the BMB2, they have a boundless potentiality to bear their witness among their neighbors or to others. They can join worship program and fellowship with mainline existing Christian churches. They may move to BMB1 box or to BMB3 box.

Azad concludes his article with the analogy of a rainbow representing the six (or seven) categories from C-spectrum, with which he generally agrees. After explaining that the colors of the rainbow actually come from three major colors (RGB: Red, Green, and Blue), he suggests a firm establishment of core identity in Christ and the harmonious coexistence of diverse social identities.

> In our country we can mainly differentiate them in to 3 categories. C1–C3 are Christian, C4 are Isai, C5 Spectrum are declining and C6 group are totally absent in Bangladesh. We may categorise it in three spectrums. C1–C3 are BMB 1, C4 are BMB 2 and reform C5 as BMBS3. We know that there need at least 6 colours for making a rainbow, but, this six or seven colours are made from RGB, i.e. 3 colours. These main 3 colours made all of the colours. We may have six even 3 categories M heritage Believers in Bangladesh. But, the Believers have been making a rainbow in the sky.
>
> Again I want to mention the category of M heritage Believers in Bangladesh mentioned by John Travis. I am agreeing with him in Broad sense. But, I do categorise those Believers in mainly three categories. We know that Light is consisting of mainly 3

colors: RGB. But, with mix-up with each other they form a spectrum of Light. Light has different weave length: Some are long
and some are short. But, those are unitedly forming a beautiful
rainbow. We do not judge them but, beautifully they are making
a rainbow. We do not want to categorizes us as BMBs1, BMBs 2
or BMBs 3. We are not belongs of Apollos or Paul's or any others
else. Our Core and collective identity is we are all in Christ. We
are not belongs to Apollo or Pauls but, we are in Christ. Our
core Identity is we are belong in Christ.[26]

Azad's conclusion provides a worthwhile reminder that we need to respect
each social identity, and also focus on the core identity of belonging in Christ.
I agree with his conclusion. In the next section, I will suggest pursuing one
paradigm for a biblical way to improve the current situation of diverse social
identity groups of Bangladeshi MBBs.

Christ-Centered Community

Another benefit of Travis's C-spectrum is its expression and pursuit of Christ-
centered community. According to Travis, "The purpose of the spectrum
is to assist church planters and Muslim background believers to ascertain
which type of Christ-centered communities may draw the most people from
the target group to Christ and best fit in a given context."[27] The spectrum
reminds us to focus not on Christianity-centered community but on Christ-
centered community. Historically, there has existed a clear boundary between
Christian and Muslim communities in Bangladesh. However, since Muslims
began coming to faith in 'Isa in the mid-1970s, several groups have emerged.
Phenomenologically, MBB groups in Bangladesh resemble a fuzzy set community rather than a well-formed boundary set, because they lack clear
boundaries and static characteristics, and see frequent moves from one group
to the other. Also, it is very difficult for one group to move to another through
outsiders' force or even by their own decision such as from Isai Muslim/
Muslim to Christian/Isai group. It is because these identities have been set
up for such a long time at both the individual and the community levels.

---

26. Azad, "Discipling, Identity, and Belonging," 34–35. Grammar as in the original.
27. Travis, "C1 to C6 Spectrum," 407.

Suppose I put the *Isai* Muslim/Muslim group on the left side of a spectrum and the Christian/*Isai* group on the right side, just as we see in Figures 6 and 7 in chapter 3, the left side (*Isai* Muslim/Muslim group) does not want to move from the left to the right side. This is because this group has enjoyed certain social benefits – such as social security – due to not being known as apostates (M01, M02, M03, L03, H08), as well as the opportunity to draw Muslims to 'Isa in a relatively less offensive manner (E04). This left-side group, however, has shortcomings, such as the possibility of falling into the danger of syncretism – mixing the gospel with unbiblical interpretation and applications – unless they keep focusing on 'Isa and the Bible (*Kitab*) (E04 and M02).

At the other end of the spectrum, the Christian/*Isai* group has some benefits such as a clearly converted identity and the possibility of focusing on the Bible and spiritual realms (H01, S01). Still, the reality is not ideal. They sometimes feel drained emotionally because of their lack of relationship with extended family members and relatives (H02, U09), and they hardly receive social benefits from the majority community, but rather have had to endure social obstacles and bans (S01, U01, U04, U05, N01, N02). So, they tend to find foreign Christian (or missionary) supporters to help with their financial and social difficulties. These difficulties and tendencies hinder this right-side group from focusing on 'Isa and growing in him.

For these reasons, I suggest an alternative paradigm that adapts the centered set with four fuzzy groups of social identity proposed by Paul Hiebert[28] and Tim Green.[29] All four groups need to keep their focus on 'Isa and the *Kitab*, wherever they are currently situated (Figure 9). The *uboi* (between *Isai* and *Isai* Muslim) identity group also needs to focus more on 'Isa instead of moving between the two sides (E02, H04, and M03) or, as Massey described C4, living "like a social chameleon, trying to maintain acceptance in two different worlds."[30] Most of the research respondents agreed that these four groups actually exist, which is why I drew this diagram with four groups.[31]

---

28. Hiebert, *Anthropological Reflections.*

29. Green, "Conversion in the Light."

30. Massey, "Misunderstanding C5," 301.

31. However, I have categorized three groups from my research findings. Further discussions and reasons will be presented in RQ 2 analysis.

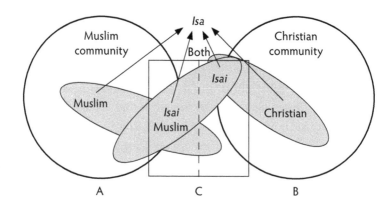

Figure 11. Groups of MBBs in Bangladesh with Centered and Fuzzy Sets Focusing on 'Isa

Also, as we see in Figure 11, it is more important for each MBB group to develop a genuine relationship with 'Isa than focus on "monitoring and maintaining the boundaries."[32] As my research has shown, H01 is situated in the Christian/*Isa* fuzzy group around position B. E04 is located in the *Isa* Muslim/Muslim fuzzy group around position A. E02 mostly stays around the C position – both *Isa* and *Isa* Muslim – but he comes and goes though all areas depending on the situation. Rather than casually assigning which position a person is located in, the first step of being a genuine follower of 'Isa should be to show 'Isa (Jesus) as the center with everyone moving toward him from every direction. This means each group needs to have a "*theo-centered directionality*"[33] or an 'Isa (or Christ)-centered directionality. This is another strength and implication of C-spectrum. In this sense, I believe the C-spectrum is still useful for understanding the reality of MBBs and for maintaining a right direction toward 'Isa. The issue of whether a certain position, such as position A, is permissible will be dealt with in the section on Analysis RQ 2 as part of a deeper discussion of contextualization.

Summary of Findings in RQ 2

Local MBBs are generally living their social lives with their majority Muslim neighbors. They have to manage aspects of their social lives such as marriage,

---

32. Yoder et al., "Understanding Christian Identity," 182.

33. Baeq, "Contextualizing Religious Form," 204.

funeral, education, and economic activities while also facing Muslims' efforts to bring them back to Muslim *somaj* by forcing them to participate in
Muslims' religious activities such as *namaz* (Muslims' formal prayer), *roza*
(thirty days of fasting: *Ramadan*), and *qurbani* (sacrificing animals). RQ 2
deals with MBBs' social activities and their participation in general Muslims'
religious activities. RQ 2 asks,

> To what extent and in what ways are MBBs integrated into the
> social, religious, and cultural fabric of the broader Muslim com-
> munity life?

Additionally, in order to understand determinant factors, I tried to find answers to sub-question 2c, which concerns the advantages and disadvantages
of MBBs' various social locations. SQ2c asks,

> What are the determinant factors that they use to decide to stay
> in their social identity and patterns of life?

To summarize the findings of RQ 2, MBBs generally want their children
to marry the same kind of believer – e.g. for an *Isai* to marry an *Isai* or an
Isai Muslim to marry an *Isai* Muslim – though some others would accept
any kind of believer for their children's marriage (U02, H04, H05) or would
leave the decision to their children (M03, S01). Also, *'Isa* followers' marriages
are different in some ways from the marriages of other Muslims, in that they
respect children's decisions (H01), view husband and wife as having equal
importance (H02), and do not practice multiple marriages (I02). Regarding
funerals, most MBBs would prefer to be buried separately from Muslims, despite the fact that this is often not possible (F02), though some said wherever
they are buried is fine (I01, I02, U12). Regarding children's education, most
MBBs pursue Christian/*Isai* education in their homes, even though some
MBBs' children have to study Islam at school (I01, N01). A foreign observer
commented that "most *Isais* are extremely concerned about the education of
their children, but not much concerned about religious education [the *Kitab*]"
(F02). Regarding economic activities, none of the respondents received any
financial benefits in exchange for having faith in *'Isa*. To get jobs, they could
portray a Muslim-like or Christian-like identity, depending on the available
position (E02, F03).

The three groups of MBBs (Christian/*Isai, Isai/Isai* Muslim [*uboi*; both], and *Isai* Muslim/Muslim) have different approaches to participation in Muslims' religious activities. Table 11 reveals the extent of participation in different activities that characterizes each social identity group.

Christian/*Isai* self-identified MBB respondents normally do not participate in any Muslim religious activities, but only Christian festivals such as Christmas. *Isai/Isai*

Table 11. Participation in Religious Activities by Three Groups of MBBs in Bangladesh

	Isai Muslim/Muslim	*Isai/Isai* Muslim (*uboi*; both)	Christian/ *Isai*
Namaz in the mosque (formal prayer)	Every Friday only (E04, M02, H08, E03); anytime invited at mosque (E04)	No	No
Roza (fasting)	Yes, but not full participation	Not usually, but sometimes if needed	No
Qurbani (sacrificing animals)	Yes, if they have money (M02)	Very few respondents (N03)	No
Eid namaz (during *Roza* and *Qurbani* Eid)	Yes	Yes, sometimes (M01, M03, E01, L03; 4 among 11)	No
Other social activities	Yes, with Muslim neighbors, but mostly with co-believers (M02, E04)	When invited by close relatives and friends	Rarely, sometimes only if invited
Christian festivals	No	Yes and no: some (H04, H05) observe Christmas on Dec. 25, but some (E01, E02, E03) do not.	Yes

Muslim (*uboi*; both) identified MBBs do not participate in most of the religious activities of Muslims, though several respondents participate in *Eid namaz* (M01, M03, E01, L03). *Isai* Muslim/Muslim self-identified believers in 'Isa might participate in Muslims' social activities such as *namaz*, Friday *jummah namaz*, and the two *Eids namaz*, but some participate only in Friday *jummah namaz* (E03, E04, M02, I04), and some only in *Eid namaz* (M03, M01, L03, E01). Participating in Friday *jummah namaz* can be a determinant factor of Muslim identity (similar to C5), and participating in *Eid namaz*, where Muslims pray in a field outside the mosque during two *Eid* festivals, is also a crucial point that demands consideration of whether it is a religious or cultural/social activity (similar to C4 or C5).

Finally, MBB respondents commented on the advantages and disadvantages of their social identity positions. These findings are summarized in Table 12.

Table 12. Advantages and Disadvantages of Three Social Identities

	Isai Muslim/Muslim	*Isai/Isai* Muslim (*uboi*; both)	Christian/*Isai*
Advantages (Benefits)	• No social obstacles and no harm for family • Living with the majority • No diminishing faith, rather getting preaching opportunities • Less persecution while there is a growing number of believers	• Flexible depending on the situation • Raising curiosity of (*Isai* Muslim) identity and using its opportunity to share the gospel	• Spiritual benefits such as assurance of salvation and peace • Clear identity such as government protection and less possibility of coming back to Islam • No need to participate in Muslims' religious activities such as *namaz, roza, qurbani*, etc.
Disadvantages (Struggles)	• Some Christians' criticism and exposure of them as Christians • Fewer opportunities to work in Christian organizations • Some persecution • Easy for faith to disappear due to lack of sacrifice and gathering	• Someone might doubt about the unknown identity • They sometimes feel guilty in terms of deceiving their Christian identity • Muslims continually try to draw them back to Islam	• Muslims' side glances and bad words • No acceptance; social ban • Lack of social relationships with the majority

The respondents offered different answers depending on their own contexts. While the Christian/*Isai* identity has certain benefits of a clear identity as well as spiritual benefits, those who self-identify as Christian or *Isai* have to endure social obstacles. Those who function with an *Isai/Isai* Muslim identity can switch their identity for their own purposes or for adapting to situations, but Muslims also try to draw them back to Islam. The *Isai* Muslim/Muslim identity may look like it has no social obstacles, but MBBs with this identity still experienced social judgments because of their faith and evangelistic activities. One of the drawbacks for them is that they could lose their faith due to their avoidance of the sacrifice involved in publicly revealing their faith and *Isai* identity, as well as the lack of dedication to regular gatherings of believers. Overall, members of these three social identity groups differ in their pursuit of two social conditions: (1) social deliverance, saving themselves from diverse social pressures, and (2) social connections, saving their belongingness to family and community they were born into and saving relationships in order to share the gospel of *'Isa*. These dominant themes will be examined in the following analysis of RQ 2.

Analysis of RQ 2

The analysis of RQ 2 in the light of other literature begins with three respondents who represent each social identity group (Table 13). These three respondents participate in the activities of the majority Muslim community to different extents and have different views of key concepts.

Table 13. Three Representatives of Social Participation

(details in Appendix 5)

	E04, *Isai* Muslim/Muslim	E02, *Isai*/*Isai* Muslim	H01, Christian/*Isai*
Points	Participation in Muslim activities with reinterpretation and opportunity	Difference between intention and obligation; searching for contentment	Clear Christian identity of children; least relationship with Muslims

First, H01 has a clear social identity as a Christian/*Isai* who has self-identified Christian/*Isai* children, and he does not participate in any religious activities of Muslims. Second, E02 has faced trouble from his Muslim wife and his mother over questions such as whether he will eventually be buried with Christians or Muslims, but he has decided to raise his child as a Christian. Marriage is one of the most difficult situations single MBBs are facing, due to the difficulty of finding a spouse who shares the same beliefs within the context of being subordinate to parents' decision (F02, F03).[34] Even though E02 does not participate in *namaz*, several other *Isai/Isai* Muslim (*uboi*; both) self-identified MBBs do so. Finally, E04 has no problem with participating in Muslims' religious activities such as *namaz* for prayer (without saying the second part of *shahada*) and *qurbani* for remembering Abraham's sacrifice and as a gospel-sharing opportunity. When he teaches his children, he focuses more on the *Kitab* and *'Isa* than on the Qur'an. In the next section, we will bring my research findings into engagement with insider movement discussions.

Engaging Parshall and Tennent's Concerns about Syncretism

Among foreign scholars and practitioners, Phil Parshall has discussed his three concerns about C5 and syncretism. In an article responding to Parshall, Travis summarized Parshall's concerns as follows:

1. Deception in Christians posing as Muslims to reach Muslims (i.e. "C5 missionaries").
2. Danger in ongoing mosque attendance past a transitional period for new believers since "the mosque is pregnant with Islamic theology"[35] and exalts Muhammad as a prophet.
3. Affirming the prophethood of Muhammad by recitation of the Muslim creed (*shahada*): "There is no god but God and Muhammad is his prophet."[36]

Parshall's first concern is relevant in the case of C5 missionaries with Christian backgrounds to become Muslim insiders to reach Muslims. This study does not address Parshall's first concern because all my respondents are from Muslim background, though one respondent (M03) participated in Christian training for several months and worked for a Christian organization for several years before quitting his job in order to follow his preference to do his ministry for Muslims as a Muslim insider. The second and third concerns, about mosque attendance and the prophethood of Muhammad, including the Qur'an issue, are discussed below in my analyses of RQ 2 and RQ 3.

---

34. Green, "Identity Issues for Ex-Muslim."
35. Parshall, "Danger!," 409.
36. Travis, "Messianic Muslim Followers," 55.

Parshall suggested several guidelines to avoid falling into syncretism. In his article "Going too far," he calls for discussion, giving an example of an excessive contextualization – such as a foreigner's conversion to Islam – and lists five guidelines.[37] John Travis responded to him in a position of supporting C5 and insider believers, suggesting seven guidelines for avoiding syncretism.[38] A comparison of the two guidelines (Table 14) is helpful for our discussion.

One interesting difference between the two lists lies in the fact that while Parshall mostly gives guidelines for foreign practitioners, Travis mostly suggests guidelines for local believers. Additionally, Parshall removed one guideline – the need for an emic view – that had been included in his previous list of guidelines.[39] The reason for this choice is not clear to me, because Parshall mentioned that "syncretism can be understood only when one takes an emic position."[40] My research agrees with Parshall's recommendation to keep an emic view and Travis's approach of valuing local believers and emphasizing their initiative.

The title of Ralph Winter's response – "Going Far Enough?" – is interesting. Even though he agrees with Parshall's points and guidelines, he challenges us to dig into more historical reasons – such as the Crusades – for the relationship between

Muslims and Christians in order to understand Muslims' discomfort with Christianity. He also suggests studying the New Testament more deeply. He argues that it does not matter whether a follower of 'Isa is called a Christian or a Muslim.[41] Just a comparison of these article titles helps us understand the kind of ongoing discussions and the questions that still need to be discussed, such as the extent we can go or we are allowed to go. John Travis once responded to Tennent's description[42] of retaining a Muslim identity after deciding to follow Jesus as "unethical." Figure 12, which is adapted from part of a figure used by Tennent, shows the C-scale as it relates to the explanation in his article. Tennent holds an evangelical view of contextualization as good when it avoids two extremes: extractionism and syncretism.

---

37. Parshall, "Going Too Far?," 667.
38. Travis, "Must All Muslims Leave?," 671–72.
39. Parshall, *Muslim Evangelism*, 57.
40. Parshall, 57.
41. Winter, "Going Far Enough?," 671.
42. Travis, "Response to Tennent"; Tennent, "Followers of Jesus (Isa)."

It is understandable why Tennent considers a C5 identity unethical. Travis, however, argues that outsiders cannot judge whether it is ethical or not, as "only they can say whether or not their conscience is violated."[43]

Table 14. Comparison of Guidelines for Avoiding Syncretism[44]

	Parshall (avoiding syncretism)	Travis (avoiding syncretism of C5)
Guidelines	• Study Islam as religion and culture • Open approach needed • Biblical teaching needed on syncretism • Constant monitoring and analysis • Gospel already syncretized with Western culture, so be aware of it as cross-cultural communicators.	• Jesus as Lord and Savior, no other name for salvation • *Injil* study (including *Torah*, *Zabur* if available) • Regular meeting • Avoiding harmful folk Islamic practices • Reinterpretation of Muslim practices as expression of love for God and neighbors • Qur'an, Muhammad, theology reinterpretation in light of Scripture. • Show evidence of the new birth and growth in grace.
My Observations	Parshall focuses on foreigners' role in avoiding syncretism. He also erased the need for an emic (insider's) approach to deal with contextualization from his previous guidelines, published in 2003.	Travis focuses on existing C5 believers and advises them to keep focusing on the gospel, 'Isa, and Scripture, as well as reinterpreting Islamic activities.

C1–C2	C3–C4	C5 (C6 too?)
Low————High	Low————High	Low————High
Extractionism	Contextualization	Syncretism

Figure 12. Evaluation of C1–C6 Spectrum[45]

So, how far is too far? Parshall often suggested not participating in activities inside the mosque.[46] Then, based on Parshall's guidelines, is it possible for a follower of 'Isa to participate in *Eid namaz* outside of the mosque in

---

43. Travis, 125.

44. I have slightly summarized the material from Parshall and Travis.

45. This representation is based on a figure used by Tennent. Tennent, "Followers of Jesus (Isa)," 103.

46. Parshall, *Muslim Evangelism*, 71.

order to retain social status and social fellowship twice a year? L03 answered that "it is social *namaz* in a field not in the mosque." So, he does not find any problem about participating in it. Then, how about local insider believers like E04 and M02, who are running several *jama'ats*, but continuing to perform activities inside and outside the mosques, either reciting "God is one and *'Isa* is Messiah" (M02) or simply not saying the second part of *shahada* (E04). The next part deals with two different paradigms for understanding the reality in our different presuppositions.

Two Perspectives

As we saw above while comparing Tennent and Parshall with Travis and Winter, there are two perspectives in the discussion and debate on the issue of contextualization and insider movement. We can describe the two perspectives as high and low contextualization, but this is not just a matter of different types or extent of contextualizing efforts. It rather comes from different theological and theoretical paradigms. Leonard N. Bartlotti, who was a long-term worker in a sensitive context, responded to the growing concern of the insider movement issues and debates by introducing the two different paradigms with his "lens" idea.[47] From Bartlotti's nine lenses, the following table summarizes five paradigms that are directly related to my research (Table 15; details in Appendix 5). The content of this table explains many things about why local MBBs and foreign practitioners take different approaches to their social identity. These differences primarily come from theological viewpoints. Figure 13 maps three social identity positions against paradigms of contextualization described in terms of Bartlotti's five lenses (see Table 15). This diagram has been adapted from Figures 9 and 11 to include two lines indicating points on Bartlotti's spectrum from radical contextualization on the left to moderate contextualization on the right. An understanding of Figure 13 will also shed light on Table 15, which compares two different paradigms with the realities of social identity among Bangladeshi MBBs.

For the section "Doing Theology," while the left side is doing "local (contextual) theologies," the right side tries to follow "Western theological tradition." As Colin Andrews suggests, in a globalizing world, contextualization of this age needs to

---

47. Bartlotti, "Seeing Inside Insider," 150.

Table 15. Two Paradigms of Contextualization Seen through Various Lenses

(Detail in Appendix 7)

Radical (high) Contextualization Left side (*Isai* Muslim/Muslim)	Theological Lens by me	Moderate (low) Contextualization Right side (Christian/*Isai*)
Bartlotti's Five Lenses		
Simple church, Jesus emphasis	Ecclesiology	Sacraments, Pauline Emphasis
Local (contextual) theologies	Doing Theology	Western theological tradition
Continuity, Fulfillment	Other Religions	Discontinuity, Exclusivism
"islams" (lower case, plural) Culturally Embedded, muslims	Islam	"Islam," Historically essentialized, Muslims, Islamic Tradition
Centered Set/Moving toward Christ	Conversion-Initiation	Bounded Set/Clear identity markers
E04, M04	Representative figure	H01, E02 (*uboi* identity)

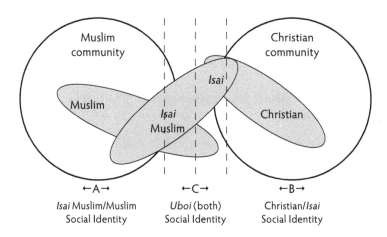

<u>←A→</u>
Isai Muslim/Muslim
Social Identity

<u>←C→</u>
Uboi (both)
Social Identity

<u>←B→</u>
Christian/*Isai*
Social Identity

Figure 13. Three Groups and Four Groups of Bangladeshi MBBs

move away "from theology to toward theologies" and "from trying to find the holy grail of contextualization models and embrace the diversity of models."[48]

---

48. Andrews, "Contextualization in a Glocalizing," 317.

Then, what is a good theology and what are good local theologies? How can we determine appropriate theologies in a certain context of Bangladeshi MBBs? How far can we proceed in our application of the biblical text? For example, E04 has a more context-based theological view, and reinterpreted faith in *'Isa* by his own judgment allowing his prayer in the mosque for reasons such as (a) worshipping the Almighty God in his contextual way without inner contradiction, (b) finding more opportunities for evangelism, and (c) saving social status. H01, however, tries to stay within his Christian/*Isai* boundary in order to participate freely in Christians' religious activities such as Christmas, since the Bangladesh government tries to protect the festivals of religious minorities from Islamic extremists and their attacks on Muslim converts. While Muslim insiders and their supporters understand that "meaning is negotiated by the local believer in his or her context," critics of the insider movement argue that "following Christ means a rejection, not retention, of Islam as embedded within Muslim cultures."[49]

We should also note that some scholars hold the view that Muslims can be "muslims" (lower case) in the sense of "cultural muslims, whose sense of religious identity is locally, ethnically, and culturally constructed," but critics of the insider movement emphasize the differences between Islamic orthodox theology and Christian theology.[50] From my research findings, the left (A) and right (B) sides have sharp distinctions, and there have been various conflicts between these two groups in Bangladesh.

Analysis of Christian/*Isai* and *Isai*/*Isai* Muslim Social Identity

The benefits experienced by self-identified Christian/*Isais* relate to the fact that they open their faith to the public intentionally or by accident. As an evangelical scholar, I am familiar and comfortable with the Christian/*Isais'* radical break from the Muslim *somaj* and establishment of a clear new identity for the security of faith. Christian/*Isais* seem to be theologically secure and in a good position to grow in their faith in *'Isa* away from Islamic theology. This would be the most secure option for MBBs who have suffered due to keeping their faith and have overcome various social pressures.

---

49. Bartlotti, "Seeing Inside Insider," 141.
50. Bartlotti, 147.

Christian/*Isai* social identity seems to coincide with what Tennent calls "a necessary rupture" following commitment to '*Isa*.[51] However, these MBBs need to solve the problem of how to heal the social rupture by reaching out to their family and neighbors (H01, S01, U02, N01). It would be better for these Christian/*Isais* to try to maintain relationships with their unbelieving family members and friends. This task is not easy work, but I believe it is possible for Bangladeshi MBBs to reconnect with their community by acting with respect and love. Careful understanding of Muslims' view of Islam and the Muslim identity is a prerequisite to keep communicating with them. In this process, it would be helpful for MBBs to develop discerning eyes for how to follow '*Isa* in their own context and avoid following Western Christian practices without considering the different contexts. This issue will be dealt with under RQ3 as part of an analysis of the four-self issue. Another important issue for Christian/*Isais* is that they are thirsty and have their need for a sense of community belonging addressed because they are still very few in contrast to the majority (H02, U09, U11, I02). We can also see the same need in the *Isai/Isai* Muslim case.

In my view, the *Isai/Isai* Muslim (*uboi*; both) identity is not a permanent position but a transitional one. Two types of MBBs fall into this category. Some of them stay in this identity for a time of waiting until they convince their family members and close acquaintances to join their new journey of finding the truth together (U10, H05). Others, however, reveal this identity to share the gospel of '*Isa* with the majority Muslims. L06 said that a high percentage of MBBs who are currently working in Muslim outreach ministry hold this identity (H05, M04, E02). They are revealed believers in their hometowns, but they do not want to introduce their *Isai* identity for the first time when they do outreach to new friends or new places (M04). They switch their social identity depending on context in the name of ministry. However, as the English proverb "you can't have your cake and eat it too" suggests, I do not think MBBs can maintain this *uboi* (both) identity for a long period. Also, it is not desirable for individuals to feel guilty or deceptive when they present themselves as Muslims or *Isai* Muslims (E02), because this sense of habitualuntruthfulness makes them feel dishonest to other persons and unfaithful in worshipping God and following '*Isa*.

---

51. Tennent, "Followers of Jesus (Isa)," 113.

In terms of their participation in *namaz* inside mosque or just *Eid namaz* twice a year outside the mosque, I tried to analyze these activities with several self-identified *Isai* Muslim/Muslims. Even though we recognize existence of two presuppositions in our understanding and two realities in the fields, questions like "which side is better?" still exist. Is radical contextualization appropriate or syncretistic? What is the way to do healthy and good contextualization in this context? Is it possible for a follower of 'Isa to participate in *namaz* outside the mosque at *Eid*, or even inside the mosque?

A Crucial Point of *Eid Namaz*

In my opinion, *Eid namaz* is the crucial point of division between the highly contextualized social identity of *Isai* Muslim/Muslims and the low contextualized identity of Christian/*Isais*. I am not simply saying that if someone participates in *Eid namaz* outside the mosque, he or she is doing a syncretistic activity as a follower of 'Isa, nor am I saying that it is acceptable for MBBs to do it because it is done outside the mosque. This assessment is only with reference to someone who has *Isai* Muslim identity because generally do not or cannot participate in this way. This is because Christian/*Isai*-identified MBBs are already revealed to the Muslim community and generally banned from joining the *Eid namaz* by the Muslim *somaj*. *Isai* Muslim, close to C4, is an ambiguous identity because they could go either way as what Massey described as "a sociological chameleon."[52]

Even if an MBB performs *namaz* only once or twice a year, it is important to discern what they think and why they do this. Why do they participate in this activity without clearly resisting it? Is the goal to relieve social pressure, to continue social connections for the sake of sharing the gospel, or both? It is difficult for foreign workers to guess how they would feel if they lost their social connections and were excluded from their families and communities. Two participants in *Eid namaz* among the five are primarily pursuing *shamajic rokka* (social deliverance) (H08, M01), while the other three are seeking social connections both to keep their social status as Muslims in this point of time and to find opportunities to share the gospel of 'Isa (L03, E01, M03).

In my analysis, their motive, timing, and places of living are more important than what they do and whether they participate or not, because some

---

52. Massey, "Misunderstanding C5," 301.

MBBs are waiting for better timing to reveal their new belief. E01 has not fully revealed his faith in *'Isa* to his family and hometown relatives because he is living in Dhaka and rarely visits his hometown. He is sharing his witness with his family sometimes and awaiting good timing to fully confess his new faith to them. He said he could fully reveal his Christian faith when he becomes self-supporting and has a family after marrying a Christian/*Isai* girl in the future. In his case, when is it a good time to reveal his faith and how can he proceed? I think he is the best person to know that. In this *uboi* (both) identity, there are many believers who live away from their rural hometown because of their work in urban areas or different places. The most important need for them is good co-believers and mentors to give them advice and spiritual nurture, thus highlighting the importance of the believers' community (*jama'at*). If *uboi* (both) identity believers get nurtured from their urban *jama'at* for a few years, they might feel encouraged and find wisdom about how they treat their hometown family and neighbors with the help of *jama'at* members. I personally think that it is better, after gaining strong faith and experiences for around one to three years with encouragement from *jama'at* members, to make relatives and neighbors listen to his witness in an understandable and respectful manner.

Three Types of Groups of *Isai* Muslim/Muslims

Then, another question remains. What about some Muslim insiders who perform *namaz* inside the mosque normally on Fridays? I extend my analysis from the previous *Isai* Muslim case. There were four Muslim insiders (E03, E04, M02, I04) who perform *namaz* inside the mosque among the ten respondents who have an *Isai* Muslim/Muslim identity. I could divide these into three groups according to their reasons for staying in this identity. First, there were unavoidable or survival insiders who were vulnerable economically and socially and continue with a Muslim identity (H07, H08, M01, M05). For those who revealed their core identity, they were too few in number in the hometown society and cannot survive by their own power. Also, some were afraid of falling into danger if they totally revealed their new faith. In my opinion, they need to pass through *'Isa's* test from the Bible about acknowledging faith in *'Isa* publicly (Matt 10:31–32). This is a test of the authenticity of faith. Also, they need to trust in God, who provides all that they need (Phil 4:19).

Second, there were strategic insiders who were hired by Christian mission organizations working among Muslims in a highly contextualized approach (M03, E03, I04, L03). Some first had a Christian/*Isai* identity and moved in response to organizations' offers, while some others were invited at the beginning stage of being an '*Isa* follower. They agreed with their organization's policy and had some passion for reaching out to the majority for the first time, and soon settled down with this social identity. M03 and L03 feel certain convictions about staying within this identity without performing *namaz* inside the mosque by their own choice, but sometimes they only participate in *Eid namaz*. E03 and I04 began with a Christian/*Isai* identity after believing in '*Isa*. E03 went to back to practicing Islamic activities in order to mingle with the Muslim *somaj* in his new town so he could share the gospel of '*Isa* and also run his local shop well. I04 went back to Islam and performing *namaz* because of the loss of his job in a Christian NGO and his disappointment with his foreign leader's misjudgment.[53] Such believers also need to pass '*Isa*'s challenge of a real disciple who takes up his cross (Mark 8:34–35), even if there are no occupational or social benefits. Also, these insider believers need to check the authenticity of their ethical consciousness of being called as a Muslim and whether they feel deceptive or not.

Actually, E04 and M02 could be called Muslim insiders or "called" Muslim insiders because they have certain convictions as '*Isa* followers and a sense of calling to maintain a Muslim identity and share '*Isa* as the Savior with their neighbors for ten to twenty years. E04 reinterprets *namaz* without any influence of Muhammad – "there is no influence and no relations with Muhammad during the *namaz*, but the only focus is on *Ibrahim* (Abraham) who is the father of a nation" – and confesses *shahada* without the second part. M02 has a son who has the same kind of belief and identity as his father. His faith and identity have lasted over twenty years. He said, "I am a Muslim and a follower of '*Isa*. This has not occurred in a few years' time. I want to live my life in this faith and identity, so do my children. In this country, the reputation of Christian identity is too bad. All things will be lost after getting all kinds of pressures." It seems to me that he wants to stay in a Muslim identity and community not because he is afraid of losing property after being

---

53. This is his own view. He did something wrong and was expelled from the organization, the exact details of which I do not know.

labelled as a Christian, but because he is thinking of his calling and destiny, uniquely combined with multiple motives: self-esteem as a Muslim in regard to honor vs. shame with his socioreligious identity at birth, the opportunity to reach neighbors, and material concerns. In my opinion, insiders like this identity and they feel that it is the right lifestyle for their children to follow (E04, M02).

Engaging deeply with C4 and C5 debates from precedent literature, I try to analyze two issues – one for C5 and one for C4. First, the two respondents (E04 and M02) that I referred to as "called Muslim insiders" above can be linked to "cultural insiders, but theological outsider" (CITO) (Jaz 2013, 56), "appropriate C5"[54], and "reformed C5."[55] However, it is hard to put them in a certain category among these three. They are not strategic insiders but cultural Muslim insiders who partially participate in socioreligious activities with general Muslims and other Muslim insiders. However, they are different from general Muslims. Even if, from our perspective, their participation in the Friday *jummah namaz* in the mosque has syncretistic points, it seems to me that they are just living their lives, negotiating and harmonizing with their context and reinterpreting their activities in light of the Bible. In my view, their participation in *namaz* activity does not remind them of Muhammad or Islamic religious allegiance, but is a form of dedication to *Mabud Allah* (Lord God) based on their reformed *shahada* (with the second part changed or omitted).

Also, these two are born Muslims, not re-converts who had first developed a Christian identity after conversion and went to back to Islam for insider ministry, which Parshall opposes.[56] They do not have an experience of religious conversion, but of a spiritual conversion of allegiance from Muhammad to 'Isa. Considering Tennent's comment that "one's religious identity with Jesus Christ creates a necessary rupture with one's *Islamic identity* or our identity in Jesus Christ would mean nothing,"[57] I suggest distinguishing an Islamic identity which opposes a Christian identity from a Muslim identity which seems not to be very contradictory to the identity of a follower of 'Isa.

---

54. Asad, "Rethinking the Insider Movement."

55. Azad, "Discipling, Identity, and Belonging."

56. Parshall, "Going Too Far?," 667.

57. Tennent, "Followers of Jesus (Isa)," 113; italics added.

Another point is that these two respondents are actively participating in sharing the gospel of 'Isa and in local *jama'at* activities. These *jama'ats* are not isolated from local *Isai* Muslim (or C4) evangelists or foreign missionaries who nurture and train them in light of the Bible. So long as they maintain connections with local or foreign Bible teachers, I think it is better to let these insiders keep having indigenous initiative until Muslim authorities expel them from the Muslim *somaj*.

During my research, I observed that MBBs who adopt an *Isai/Isai* Muslim (*uboi*; both) or solely *Isai* Muslim identity – which is closest to C4 – are not only hard to find, but also have a tendency to move toward the C1–3 side rather than staying in the same position. MBBs seem to have no problems with developing a proper Christian theology if *Isai* Muslim identity move toward the Christianized direction. However, it does not match the ideal of C4 maintaining both culturally appropriate practices and outreach engagement. But, the reality I observed in my research is very similar to what Massey described of this downsliding tendency:

> C4 identity (being neither Christian nor Muslim) is a very difficult position for MBBs to maintain. The more they behave like gentile Christians, the more they will be trusted by C1–C3 believers but distrusted by Muslims. Unfortunately, the more they retain their Muslim culture . . . the more suspect [*sic*] they tend to be in Christian communities. Theoretically, C4 MBBs should not have to enter C1–3 communities at all. Practically, however, their paths tend to cross more often than C4 advocates would prefer, and so begins the process of Christianization which inevitably pulls Muslims "out" of their community and "into" some forms of Christianity.[58]

The following comment from F04 seems to agree with what Massey described above: "We are trying to pursue and be in C4 but they (local MBBs) are moving to C3 and C2 side." I am not going to criticize this tendency, but rather just report the reality. Engaging this tendency and tension is another important task for ministry among Muslims.

---

58. Massey, "Misunderstanding C5," 301.

In addition to the analysis above, we can draw an interesting comparison between two former mosque imams. S02's faith and baptism were accidentally revealed to the Muslim *somaj*. He was expelled from his mosque job, and joined the local Christian outreach (mission) organization that led him to have Christian faith. He became a Christian with a Christian social identity after his baptism was revealed. However, his maladjustment to the organization and disappointment between him and the director drove him out of the organization. Members of the Muslim *somaj* are still warning, or sometimes threatening, him not to influence his neighbors. His communication with me is currently cut off, and I personally worry about his safety.

On the other hand, E04 came to faith in 'Isa through an organization that teaches 'Isa from the Qur'an. Even though he was revealed as a follower of 'Isa and endured several social judgments, he kept his social identity as a Muslim by participating in Islamic socioreligious activities. Whenever E04 faced social judgment, he escaped by citing the qur'anic verses and connecting his faith in 'Isa with the Qur'an. I cannot judge at this moment which social identity and case is a better option or more desirable between the two former imams.

This kind of case leads us to the RQ 3, which addresses respondents' views of Muhammad, the Qur'an, and the MBB community. Is their view of Muhammad and the Qur'an permissible and healthy as a follower of 'Isa? With these viewpoints and the issue of participation in *namaz*, I will suggest my own analysis of healthy contextualization. Finally, one other important point remains: Are MBBs' new faith communities (*jama'ats*) healthy and able to take care of themselves in the long run?

Summary of Findings in RQ 3

The findings in RQ 3 can be summarized in two parts: (1) MBBs' different perspectives from other Muslims on four issues, namely, Allah, 'Isa, Muhammad, and the Qur'an, and (2) social identity in view of four-self community. Research question 3 asks:

> To what extent and in what ways do MBBs think there is continuity and discontinuity between their own beliefs and practices and those of Muslims around them? Do their views affect

whether, or how, they share the gospel with Muslim and self-standing (four-self) faith community in the long run?

When it comes to MBBs' perceptions of the four theological issues, the respondents generally agreed with Muslims' view of Allah as a creator, almighty, and merciful. However, some MBBs considered Allah as the one who is near them (H05), close to the biblical understanding of God's transcendence and immanence. For the concept of *'Isa*, their answers addressed three main points: *'Isa* as Allah (or Allah's son), *'Isa* as a Savior, and his not coming back as a disciple of Muhammad. Many Christian/*Isai* self-identified MBBs answered that *'Isa* is Allah (or Allah's son), who has divinity. The view of *'Isa* as a Savior from sins and someone who brings them to heaven is found across the spectrum of MBBs. Several MBBs corrected Muslims' wrong concept of *'Isa* as someone who will come back as a disciple of Muhammad (H01, U04, U09). Regarding Muhammad and the Qur'an, the respondents generally agreed that Muhammad is not a savior but only a prophet, a warner, or an introducer of the gospel, and the Qur'an is not the divine heavenly book. However, some who have an *uboi* or *Isai* Muslim/Muslim identity consider the Qur'an as one of the four heavenly books (*Torah, Zabur, Injil,* and the Qur'an), but they value and read the other three *Kitabs* (especially *Injil*) more (E02, M01, M02, M03).

Regarding the four-self issue, I found that most of the respondents, including foreigners, generally agreed on the need for four-self practices in their *jama'ats* and the Bangladeshi MBB community. Respondents offered many helpful comments on the reality and situation of Bangladeshi MBB *jama'ats*, mentioning issues such as the historically situated dependency and pragmatic mentality of Bangladeshi people (L01, L05, F03).

Self-propagation is generally practiced in the Bangladeshi MBB community, according to the respondents' statements (90% are voluntarily sharing the gospel), often through the use of Islamic commonalities like the stories or verses of the Qur'an (89% of MBBs).

The concept of self-support, however, is hardly actualized in Bangladeshi MBB society because of the effect of traditional Christians' dependency culture (F04) and the low economic conditions of MBBs (F01). Two opinions related to the lack of offering/tithing habits among Bangladeshi MBBs (L02) and the need for becoming self-supporting (I02, F01) are worth mentioning.

Jama'ats of most of the respondents are trying to practice some form of self-governance, such as rotation of weekly preachers from among the members (I01) and local leadership meetings (N01). Considering the reality of Bangladeshi *jama'ats*, however, self-governance is still minimal due to the lack of knowledge and attitude of building up one another (L02, F03, and F09).

Questions about the application of the word of God, MBBs' preference of foreign or local teachers, and ways to influence the majority society were designed to reveal the extent of self-theologizing. Respondents reported that they prove their new life through their changed behavior by applying Scripture in their daily life and by the power of prayer (N02, U03, U11). Most show a preference for foreign teachers due to their trustworthiness. When asked how to impact the majority, the respondents answered in three ways: more connection to the majority, more good works, and clear conversion and identity.

Analysis of RQ 3

Analysis of Viewpoints of the Four Issues

Religious terms such as Allah, *'Isa*, Muhammad, and the Qur'an are very important concepts to Bangladeshi MBBs. For them, the term "Allah" is not to be discarded after following *'Isa*, but they continue to use it to keep their focus on worshiping the only Almighty God. Before their faith in *'Isa*, MBBs referred to Allah as the one and only divine being who created all things over all; after believing in *'Isa*, they keep referring to the one who created them as Allah, and they understand that Allah has saved them through *'Isa*. I agree with Scott Hedley's comment that Muslims and Christians are literally referring to the same God, the one Almighty God who created all, but their understanding of God is much different in many senses in terms of the God of Trinity, love, and granting of salvation through his son.[59] This is the

---

59. Scott Hedley, self-introduced as a Bible translator in Asia, reviewed two books by insider movement critics – *Insider Movements* by Jeff Morton (2012) and *A Theological Analysis of Insider Movement Paradigm from Four Perspectives* by Doug Coleman (2011) – online. Hedley commented on the referent issue. "Both authors also seem to believe that Muslims and Christians worship a different God. But here they seem to confuse the referent with the sense. Both Muslims and Christians refer to the same referent, God, the Almighty, the One who created all that is not God. But both religious groups have a different understanding, a different sense, of that same referent." Hedley, "Helpful for Those Wanting."

way in which most of my respondents are currently thinking of the concept of Allah, the creator. In this sense, Bangladeshi MBBs have no problem calling the almighty God Allah or *Mabud* Allah – they frequently add "Mabud" which means Lord before Allah following the *Kitab*'s (*Mussolmani* Bible's) usage – though self-identified Christian/*Isais* sometimes use the traditional Bible term for God, *Issor*. The term *'Isa* is used the same way for Allah. Even though Allah and *'Isa* are in the Qur'an, Bangladeshi MBBs are already familiar with these terms because they find these terms whenever they read the *Mussolmani Kitab* (Bible).

Process of MBBs' Conversion and Negotiation of Social Identity

My findings indicate that most of the MBB respondents have gone through a process of comparing the Qur'an with the Bible and *'Isa* with Muhammad, even if this is only a tiny part of their journey. For example, even though H01 received *'Isa* through the Bible alone, he needed to take the step of looking at the Bible and the Qur'an comparatively a few years after his conversion. This comparison is a normal process through which Bangladeshi MBBs come to faith in *'Isa*. This is similar to Tippet and Hibbert's understanding of periods of awareness, decision, and incorporation. First, Muslims were exposed to the gospel through small booklets or contact with believers who introduced *'Isa* by recommending these small books or sharing their faith verbally. The small books, such as the booklet "The Way of Going to Heaven," are mostly composed of verses from the Qur'an and the Bible (*Kitab*). Second, after looking at such booklets, individuals show their interest in learning more about *'Isa* and decide to follow him. In this stage, both introducers and receivers are important. Who introduces the gospel of *'Isa*? What is the introducer's current social identity? What does the introducer already know about *'Isa*, and what is their view of the Bible and the Qur'an? Receivers' prior knowledge of the Qur'an and their perspectives are also important. Third, receivers of the gospel of *'Isa* form their new core identities and negotiate social identities in the light of these dynamics.

Those who received the gospel of *'Isa* from Christian/*Isais* and through the Bible perceive *'Isa* as closer to the divine being or the divine being himself as close to him (H05), as a son of God (U03, U05), as Allah himself (I01, I03, E01, S01), or as the savior. Their views of *'Isa*, based on the Bible, are diverse.

On the other hand, those who received the gospel of *'Isa* from *Isai* Muslim/ Muslims have views of Jesus limited to his identity as the Messiah, the Savior. E03, however, added his own observation about *'Isa* based on his reading of the Qur'an: "*'Isa, Ruhullula* (Spirit of Allah) and *'Isa, Kalema* (the Word)."

Analysis of MBBs' Views of Muhammad and His Prophethood

All of my MBB respondents view Muhammad as an insignificant figure for their salvation, in contrast to their high exaltation of *'Isa*. In response to the question about Muhammad, though eleven of forty-three respondents (25%) described him as a prophet, Christian/*Isai*/*Isai* Muslim self-identified MBBs understand this as a respectful expression in terms of the qur'anic verses that are related to the Bible. Three Christian/*Isai* self-identified MBBs mentioned that Muhammad is a prophet but used qualifiers such as "one kind of" or "in some senses." They view him as a prophet sent to introduce *'Isa* (U09, H04, H01) or warn people to come to monotheism (H01). Phil Parshall discusses the variety of statuses and roles of prophets in Islam.

> In the Islamic religion, prophets are men especially appointed by God to be His messengers. Theoretically, all prophets are to have the same status. In practice this is not true. Certain prophets are accorded special status by all Muslims. It is reputed that there are 124,000 prophets. Of these, 313 are called apostles, 9 are called "possessors of constancy," 8 are rasuls (those having a separate people for whom they are responsible), 6 are lawgivers, and 6 have special qualities. Only 28 of the 124,000 are mentioned in the Quran.[60]

Christian/*Isais* use this understanding of prophets to introduce *'Isa* to Muslim acquaintances. They start by discussing the line of around twenty-eight *nabi* [prophets] between Muhammad and *'Isa* mentioned in the Qur'an. Muhammad is higher than *'Isa* for general Muslims, but this is soon reversed when someone comes to believe in *'Isa* as the Savior. David Garrison's interviews with insider believers in eastern South Asia (including Bangladesh) support this finding.

---

60. Parshall, *Muslim Evangelism*, 150.

Westerners mistakenly suspect that Muslim-background believers wrestle with the loyalty demands of Christ and Muhammad, but this was rarely the case. For the Muslim-background believers I interviewed, Muhammad was not a rival to Christ. They knew that Muhammad never claimed deity or status as a savior; he faded into irrelevance once a Muslim accepted that Jesus was, in fact, Allah's provision for salvation.[61]

The question Harley Talman raised in his article "Is Muhammad also among the prophets?" can be answered in two ways based on my respondents' comments.[62] I would answer negatively if Muhammad is viewed as one of the line of prophets who wrote the divinely inspired word of God, such as Isaiah and Jeremiah. There is some possibility for a positive answer, however, from the perspective shared by my MBB respondents, who view him not as a rival to Jesus but as a normal person who can be respected for introducing 'Isa, pointing in the right direction toward the previous Kitabs, and warning people to turn toward monotheism.

Analysis of MBBs' Views of the Qur'an

MBBs' views of Muhammad are connected to their views of the Qur'an. Most of the Christian/Isais interviewed for this research view the Qur'an as a book of collections drawing from the previous Kitabs and a pointer to the previous Kitabs, especially the Injil. They view the Qur'an as a book of introduction and warning. Some Isai Muslim/Muslims (E04, M01, M01, M02, M03, L03) and several Isai/Isai Muslims (E02, H04) believe that the Qur'an is one of the four heavenly books, but this does not mean it is a divinely inspired book because they do not accept thepoints that contradict the previous Kitabs. They only believe the points it has in common with the Kitab (L03, E04, M03), or they value the Kitab more (M02, I04, H08).

Another question arises at this point: Does the authenticity of the Bible over the Qur'an need to be taught to MBBs, or is it self-evident to them when they read it? Should Christian leaders forbid them to read or use the Qur'an but only the Bible? For most of my MBB respondents, the Qur'an is the initial introducer of 'Isa and a tool for introducing the gospel of 'Isa to their Muslim

---

61. Garrison, *Wind in the House*, 116.
62. Talman, "Is Muhammad Also"?

acquaintances, since general Muslims do not want to hear Christian biblical verses directly.

I think that, for MBBs, the Qur'an is useful for promoting initial interest in the gospel of 'Isa, but there is a need to develop biblical Christology at a deeper level. Fred Farrokh criticized the Insider Movement Paradigm (IMP) as bringing about qur'anic Christology, which which does not have the same depth as biblical Christology. He also blamed this paradigm for creating a hybrid Christology and allowing believers to keep participating in Islamic activities inside the mosque.

> Historically, Christian mission efforts have sought to lift Muslims from the Q line [qur'anic Christology] to the B line [biblical Christology]. The IMP departs from this paradigm through the creation of a new hybrid position represented by the IM line [between the two lines]. These Muslim insider believers are encouraged to remain inside their socioreligious community . . . which requires some level of affirmation for Muhammad and the Qur'an.[63]

I agree with his point, but I also believe that we need to trust the Holy Spirit enough to let MBBs study and research the Bible, or sometimes the Qur'an, freely on their spiritual journey, even as we keep encouraging them to live their lives in light of the Bible.

Another interesting point to note is that Parshall and Tennent, who opposed the insider movement paradigm and practice, do not oppose the use of the Qur'an as a tool for evangelism or comparative study of the Bible and the Qur'an. Parshall allows the use of qur'anic passages that affirm a high view of Scripture and introduce 'Isa. "In sharing Christ with a Muslim, one should make careful use of Quranic passages that point to a high view of Scripture."[64] "The Qur'an refers to Jesus in other ways that may help bridge the gap: Spirit, Prophet, Apostle, Preeminent One, Example, Sinless One, and Miracle Worker."[65] Tennent also acknowledges that MBBs should be able

63. Farrokh, "Indigenous Perspective," 5–6.

64. Parshall, *Muslim Evangelism*, 148.

65. Parshall, 155.

to retain the Qur'an, as long as the Bible has the authority to reinterpret the verses in the Qur'an:

> It is true that the Qur'an is not nearly as offensive to Christian doctrine as is sometimes supposed. However, the only way MBBs have successfully been able to retain the Qur'an (or some portions of the Qur'an) is if the Bible is used as the hermeneutic to constantly re-direct, re-interpret and clarify various texts in the Qur'an.[66]

In this sense, I also agree that it is valid to use the Qur'an for sharing its common points with the Bible to Muslim neighbors and for developing MBBs' faith in various ways.

The Qur'an operates in three steps of MBBs' faith journey toward 'Isa. First, Muslims who have heard interesting stories of 'Isa and the other three *Kitabs* start to think about reading the *Kitab* (Bible) because the Qur'an commends them to read the previous *Kitabs*. Second, they find the authenticity of the Bible and the true way of salvation in 'Isa when they read the Bible, and they come to value the Bible more highly than the Qur'an. Third, they find the common points between the Bible and the Qur'an and use them to share the gospel with their Muslim neighbors. David Garrison observes that many South Asian MBBs, like those in Bangladesh, came to faith in 'Isa initially through the Qur'an. He argues that understanding gained this way is initially limited, yet sufficient for those beginning to live as followers of 'Isa who can be guided and with whom follow up can be done in their long-term spiritual journeys.[67] "Granted, their initial understanding of Jesus was limited and doubtless would not pass a theological quiz, but it was sufficient to drive them to the living Christ who saved them and guided them to the Bible, from which their faith has gained clarity and understanding."[68] In this journey, practical guides based on social identity are required for those who have the same social identity as the new believers because Christian/*Isais* have relatively higher view of 'Isa and the Bible than *Isai* Muslim/Muslims do.

---

66. Tennent, "Followers of Jesus (Isa)," 114.

67. Garrison, *Wind in the House*, 117.

68. Garrison, 117.

In this regard, one weakness for *Isai* Muslim/Muslims is that Muslims' open and communal society normally does not allow *Isai* Muslim/Muslims (or Muslim insiders) to freely focus on reading the *Kitab*. I would therefore suggest that they announce their new faith identity as a follower of *'Isa* at some point and then find more opportunity to read the Bible. By doing so, they will quickly and inevitably come to value *'Isa* and the Bible more highly than Muhammad and the Qur'an.

I want to conclude by affirming F04's comments about how to nurture MBBs to value the Bible more highly. He emphasized the need for more opportunities to read the *Kitab*.

> The matter of giving more value to the *Kitab* is connected to how much they read these four *Kitabs*, including the Qur'an. If they read the *Kitabs* more, they raise the value of the *Kitab* naturally. In rural areas, most of the houses are open to neighbors, so it is hard to put the *Kitab* even in leaders' houses. It is difficult for them to read the *Kitab*, but when they read it, we hope they get to realize the fact that it is worth reading more. There are few smartphone users among Bangladeshi MBBs, but it is a good idea that they use the general mobile because it is also possible to listen to the *Kitab*. It would be better for them to use the Qur'an as a helper to get closer to the *Kitab*.

Assessment of Insider Believers

My overall assessment is that *Isai* Muslim/Muslims' view of the Qur'an and Muhammad is not enough, and participating in *namaz* inside the mosque has syncretistic points in terms of the possibility of mixing the biblical view and the limited qur'anic view of *'Isa* and God. It is also difficult to provide indigenous forms with biblical meaning or put biblical meaning into indigenous forms. Unlike several other *Isai* Muslim/Muslims who have moved around Christian and Muslim boundaries, I would consider E04 and M02 as Muslim insiders who were called to be followers of *'Isa* in the communities they were born into. They have reinterpreted indigenous forms of *namaz* through the lens of worshiping and praying to Allah in their communal way, and they see this as a way of submission to God (E04). M02 and his adult son believe themselves to be full Muslims who fulfill Allah's will. Even though they have been revealed as followers of *'Isa*, they are currently less persecuted because they have the good reputation of being generous and helping the poor, and they occasionally gather with believers in their community (*jama'at*). Both are not receiving any regular pay from foreign missionaries.

E04 and M02 do not consider Muhammad to be a significant figure in terms of reinterpretation or not uttering the second part of *shahada*. We are reminded of the points that Gene Daniels raised about differences in understanding between Muslim insiders who say the *shahada* in spite of omitting the second part and receptors among general Muslims who interpret insiders' act according to their own understanding. This may raise concerns because *shahada* is proclaimed when people perform *namaz* [formal prayer], and general Muslims only see whether insiders perform it or not, regardless of whether they confess the second part. I believe, however, it does not seem to cause many problems for E04 and M02. The reason for this is that they influence two different groups: their co-insider believers or disciples, and their Muslim neighbors. E04 and M02 teach their co-believers to reinterpret the role of Muhammad and the Qur'an as a new way of worshipping *Mabud Allah* (Lord God) and believing in *'Isa* in their context. Meanwhile, they give their Muslim neighbors some sense that they belong to their *somaj* (religious community) by sometimes performing *namaz* inside or outside the mosque at *Eid*. I believe, as long as they do not contradict their consciences in their *reinterpretation* of Muslim identity and activities, they can stay in the community until the Muslim *somaj* forbids them from coming to the place where Muslims meet for religious activities.[69]

Furthermore, E04 and M02 do not value the Qur'an over the Bible, but instead focus on the Qur'an's account of *'Isa* and its similar elements with the *Kitab*. With the eye of a missiological anthropologist, I recognize these respondents as co-believers who follow Jesus in their context. I have a feeling that their faith in *'Isa* is not fake, and that their present lives as sharers of the gospel of *'Isa* proves their faith in some sense. I would summarize their understanding of their journey as follows: they admit that they had some lessons from outside teachers, but both respondents were born here, began to follow *'Isa*, witnessed voluntarily, agreed with some teachings from locals and foreigners, chose their identities for themselves, and continued to struggle,

---

69. Actually they have gone through diverse kinds of persecutions and social judgments.

suffer, and enjoy life as followers of *'Isa* in their own context without being labelled as Christians. Garrison's observation seems to agree with the local initiatives of the movement:

> It is true that a handful of Western missionaries have encouraged some of the Insider leaders, providing them with counsel and support, both missiologically and materially, but this occurred only after the movements had already taken root and begun to grow. In their fundamental opposition to what they perceive to be Christendom and the West, these Insider Movements have little tolerance for foreign control or even influence from the West.[70]

As F04 mentioned, helping MBBs and Muslim insiders to keep focusing on the Bible (*Kitab*) rather than the Qur'an is the key for growing their faith in the biblical *'Isa*.

My assessment of Muslim insiders is limited to the individuals interviewed. Several limitations exist because I had very few interviews with Muslim insiders and could not visit all of their locations due to security concerns. I only visited M02's house in the village and met E04 several times in Dhaka. I could not, therefore, personally prove the existence of regular gatherings of *jama'ats* or investigate their Muslim neighbors' responses. It is difficult to generalize and apply my findings and assessments to all insider movements, but I think this study has implications for consideration of this issue.

Analysis of Four-Self Community

The second part of my analysis of RQ 3 begins with our three representative respondents of different MBB social identities (H01, E04, E02). The practices of their *jama'ats* are summarized below (Table 16). Generally, these three representatives offer different pictures of practicing *jama'ats*.

H01's *jama'at* tries to be self-dependent in the four areas in terms of reaching out to neighbors, sustaining his own work, organizing leadership programs, and making disciples of MBBs in various social identity positions. He encourages believers in his *jama'at* to be open about their identity and endure social pressure as he has. But because he also thinks about links to

---

70. Garrison, *Wind in the House*, 113.

the majority and security for believers in his *jama'at*, he also advises new believer's family to not reveal themselves quickly, but rather be a witness first in their present social position and slowly come to Christian/*Isai* identity.

Table 16. Three Representatives of Four-Self in Their *Jama'ats*

(details in Appendix 6)

	E04	E02	H01
Background	Started several *jama'ats* in different areas. Trying to be self-dependent, welcomes cooperation for training. Teaching how to use the Qur'an to leaders	His village *jama'at* always needs him; lack the four-self areas. His city *jama'at* depends more on foreign initiative in terms of self-supporting and governing.	*Jama'at* in his house. Trying to be self-dependent in all four areas and tries to reach out to the majority with an *Isai* Muslim approach.

E04 started his *jama'ats* around ten years ago. The *jama'ats* are also governed by independent principles with regard to sharing 'Isa through the Qur'an. He manages his living and working expenses on his own, teaches his disciples to teach others, and makes a theological circular system from the Qur'an to the *Kitab*. E04 *jama'ats* are not receiving operational support, but he opens them to foreign teaching and foreign support to help in training his disciples. The *jama'ats* of H01 and E04 also have shortages, in the eyes of foreigners, in terms of funding and teaching, but they provide good examples of progress in applying the four-self dynamics.

E02's two *jama'ats* are good examples of typical MBB *jama'ats* in Bangladesh. For his rural *jama'at*, it is hard for him to find a proper leader to manage it, and the members are passive and reluctant to gather, financially contribute, or teach others. There is little or no opportunity or energy to apply the four-self idea to his village *jama'ats*. For his urban *jama'at*, there are active disciples of 'Isa in terms of regular gathering, offering, sharing, and teaching by foreign and Bangladeshi believers based on the work of an NGO. However, once the NGO work finishes and/or the Bangladeshis lose their jobs, the *jama'at* will most likely change to some extent.

Dependency and Money Issue

A dominant theme in the responses about the four-self faith community and collective identity of MBBs is the money issue, which is deeply rooted in complex factors of worldview and a historical context of dependency. To analyze this situation, it is necessary to start from a general historical background of self-issue in the specific Bangladeshi context. Hiebert's writing on "the fourth self" provides a historical background on whether or not the three-self principle developed by Anderson and Venn had been applied properly by young churches. Concerning self-propagation, indigenous young churches pioneered by foreign missionaries were not likely to reach their neighbors through local believers' efforts and money. Instead, local churches naturally considered evangelism and mission work as missionaries' responsibility.[71] Anderson and Venn's argument that local churches have to be involved in evangelistic works and missions brought little disagreement, although they could not follow the methods used by missionaries, such as expensive evangelistic events. Soon, local believers started to concern themselves with reaching their neighbors. Self-support, however, was more difficult for local believers to practice. Missionaries have already operationalized many kinds of evangelistic projects and social works, so money was much needed. "Some of these were closed, and they continued some to operate on levels more in line with their own financial abilities."[72] Self-governance raised more debate because local churches began to require missionaries to turn over leadership roles. Actually, it was not easy for missionaries, who believed local leaders were immature, to transfer their ecclesiastical authority to the local believers.[73]

Analysis of Tendency of Bangladeshi Churches and MBBs

Comparing Jennings's historical research with many interviews with Bangladeshi local and foreign workers and our respondents will help us analyze the issue seriously.In the over two hundred years' history of Bangladeshi Protestant churches, dependency stories have played out for several reasons: a huge gap between foreigners' economic capability and that of local believers, hierarchical structures from a denomination's (or foreign mission's) headquarters to a local church, and patron-client relationships.[74] Also, be-

---

71. Hiebert, *Anthropological Insights*, 194.

72. Hiebert, 195.

73. Hiebert, 194–95.

74. Jennings, "Muslim Background Believers," 57.

cause of traditional Christians' dependent tendency, a popular notion that "Christianity means easy money and jobs" has developed.[75]

As we saw in the review of Stephenson's research in chapter 3, Bangladeshi Muslims are also subject to four major cultural tendencies: "hierarchy, collectivism, patronage, and shame."[76] For MBBs, it might be difficult for them to throw off the strong historical habits of a dependent culture among Bangladeshi Muslims and Christians. Even if some MBBs desire to build up a self-sustaining *jamaʿat*, this is hard to actualize because this effort has rarely been practiced and missionaries who could support poor local churches have been still around them (F04, F10, L04). Nevertheless, we found many MBB respondents who are willing to reach out to their families and neighbors due to their life-changing conversion experience from Islam. Bangladeshi believers are also prone to their historical mentality of seeking personal survival and interests first, as well as contending with others for power. These tendencies have also been obstructions in the process of building up self-supporting and self-governing churches (F03).

Looking at the issue through several foreigners' statements, it seems that the Bangladeshi church has become a society with a big leader who has drawn big investments from outside (F10). Moreover, the Bangladeshi culture of ruling over the low-class and serving the high-class makes it difficult for missionaries to transfer leadership to local believers (F03). On the other hand, several MBBs expressed their dissatisfaction toward MBB leaders in Bangladesh. It is often mentioned that this was because the leaders are trying to get more funds from the outside, but once they get the funds they do not sincerely care for local believers (E02). However, looking at the issue from the Bangladeshis' perspective, it seems that indiscreet and hasty missionary support made Bangladeshi MBBs greedy for money.[77] Some MBB leaders uncovered their hidden antipathy and embarrassment about foreign organizations and missionaries who have made mission work a kind of religious business (L04, L05). This raises another important and debatable issue of whether the patron (foreign missions)-client (local evangelist) relationship is appropriate in Bangladesh. Concerning the early stages of MBBs in Bangladesh, one MBB

---

75. Jennings, 62.

76. Stephenson, "Messiah of Honor," 2.

77. Jennings, "Muslim Background Believers," 58–60.

commented on foreign missions' activities saying, "They don't cook curry but they come and divide it up."[78] Several organizations' hasty investment in mission work without healthy accountability made local leaders greedy and encouraged them to write false reports.[79] Both foreigners and Bangladeshis need to take responsibility for their respective actions and reactions in the area of dependency. In this situation, how can we develop a three-self model? Furthermore, how can we move to the fourth self (self-theologizing), which gives new MBB churches authority to interpret and apply their own theology?

Several Ways of Building Four-Self Community

First, Robert Priest found that the four-self criteria do not exist separately, but rather are connected and working together. Even though there have been debates regarding separate variables of each of the four criteria, Priest's research has proven that four-self dynamics represent "a single unitary construct," with the elements showing positive correlation with each other.[80] Therefore, following the maturity of a three-self Bangladeshi MBB community, they can also strive toward element of self-theologizing, which makes local church leaders and theologians "feel free to explore their theological perceptions from their own contexts."[81] Hiebert agrees that self-theologizing is needful in spite of possible dangers like theological errors, so local believers can mature deeply in their context through trial and error.[82]

The benefit of working toward self-theologizing is "not only indicating the right to do one's own theology or theological reflections but also allowing for equal partnership in globalizing theology."[83] I believe this is also applicable in Bangladesh. The more MBB communities participate in this process, the better the outcome will be in this self-theologizing activity. Hiebert's suggestion of building up "transcultural theology," which discerns cultural bias and examines the universality of the Bible, can be also a useful guideline for avoiding syncretism and nurturing the fourth self.[84]

---

78. Jennings, 58.
79. Jennings, 58.
80. Priest, "Researching Contextualization," 311–16.
81. Trull, *Fourth Self*, 5.
82. Hiebert, *Anthropological Insights*, 195.
83. Trull, *Fourth Self*, 5.
84. Hiebert, *Anthropological Insights*, 216–24.

Second, when we look at the three representative respondents (E04, E02, H01) through Hiebert's insights – focusing on producing new believers and building up local theologians[85] – we can move to develop the fourth self. First, we should analyze what made it possible for Muslims to respond to the gospel. Following L01 and L03's suggestions of sincere study of Islam and Islamic tune/tone, we can research Muslims and study when they respond to the gospel. We may then utilize similar opportunities to communicate with various kinds of Muslims in order to convey the gospel in this context and nurture them in light of the Scripture. Second, how do we prepare and develop the future of the Bangladeshi MBB community? It must be through building up local leaders and indigenous theologians[86]. Also, they can learn from theological applications from similar Muslim majority contexts like Iran and Pakistan, or from different but corresponding Majority World contexts such as African and Korean theologies. For African applications of indigenous theological education, *The Fourth Self* shows the results of dealing deeply with both context and Scripture in theological education.[87] For Korean applications, self-theologizing is currently mentioned quite often in publications such as *Current Mission Trends*.[88] The responsibility for this task belongs not only to Bangladeshis, but also to all believers in Christ around the world.

Finally, the most important question remains about who will and who can do it. In two recent dissertations about MBBs in Malaysia and immigrant converts in the United States and Canada, John Cheong and Alan Totire both argued that we need Barnabas-like persons.[89] According to Cheong,

> Every church needs such a "Barnabas" to receive genuine Malay seekers looking for Christ, the fellowship of Christians or spiritual food for their growth. Ideally, such persons should have sound judgment, not a novice, experienced in Malay/Muslim ministry, faith-filled and courageous in the Lord. Such persons need not be confined to experts.[90]

---

85. Hiebert, 215.
86. Hiebert, 215.
87. Trull, *Fourth Self*.
88. Moon, "Self-Theologizing."
89. Cheong, "Socio-Religious Identity"; Totire, "Investigation into the Identity."
90. Cheong, 311–12.

Totire agreed about the need for a person like Barnabas, saying,

> For people like Grace . . . what they missed was a "Barnabas"
> person – someone who reaches out to them, introduces them
> to the church, explains the organizational structure of the
> church, and includes them in a small group where discipleship
> combined with cultural issues can be discussed. Similar to the
> role of Barnabas in the Bible, known for being the "Son of en-
> couragement," a Barnabas Person would be an encourager and
> an advocate for newcomers, particularly if that person is from
> another country or religion. This Barnabas Person would be
> culturally intelligent and does not have to be an expert in Islam
> per se. After all, most churches may never have a Muslim come
> to their congregation, but other ethnicities and cultures may
> also benefit from such a person.[91]

Need for a Barnabas

During the research, I had dreamed of being a Barnabas myself, because a
person like Barnabas is especially needed in a context like Bangladesh. First,
Barnabas was an introducer who approached others before they asked for
him. He saw the veracity of Saul's faith, and introduced Saul to the apostles
for letting him do his job as God called him. Barnabas was a missionary sent
by the Jerusalem church (foreigner) and he had faith in Saul (a local believer)
before he asked for help. Acts 9:26–27 says,

> When he [Saul] came to Jerusalem, he tried to join the disciples,
> but they were all afraid of him, not believing that he really was a
> disciple. But Barnabas took him and brought him to the apostles.
> He told them how Saul on his journey had seen the Lord and
> that the Lord had spoken to him, and how in Damascus he had
> preached fearlessly in the name of Jesus.

Second, he was a team worker. He invited Saul to work together with him.
This yielded great results. In a year, the church in Antioch grew enormously
both in numbers of believers and reputation by their maturity. Acts 11:25–26

---

91. Totire, "Investigation into the Identity," 238.

says, "Then Barnabas went to Tarsus to look for Saul, and when he found him, he brought him to Antioch. So for a whole year Barnabas and Saul met with the church and taught great numbers of people. The disciples were called Christians first at Antioch."

Finally, Barnabas was a real encourager who empowered others. Paul was stoned and almost died, but the next day he got up and left for another city to preach. How could Paul get up and move to another city so quickly? Reading between the lines of these passages, I imagine that Barnabas's encouragement helped him go back to work. Acts 14:19–20 says, "They stoned Paul and dragged him outside the city, thinking he was dead. But after the disciples had gathered around him, he got up and went back into the city. The next day he and Barnabas left for Derbe." Among Bangladeshi MBBs, these kinds of persons are very much needed. The context of Bangladeshi MBBs is a society that rarely introduces other MBBs nicely to others because they can be seen as competitors for limited opportunities and funds. Also, this is a context in which they cannot usually do teamwork because they easily play power games regarding who is better and powerful (F10). If we consider the relationship between a foreigner and a local worker, it is hard to have equal authorities in teamwork because a foreigner must be an investor and a local worker is a beneficiary. Finally, this is a context in which they themselves like to use power, but don't know how to build up and empower others (L02, F03, F09). In this sense, a radical turnabout is needed in three cases: from self- and my group-centered to other-concerned; from individual-centered to partner(or team)-centered; and from exploiting others to empowering others. Once Barnabas figures begin to work in Bangladesh, whether foreign or local, new hope will emerge.

Comprehensive Analysis

Once I analyzed each of my three research questions and findings separately, I decided to come up with a comprehensive analysis of the three issues. These three can be concluded only after synthesizing all three research findings and analysis: social identity in the middle of core and collective identity; the need for time for local initiative and the value of moving forward in this direction; and the need for studying and interacting with Islam and the Qur'an more seriously.

First, social identity is not formed in a vacuum without core and collective identity. These three layers of identity interact and influence each other. In RQ 1, we examined the motivation behind a new core identity and its connection to social identity, and we found that the formation of MBBs' core identity, as well as their negotiation of social identity and positioning within a certain social group, is influenced by diverse factors such as gospel introducers and social surroundings. In RQ 3, we found that their religious community (*jama'at*) forming a collective identity is important for the stability of MBBs' core and social identities. For example, E02 had sought to address his needs for participation in religious festivals and communal sense of belonging. He had Christian/*Isai* identity before, but after joining his organization and its related *jama'at*, he has not participated in any Christian festivals such as Christmas or Easter. This is because his *jama'at* and organization pursue an *Isai* Muslim identity to reach out to Muslims, and the organization's director believed that these Christian festivals came from pagan traditions and tried to get rid of the impression of Christian religion. So, E02 did not participate in either Christian festivals or Muslim *Eid* festivals. It is not easy for MBBs when their desires to feel a sense of communal belonging are neglected. Therefore, I think it is better for the three layers of identity to be consistent and harmonious in order to develop a stable identity and sense of belonging. If this does not work, they will soon be drained because of the lack of integrity and satisfaction in their identity.

Second, we need to keep encouraging MBBs' initiatives to reach out to their own people and to build up their own context-appropriate churches, even though this takes time. Two findings encouraged us about local initiative. The first is that 90 percent of MBBs are voluntarily sharing the gospel of *'Isa* with their families and friends. This is a good starting point. The second is that all participants, including foreign respondents, agreed with the direction of building up four-self faith communities. Even though the present reality of local initiative is not enough, we are at least going in the right direction toward *'Isa* and toward four-self communities. We have to be very cautious in bringing foreign funds for diverse development and outreach projects. As L04 and L05 mentioned before, this brings a very real possibility of danger and inappropriate control of local believers through the power of foreign funds coming with foreign theology and foreign ministerial goals. However, I also

agree with F01's comment that "you can't live with and without [money],"
suggesting waiting until material and spiritual growth have progressed:

> We have to move forward working with some of the strengths
> and weaknesses [of money] and we try to build when the
> churches grow in numbers and in maturity with growth of GDP
> of Bangladesh. And then some of these problems get solved
> on their own. But, until that happens, we can do nothing. If
> the number of believers grows from 20 to 200 or 2,000, we can
> get manpower and some financial resources too. We can draw
> totally different pictures.

In this sense, it is necessary to resettle the purpose of ministry and way of
bringing foreign investment for ministry in Bangladesh from foreign initiative to local initiative, moving, for example, from seeking foreign funds first
to finding local potential; from direct control from foreign headquarters to
communication between foreign and local leadership with mutual respect;
from partnership for fulfilling foreigners' own ministerial purpose and policy
to partnership for building up local leadership by their own calling and long-
term plan of establishing context-appropriate churches and Christ-centered
communities. It will take time, but it is also rewarded. As Galatians 6:9 says,
"Let us not become weary in doing good, for at the proper time we will reap
a harvest if we do not give up."

My last suggestion is that we need to deeply study Bangladeshi Muslims
and Islam. The first motivation to do this is that it is worth remembering that
most Bangladeshi MBBs, including my respondents, were first exposed to the
gospel of 'Isa through qur'anic verses. The second motivation is related to two
implications of self-theologizing: learning Bangladeshi Islam and Muslims
and learning the unique tunes. I agree with L01's point that the purpose of
study "is not for studying their negative parts, but for interacting with them."
As he suggested, we need to learn and interact with Islam more as a subject in
the MBBs' or Christians' seminary or Bible college. The more we understand
Bangladeshi Islam and Muslims properly, the better we can share the gospel
with them in appropriate ways. I also agree with L03's point that "religious
teaching has a unique tune. Even between similar words, there exist differences. Bangladeshis cannot eat [absorb] that when foreigners teach their
own tune such as European style of preaching or direct translated teachings

from English to Bangla." We need to learn the unique style and tune that the majority Bengali Muslims have acquired religiously. This is a good way to communicate the gospel of 'Isa to them in the familiar manner they have learned from their early days.

These two comments accord with Parshall's first guideline for "avoid[ing] syncretism while engaged in Muslim evangelism": "Islam as a religion and culture must be studied in depth."[92] L01 and L03's comments are also very relevant to Martin Accad's call for "developing a Christian and biblical theology of Islam."[93] Harley Talman's research into the possibility of Muhammad's prophethood is also relevant to one type of effort to appropriately understand Muslims and the religion of Islam from a Christian perspective without easily discarding or ignoring them.[94]

Finally, I will introduce Harold Netland's three urgent calls for inquiry into a proper theology of religion by evangelicals, especially in reference to Islam and a Muslim context.[95] Netland argues that evangelicals:

1. Need to think more carefully about what we mean by religion and the religions.
2. Will need to find theologically and culturally appropriate expressions of Christian witness in contexts of religious diversity.
3. Must develop appropriate forms of apologetics for interreligious contexts.[96]

Following Netland's urgent request for the establishment of an appropriate evangelical theology of religion, I also believe that developing the theoretical and practical understanding of Bangladeshi Muslims and their religion of Islam is connected to our two great rationales: to follow the Great Commission (to make disciples) and the greatest commandment (to love God and neighbors). First, it will help us make fully devoted disciples in the Bangladeshi Muslim context through studying and connecting the Qur'an to the Kitab. Second, it will help us love our Bangladeshi Muslim neighbors, have good relationships with them, and deeply understand one another with

---

92. Parshall, "Going Too Far?," 667.
93. Accad, "Towards a Theology," 192.
94. Talman, "Is Muhammad Also?"
95. Netland, "Evangelical Missiology and Theology," 7–10.
96. Netland, 7–10.

mutual respect. This study of Bangladeshi Muslims and Islam will surely help continuing discussions of the insider movement, contextualization, and syncretism, including the tension of how far we can go and where we should stop. There remains a continuing need to study Muslims and the religion of Islam from a Christian perspective.

CHAPTER 6

Conclusion and Implications

This research explores the social identity of Bangladeshi Mbbs (Muslim Background Believers) in light of contextualization.

Summary of Chapters

To begin the discussion of the concept of contextualization, chapter 1 provided a brief sketch of this study in terms of research problems, contextualization among Muslims, and the social and historical context of Bangladeshi Mbbs. The two unique contexts of Bangladeshi Mbbs – struggling social status and relative economic shortage – affect their coexistence with the majority Muslim community.

Chapter 2 described the qualitative research method employed by this study to gather data by means of interviews and observation. A total of fifty-eight respondents – including forty-eight Bangladeshi Mbbs who were diversely self-identified and ten foreign workers who have worked at least ten years in Bangladesh – were interviewed.

Chapter 3 examined four areas of literature related to this research. From religious dual belonging, discussions were continued to the insider movement and C4 and C5 debate. Tim Green's social identity theories and practical research related to Bangladeshi Mbbs were introduced. Finally, several Bangladeshi studies and research completed in Bangladesh were engaged with another important issue of four-self Mbbs' community.

In chapter 4, research findings were presented question-wise. Regarding RQ 1's inquiry into new social identity formation, Mbbs' faith in *'Isa* grew gradually in response to multiple factors, primarily cognitive and affective.

Their social identity is formed after their initial dedication to 'Isa; they mainly follow their gospel introducers' social identity, but also frequently change. We can identify three social identities: Christian/*Isai, Isai/Isai* Muslim (*uboi*, both), and *Isai* Muslim/Muslim. Regarding RQ 2, MBBs generally try to involve in different ceremonies and have different views of the four social activities of marriage, funeral, children's education, and finance compared to majority Muslims. Among Bangladeshi MBBs, there have been different degrees of participation in Islamic religious activities such as *namaz*. Only self-identified *Isai* Muslim/Muslims participate in *namaz* frequently, though they have their own interpretation of them. Regarding RQ 3, MBBs generally did not regard Muhammad and the Qur'an as very significant compared to 'Isa and the Bible (*Kitab*), but for them the qur'anic verses which connect to 'Isa and give direction to the *Kitab* are still usable for introducing the gospel of 'Isa, as many of them were introduced to 'Isa through the Qur'an. Regarding the four-self faith community of MBBs, while the reality is far from the ideal of a self-sustaining community, there is reason to be optimistic due to the large percentage of MBBs who practice self-propagating activities (90%) and their pursuit of actualizing the four-self direction in the long run. That said, it is also necessary to wait for the development of heathy partnerships.

In chapter 5, the research findings relevant to each RQ were analyzed. First, MBBs' gradual process of dedication to 'Isa includes a period of social identity negotiation. Although the three categories of Bangladeshi MBBs identified in this study differ from the six categories of the C-scale, the C-scale is still useful and relevant to the Bangladeshi MBB context, and valuable for its direction toward Christ-centered community. Second, two different paradigms vis-à-vis contextualization are reflected in different levels of participation in Muslim religious activities by followers of 'Isa. Although "called Muslim insiders" among self-identified *Isai* Muslim/Muslims participate in mosque activities, they tend to reinterpret the ritual and creed in their own way, differentiating their views from general Muslims' notion of Muhammad and the Qur'an. It was suggested that they develop the habit of reading the Bible more than the Qur'an in order to follow the word of God. Third, while there exist good intentions to build a self-sustaining community by developing the four "selfs," chronic problems of money and dependency hamper the fulfillment of this ideal. We also identified the need for a real encourager or Barnabas-like person. Finally, a comprehensive analysis presented three needs: (1) the need to study all three layers of identity, (2) the need to develop local initiative, and (3) the need for deeper study of Bangladeshi Muslims and Islam.

Implications for Bangladeshi Local Believers from Muslim Backgrounds

In spite of their very real physical needs, Bangladeshi local believers from Muslim background need to overcome the mentality formed from a long time of putting their own "survival" first, and instead take care of each other, live sustainably, and encourage others. This kind of mentality is practically applied to them as different social identities and responses to the context they are facing. They also must remember that they have the full potential to think critically and apply their findings appropriately in light of Hiebert's three criteria of "the Bible, the Holy Spirit, and a discerning community."[1] The more they focus on Scripture, the better they can practice right decision-making in light of it. The Holy Spirit will guide them as he has guided them for a long time. Local leaders must not only become good teachers, but also good questioners who lead believers to engage their context with Scripture.

In some sense, different groups of MBBs need to accept their own imperfections before they fully judge others, because each one has its own "plank" (Luke 6:42). Even though the *Isai* Muslim/Muslim social identity has the most theological danger of falling into syncretism and suffers from ethical opaqueness due to hiding believers' core identity, all groups face certain temptations to mix their faith with other things, including materialistic worldviews, the dishonest culture of Bangladeshis and existing churches, and following foreign theological traditions without reflection. Therefore, it is essential to develop a discerning believers' community in each social identity group, to share encouragement both within and between each group, and to practice dutiful regular gathering, just like the believers in the early church did (Acts 2:46). After all, without respect and love, even excellent theological knowledge can only be "a clanging cymbal" (1 Cor 13:1). Based on this premise, the effort to communicate with the majority and communicate with the Master is needed for us to strengthen ourselves for this task day by day.

---

1. Hiebert, "Critical Contextualization," 293.

Implications for Foreign Practitioners and Organizations in Bangladesh

For foreign mission workers, a humble observation of what we have done wrong – such as trying to control the ministries (or movements) by using economic superiority and implanting Western (or foreign) theological perspectives – and what we should change is the first step toward improvement. Added to this, a sincere concern for the development of MBB society over the long term is essential. A short-term fix is not a proper answer for a long-term problem. The history and current situation of Bangladeshi MBBs is an example of this, especially in light of the problems of financial dependency and lack of autonomy. It is possible to correct this if believers, both foreign and local, cooperate with each other for the long-term development of a healthy MBB society. For this, foreign organizations need to find a way to help local believers bring their own resources, take initiative, and develop their community by their own potential, and also to keep encouraging MBBs to meditate on and apply Scripture through their own eyes. Individual and piecemeal solutions are not enough, but a cooperative open network of listening to one another's voice – between foreign workers and organizations and between Bangladeshi believers and organizations – would be one kind of solution for moving a step forward in healthy contextualization and the application of four-self dynamics to the future of MBB society in Bangladesh. We need Barnabas-like persons who will be a bridge and encourager, empowering locals and uniting all believers (foreign and local) in Bangladesh, so that they will "Stand firm in the one spirit, striving together as one for the faith of the gospel" (Phil 1:27).

Recommendations for Further Research

My research dealt with a diverse range of issues related to Bangladeshi MBBs' social identity vis-à-vis contextualization. This area of study can be divided into various topics, and more work is needed to dig deeper into each of the issues. I suggest the following possible further research topics.

First, social identity research from diverse contexts is needed, because every context is different. It is good to read a book like *Longing for Community*, which contains diverse case studies of social identity issues among MBBs around the world. Different issues arise among the Pakistani MBBs studied by Tim Green[2] and the Mbbs in Arab countries studied by Kathryn Kraft,[3] but their findings intersect because Muslims contexts around the world share many points of similarity.

Second, more emic research is needed to gather in-depth interviews and long-term observations within a specific group of Muslim background believers. This will require the building up of long-term relationships between the foreign researchers and local believers until they trust each other. On the other hand, for knowing each other deeply, comparative and intersecting interviews addressing subjects such as Muslims' opinions of MBBs or MBBs' opinion of Muslims must be invaluable for digging deeply into this topic.

Third, unlike my research on all three social identity groups, it would be helpful to study each different group of MBBs to find practical examples of solving specific problems. For example, for the Christian group to mature, it would be valuable to understand how this group solves the problems and obstacles of cultural differences between existing Hindu-background Christians and MBBs and daily grow in faith in the Lord.

Fourth, researching Bangladeshi MBB identity vis-à-vis Bengali ethnic or Bangladeshi national identity would be helpful. While Bangladeshis commonly share their culture and values as Bengalis or Bangladeshis beyond religious boundaries, each religious group has its own uniqueness vis-à-vis the common Bengali identity. In addition, it would be interesting to research differences between Bengali and Turk or Malay believers, whose ethnic identity and religious identity are regarded as generally identical.

Fifth, as a social science subject, it would be good to examine topics like the government's policymaking role in protecting MBBs from social bans and developing the human rights of religious minorities. Data could be gathered from diverse positions such as government representatives, social persecutors, and victims, and researchers could investigate the motives of offending persons, the victims' responses, and government officials' attempts to deal with the issue properly.

Finally, several MBBs who are currently studying the subject of contextualization and MBBs' social identity confess that there is lack of resources and documents available to them because researchers don't publicizetheir findings

---

2. Green, "Issues of Identity."
3. Kraft, "Community and Identity."

and suggestions. While I understand the situation of keeping respondents' data secure and avoiding possible conflicts that might arise if the research is shown to the public, it would be good if future researchers could freely access and study previous research works on contextualization and MBBs' social identity. Moreover, it would be helpful to research more open approaches that engage Muslims to give attention to 'Isa, such as interreligious dialogue and comparative study of both religious books.

Glossary

Anushari. Follower.

Cutna anusitan. Circumcision ceremony.

Eid Festivals. There are two big festivals for Bengali Muslims: *Roza* (fasting) *Eid* and *Qurbani* (sacrifice) *Eid*.

Eid namaz. Muslims perform *namaz* in the field, rather than inside the mosque, on the morning of *Eid*.

Hadith. Collection of books and reports containing Muhammad's words and deeds.

Hartal. National political demonstration.

Hujur. Islamic teacher.

Iman. Faith.

Imam. Muslim preacher. It is also used to refer to *Isai* or MBB preacher.

Imandar. Believer.

Injil Sharif. Four Gospels or New Testament.

'Isa. Many Jesus-followers in Arabic and Muslim contexts call Jesus *'Isa*, which is his qur'anic name. Bangladeshi MBBs normally call Jesus *'Isa* rather than *Jisu* (the name used for Jesus in the Bible translation used by traditional Hindu-background Bangladeshi Christians).

Isai. A follower or believer of *'Isa*.

Jama'at. Arabic word for "group" or "congregation." MBBs in Bangladesh normally use this word to refer to house church gatherings of believers from a Muslim background. It has been used primarily by Islamic groups or Muslim organizations or movements such as *Jamaat-e-Islami*, a South Asian Islamic movement based in Pakistan, Bangladesh, and India. However, several Christian groups in predominantly Muslim areas – such as *Jama'at-e Rabbani*, a Christian Assemblies of God organization in Iran – are currently using the word *jama'at*.

Jummah (namaz). Muslims' Friday worship meeting or *namaz*.

Kitab. An abbreviation of *Kitabul Mokaddos* (a translation of the Holy Bible in *Mussolmani* Bangla). The name *Kitabul Mokaddos* refers to the four "Holy

Books" which are displayed on the front page: *Taurat or Torah* (Pentateuch), *Zabur* (Psalms), *Nabider Kitab* (holy books of Prophets), and *Injil* (Four Gospels or New Testament). Unlike the earlier Bangladeshi Bible, which employed adaptations of Hindu-background terms used by William Carey around two hundred years ago, *Kitab* adapts terminology used by Muslims. *Kitab* was published by the Bangladesh Bible Society book-by-book, beginning with the gospel of Mark and the whole *Injil Sharif* (book) in 1980, and continuing with the other books of the Bible. Muslims do not accept *Kitab* – or any other Christian Bible – as a holy book, but rather insist that it was modified from the original revelation by Christians. Traditional Hindu-background Christians also did not like this translation when it was first published because they saw it as distorting the language used in their Bibles. However, this Muslim-friendly version of the Bible is commonly used by Bangladeshi MBBs. Much of the figural and theological vocabulary used in this translation differs from the terminology in traditional local Bibles: this includes the words used for God (*Allah* rather than *Issor*), Son of God/Allah (*Ibnullah* rather than *Issorer Putro*), Jesus (*'Isa* rather than *Jisu*).

Kitabul Mokaddos. Full form of *Kitab*, which is a translated version of the Bible that uses Muslims' terminology. There are two versions currently being used by the BBS (Bangladesh Bible Society) and BACIB (Biblical Aids for Churches and Institutions in Bangladesh).

MBB. An abbreviated form of Muslim Background Believer. With the exception of some second-generation MBBs, most MBBs are born to Muslim parents and grew up following the rules and regulations of Muslims. They have converted from their previous way of life in Islam to follow Jesus.

Mosiho. Bangla word for "Messiah." Jesus the Messiah (Christ) can be translated as *'Isa-al-Masih* in other Muslim-majority countries, but Bangladeshi MBBs simply say *'Isa Mosiho* to refer to Jesus Christ.

Mukti/muktidata. Freedom (deliverance)/redeemer.

Mussolmani. Muslims.

Nabi. Prophet.

Najat/najatdata. Salvation/savior. Equivalent to *trankorta* in traditional (Hindu-background) language.

Namaz. A formal prayer performed by Muslims five times a day. During two *Eid* festivals – *roza* ("30 days of daytime fasting") and *qurbani* ("sacrificing animals for remembrance of Abraham's act"), Muslims gather and perform *Eid namaz* together in a field rather than inside a mosque.

Pak-koshol. Holy bath. Sometimes used to refer to baptism.

Qurbani. Sacrifice of an animal. Sometimes used to refer to the atonement [of Jesus].

Rasul Allah. Prophet or messenger of God [Allah].

Roza. Fasting.

Salat. Muslims' formal prayer. Has the same meaning as *namaz*.

Shahada. Islamic confession of the creed "God [Allah] is one and Muhammad is the messenger of God." Muslims normally recite it out loud in Arabic in their formal prayer [*namaz*].

Somaj. A religious community and society. It is sometimes translated as "religious assembly" or "congregational committee." It can be used to refer to a Muslim *somaj* or an *Isai somaj*. In some cases, a religious majority's *somaj* (such as Muslims in Bangladesh) can put pressure on a religious minority community (such as MBBs). *'Isa* followers from a Muslim background are generally put under social pressure by the Muslim *somaj*.

Suparis/Supariskari. Intercession (mediation)/mediator.

Sūra al-Fātiḥa. The first *Sūra* (book or chapter) of the Qur'an.

Tawhid. Islamic law.

Touba. To repent publicly (or privately); confession of falsehood.

Ummah. Muslims' community.

Ummot. Disciple.

Zakat: Almsgiving, one of the five pillars of Islam.

Informed Consent Letters

Thank you for your willingness to interview with me. The research is being conducted by Peter Kwang-Hee Yun, who is currently a PhD student in Intercultural Studies at Trinity International University, USA. The research which you are about to participate in is designed to investigate your social identity as a Muslim Background Believer and social integration with other Muslims in your community. In this research you will be asked a series of questions regarding three issues: your social identity change by conversion, social integration with the community, and continuity between two religions.

The interview will take one or two hours and will be recorded. At no time will your name be reported along with your responses. Please understand that your participation in this research is totally voluntary and you are free to withdraw at any time during the study. I am asking you to permit to tape record this interview. If you do have something that you do not want to be recorded, the recorder will be stopped. Please be assured that any information that you provide will be held in strict confidence.

Interview Questionnaire for Mbbs

RQ1. New Identity Formation and Factors

Background of family and community. Tell me about your family and community background. Members of your family? Community religion? Class/Work?

Background to conversion. Tell me about before and after your conversion. When and how did you come to know about 'Isa and decide to be a follower of 'Isa?

Others' response and recognition. Tell me about the initial and present responses of your family and neighbors after your conversion. Do these responses affect your identity as an 'Isa follower? Tell me about other Muslims' recognition of you. What do they recognize you as and call you? Has their identification of you changed since your conversion up until now? How do you answer when you are asked about your religious identity? Tell me some stories about it.

Identity inner/outer change. Have you changed your thinking after conversion? What have you struggled with about your being/identity since your conversion? Have you changed your language and behavior after your dedication to 'Isa? Have other people recognized your changes?

Self-social identification. Tell me about the extent of your self-social identification as a Muslim, or a Christian, or somewhere between the two? Can you put your social belonging in the chart? Do you think of yourself culturally as a Muslim or Christian? Have you sometimes felt the need to change your social identity in different circumstances? If yes, when and why?

Identity changing factors after conversion. Do your family members influence your identity? What other factors make you change your identity most beyond family, such as theological education, relationship with other believers, financial situation, etc.?

RQ2. Social Identity and Social Integration

Marriage. What happens to the followers of 'Isa when they get married? Is their wedding different from someone who is not a follower of 'Isa? For you, who do you prefer your children to marry – other followers of 'Isa, Muslim, or Christian? Is it important that your children marry someone who is also a follower of 'Isa?

Funeral. What happens to the followers of 'Isa at their funeral? Do they do everything that Muslims do, or are there activities that you do not do? Which place do you want to be buried in, Muslim or Christian graveyard?

Education. How do followers of 'Isa educate their children? Do they attend regular schools with other Muslim children? Are there any activities in school you do not allow your children to participate in? Do you educate them differently from other Muslims at home?

Economic activity. How do you manage your life economically? Do economic factors affect your identity? How does your identity affect economic situations?

Participation and Hesitance of participation. What kinds of social/religious activities do you participate in without hesitance? Should followers of 'Isa participate in traditional Muslim activities or not, such as *namaz* (formal prayer), *qurbani* (animal sacrifice), circumcision, etc.? Are there some practices of Muslims that you will not participate in? Do you have any reasons not to join?

Treatment. Can you tell me about an experience with other Muslims in which you did not feel accepted? Can you tell me about any time someone treated you badly because you are a follower of 'Isa?

Legal/Social Identification. What is your legal/formal religious identity? What do you mark when you need to mark your religion such as opening a bank account or enrolling your children's in school etc.? If you respond differently in diverse situations, how do you decide?

Determinant factors of identity. Who has been influential in helping develop your specific social identity and do you have significant moments and reasons that have influenced your social patterns of life?

Benefits and weaknesses. Have you experienced pride in your social identity? Have you been regretful because of following 'Isa in your life? Do you think there are some benefits and weaknesses for your social identity?

RQ3. Continuity and Continuing (Self-sustaining) Community

Conception of God and Jesus. Do you think followers of 'Isa and Muslims have similar beliefs about God and Jesus? What do you think are the differences between God and Jesus?

Conception of Muhammad and the Qur'an. Do you think followers of 'Isa and Muslims have similar beliefs about Muhammad and the Qur'an? What do you think about Muhammad and the Qur'an?

Sharing faith and self-propagating. Are you actively sharing your faith with Muslim neighbors? Do you build upon Islamic commonalities with Christianity in sharing your faith, or do you avoid using commonalities? If yes, what are they? How do you use them?

Self-supporting. Do you and your *jama'at* get funds from outside? What percent of your budget is supported by outside funds? Are you and your community trying to become self-dependent? If yes, what are you doing and planning so as to become self-supporting?

Self-governing. How does your *jama'at* build up leaders? Who determines leadership selection and decides *jama'at* activities? How do new potential leaders develop their (spiritual) leadership?

Self-theologizing. How do you and your *jama'at* meditate and apply the word of God (*Allah*)? Does teaching and preaching in the *jama'at* reflect everyday reality of living within a Muslim community? From whom do you prefer to learn theology and the Bible, well-educated foreign missionaries or local leaders?

Interview Questionnaire for National/Foreign Leaders

Dear national leaders of believers from Muslim background or Foreign workers,

I appreciate your consideration and your generous acceptance of my interview request by email (or phone). I have been working here in Bangladesh for several years and hoping to contribute to a better future in Bangladesh in his perspective.

I am Peter K. Yun, who is currently a PhD candidate in Intercultural Studies at Trinity International University, USA. The research which you are about to participate in is designed to investigate Bangladeshi Muslim Background Believers (MBBs)' social identity, social integration with other Muslims, and their believers' community. Regardless of local MBBs' participation in my research, I sincerely request you to give your (national or foreign practitioner's (leader's)) perspective regarding this issue with as much detail as possible in an honest manner. In this research, you will be asked a series of questions (10 questions in total) regarding three issues: MBBs' new social identity formation, social integration, and social identity with community in future.

Your interview content will be considered as confidential. If you want me to use a pseudonym for your name and organization, please tell me. I strongly believe that your cooperation is not only very much valued to my research, but you are also helping in building up the kingomd of our Lord through this research and its application to our works. Please send me any questions for clarifying my intention and send me email response to yunpeter7@gmail.com.

Part 1. New Identity Formation and Factors.

As far as you know, what do you think is the most important reason(s) for Muslims to come to faith in *'Isa* (Jesus) in Bangladesh? How did MBBs' initial (core/spiritual) identity change happen from that of Muslims? If you know several cases, please name the reasons briefly.

As you see three pictures of the social identity chart in my the attachment (or last page), do you agree with the last chart (4 social identities) in the situation of Bangladeshi MBBs? Then, can you tell me where your associating/cooperating MBBs belong to in the chart? Can you tell me why they have this kind of social identity (for example, Christian, *Isai*, *Isai* Muslim, and Muslim)? Do you think their current social identity position has been much influenced by foreign workers' (mission organization and missionary) intention and policy or national/indigenous choice?

If you see that your associating MBBs move from one social identity position to another, why do you think they make that shift? What do you think is the most important reason(s) for them to move to a different social identity position?

Part 2. Social Integration.

Among the four important social issues like marriage, funeral, education, and finance, what do you think is the most important issue for development of MBBs' social identity? What issue among these makes them struggle the most? Have you influenced them in some way in this matter? If you have some experiences, then please tell me.

How do MBBs who are related to you participate in three religious activities such as *namaz* (5 times prayer), *roza* (30 days fasting), and *qurbani* (sacrifice) and how do you teach or influence them to respond to this religious/social practice? Does it depend on MBBs' personal decision, local faith community decision (*jama'at*), or the guidance of foreign workers like you?

As you may know Paul Hiebert's concept of Critical Contextualization and his suggestion of a four-step linear process: exegesis of the culture, exegesis of the Scripture, community-wide critical evaluation of cultural practice in light of Scripture, and the community to arrange any new practices into a contextualized ritual. Do you think this process is needed in the Bangladeshi MBBs' context? Then, have you applied this related concept to your works? Please tell me your experience and view.

If you and your organization support a certain social identity position, could you tell me the position? For developing individual MBBs (and their community) in this social identity position, what do you think are the benefits and weaknesses of the group they belong to (for example, Christian, *Isai, Isai* Muslim, or Muslim)? If it has some weakness, how have you (or do you) supplement(ed) it?

Part 3. Social Identity with Continuity and Continuing Community.

How do you want to develop/nurture a perspective of MBBs about three/four important subjects such as Jesus, local believers' community (*jamaʿat*), and the Qurʾan (Muhammad)?

As you may know Rufus Anderson and Henry Venn had developed three-self idea (Self-propagating, Self-support, and Self-governing), and Paul Hiebert added a fourth self, called Self-theologizing. Do you think it (Four Selfs) is worth applying and possible to apply in Bangladeshi MBB community? To what extent and what ways are they/you applying the concept in your related field?

Self-Propagating -

Self-Support -

Self-Governing -

Self-Theologizing -

Could you assess these four selfs in your (and Bangladeshi) current MBB community situation a little more? What do you think is the most difficult part to apply in this MBB community? How do you think we need to apply or correct more the part(s) in the four-self idea for the future of MBB community in Bangladesh? If you can arrange the four selfs in order of significance and urgency in Bangladesh, could you tell us your opinion and reason?

Thank you for your views and cooperation.

Table 17. Groups of Believers from a Muslim Background in Bangladesh

Christian	Isai	Isai Muslim	Muslim
Completely assimilated in the traditional church with its festivals, language, and social relationships. They no longer have any contact with their Muslim relatives.	Mostly live in the Christian community but preserve a little contact with their Muslim relatives, visit them at *Eid* and so on. They switch between Christian and Muslim terminology according to the group they are with. The Christians tend to understand the need of *Isais* to compromise in this way; their Muslim relatives view them as heretical but not beyond the bounds of social contact.	Mostly in the Muslim community but they preserve a little contact with Christians. They use Muslim terminology. Many in the Christian community view them as "fake Christians." Muslims view them as an odd kind of Muslim, but acceptable within the range of Muslim sects.	Remain within the Muslim community, follow Muslim customs, celebrate Muslim festivals, and use only Muslim terminology. They have no contact with Christians. They are considered as Muslim by the Muslim community and also by the Christian community. There are two kinds in the group: one is Muslim but do not attend the mosque or carry out the *Eid* sacrifice. Full contact with Muslims, but considered as slack in religion. Believers in this group meet for fellowship with each other. The other is secret believers who still observe religious Muslim practices.

It is written by Tim Green with the help of Abu Taher's comment. See Green, "Identity Choices," 53–68.

Three Representative Cases of Social Identity for RQ 1

		E04	E02	H01
Family Background		Muslim whose grandfather was a *haji* (one who was Mecca pilgrim) and father was an imam.	Muslim family whose mother was working in a Christian pastor's house as a housemaid.	Muslim who worked making *lungi* (man's comfortable skirt). Followed most of the Islamic laws.
Background of Change (Conversion)		When in class seven, bought a book at a cheap price and knew something about *'Isa Mosihi* from Bible and Qur'an verses. When house was burnt, found one *Injil Sharif* in a suitcase. From that time, desire to know more has grown. The next year, joined one-week training course, which teaches about *'Isa* as Savior through Qur'an. Trainers were satisfied with his positive response. After coming back from the training, he and several others were baptized in his home town.	As a child, joined the house worship and learned biblical teaching sometimes. Not allowed to go to church by Muslim mother. Tried to be baptized but they denied and asked him to wait because he was a Muslim. Also, after finding false report about culture and struggling for several years, came to city and worked with foreigners. Through discipleship with them, confessed sins and felt some changes from his inner being to even outside circumstance.	Feeling of uncertainty and doubt about Islamic way of salvation. Purchased a small book but did not understand it due to Hindu-background Bible language. After ten years, he met an evangelist as his customer and bought one Bible from him. In his expression, with the help of the Holy Spirit, he could understand most of the language and believed in Jesus. Afterwards, he began to open one spot of his shop to gather together as a *jama'at* even before taking baptism.

	E04	E02	H01
Family and Community Response	Because his father was imam and he has prepared to be an imam from childhood, he started work in themosque as a local imam to preach about 'Isa for five years. Received social judgment three times, but not harmed because of self-dependence. Now a free preacher, sometimes in mosque, or in church.	Because of the good reputation of Christians in his hometown, such as caring for the poor, and working in a Christian NGO for several years, he did not receive much persecution.	Expelled from family. Persecuted by bad words and deeds of Muslim majority in the village. Some Muslims took his goods on purpose or did not pay for their purchases. Thus, he decided to get baptism certificate to prove that he is a Christian because police can protect him and his family from unreasonable persecution.
Motive of Present Social Identity	*Isai* Muslim, but some see him as a Muslim in his local area, while some others also see him as a Christian when he preaches the Bible to the other tribal Christians in the town.	Was encouraged to be an *Isai* Muslim following organization's heart to reach out to Muslim neighbors. When he goes to the village where the organization works, sometimes introduces himself as a Muslim because of mostly dealing with village Muslims and not wanting to fall into trouble.	In order to communicate with the majority Muslims, uses *Kitabul Mokaddos* (Mussolmani Bible) and he also identifies as *Isai*.
Social Identity	*Isai* Muslim/Muslim	*Isai*/*Isai* Muslim (*uboi*; both)	Christian/*Isai*

Three Representative Cases
of Social Identity for RQ 2

	E04	E02	H01
Social Integration of Family (marriage/child education, etc.)	Judged by society several times because of his faith in 'Isa. Hopes to marry his children to 'Isa-following girls. Has taught children the Bible and sometimes the Qur'an before, but now mostly teaches the Bible.	Married a Muslim woman. Tries to bring up his son as a Christian schoolboy. His mother (still Muslim) asks a question about her son's burial saying "Where do you want to be buried? With Muslims or Christians?"	Children studied Christian religion and clearly identified themselves as Christians. Elder son married an MBB whose parents do not agree with her marriage. His daughter-in-law needed to go to court to change her religion before marriage.
Participation in Muslim Rituals	Has joined Muslim prayer (*namaz*) in mosque sometimes, but for the last part of the prayer, finishes only saying that God is one (not mentioning the next part about Muhammad). During the sacrifice festival, remembers Ibrahim's (Abraham's) faith, using this as an opportunity to preach 'Isa as a lamb of God to Muslims.	Visits Muslims' homes at *Eid* festival, but does not want to participate in any religious activities like *namaz* or *qurbani* because he thinks these are Islamic. Because his organization and city *jama'at* do not want to celebrate Christmas, sometimes feels the desire to celebrate Christian festivals.	Does not participate in Muslim religious and social activities because he believes rituals are Islamic. His neighbors do not invite him to their social activities like marriages and funerals because they have jealousy and hatred toward him as a convert from Islam.

	E04	E02	H01
Social Association and Legal Identity	When he was subjected to social trial (judgment) several times by Islamic foundation and others, the effect of verbal punishment was dismissed automatically because his economic condition was good and had a good reputation for serving the poor in village. Advantage of position: social integration and opportunity to share 'Isa. Disadvantage:some people hate him due to his being an 'Isa follower.	Advantage: got a job in Christian organization because of being baptized and experience of working with Christians. Disadvantage: Feels guilty when he needs to introduce himself as a Muslim, even though he agrees with the literal meaning of the term which is "who submits to God (Allah)."	Sometimes if he was invited, he did not go in order to avoid possible fights with hot-tempered Muslim guests. But, legally, he is allowed to hold Christmas festival to invite police to give them opportunity to hear the good news and eat good food. Advantage: legal protection from government. Disadvantage: some hate him due to his conversion from Islam.
Belief about Jesus and Bible	'Isa (Jesus) as the Savior, but he focuses on similarity, not wanting to criticize or dwell on the difference between the Qur'an and the Holy Books.	'Isa (Jesus) as a Savior; most of time he meditates on the Bible himself and with his foreign leader.	'Isa (Jesus) as a spiritual son of God in contrast to local Bangladeshi Muslims' belief in 'Isa as a prophet and one who is coming to the world again as a disciple of Muhammad.
Belief about Qur'an and Muhammad	Muhammad as a prophet like other prophets in the Bible. Qur'an as like other holy books such as the *Torah*, *Zabur*, and *Injil*.	Muhammad as a warner and a prophet. Does not want to look down on the Qur'an in comparison to the Bible (*Kitabs*).	Muhammad came to this world to introduce the good news and be a warner of judgment.
Point	Participation in Muslim activities with reinterpretation and opportunity.	Difference between intention and obligation. Searching for contentment.	Clear Christian identity of children, least relationship with Muslims.

Three Representative Cases
of Social Identity for RQ 3

	E04	E02	H01
Self-propagating	He willingly preaches *'Isa* as the Savior through the Qur'an and the Bible. He formed many *jama'ats* and circuit every week, and his disciples and believers of the *jama'at* have similar identity with him.	He has two *jama'ats* which he involves with: one is a village *jama'at*, and the other is a city *jama'at*. He couldn't care for village *jama'at*, so they are passive, but several members share the gospel in urban *jama'at*.	He is willing to share the good news to his majority neighbors, sometimes using the Qur'an as a tool for easily acceptable bridge to introduce the good news.
Self-supporting	Each *jama'at* consists of 2–3 families (5–8 persons). He teaches them offering and tithe, and sometimes *jama'at* members buy blankets and distribute to the needy. However, because of their financial insufficiency, it is not enough to hold training. In this sense, he can get some benefit from cooperation with foreign workers.	Village *jama'at* always wants his leadership and teaching to run it, but he does not have much time to visit his own village. City *jama'at* looks self-supporting, but he feels it is not because major portion of offering comes from foreign workers' tithe.	He is running a local *jama'at* in his house himself, without outside support. He has plan to self-support in the long term such as buying or selling land given by donation and doing different kinds of business. With benefits (tithe of income) of these businesses, he wants to do diverse ministries.

	E04	E02	H01
Self-governing	He seeks to find knowledgeable followers and someone who is able to teach others and guidance in the right way. Most leaders of *jama'ats* have been selected by members of *jama'ats*. They can choose a proper leader through discussion.	His urban *jama'at* – Feeling that it is founded by foreign initiative but foreign leader tries to empower local leaders. Rural *jama'at* – too far to train leaders. He has connection to Christian church in his hometown but worry about cultural difference.	Members of *jama'at* gather once a week and open several seminars each year (like family or leadership seminars) and invite good speakers around the country. Candidate of leader is someone who comes to *jama'at* every week and willing to serve and share the gospel.
Self-theologizing	He starts from teaching the Qur'an to connect it to teaching the Bible and once one becomes a leader of the *jama'at*, he trains them for both evangelism and discipleship.	For applying four-self, he believes that the first step is to see the change in their life before preaching the good news because he saw that many Christians or MBBs who are involved in evangelistic work have materialistic mindset (religious business).	He is thinking to build up several ongoing (or new) disciples from Muslim society (like *Isai* Muslims) to be a light in the process of coming toward *Isai*/Christian and draw his family and neighbors to the gospel step by step.
Point	Started several *jama'ats* in different areas. Trying to be self-dependent, cooperation welcomed for training. Teaching the leaders how to use the Qur'an.	His village *jama'at* always needs him, finds lack of four-self areas. His city *jama'at* depends more on foreign initiative in terms of self-supporting and governing.	*Jama'at* in his house. Trying to be self-dependent in all four areas and developing strategies to reach out to the majority through the social identity of *Isai* Muslims.

Two Paradigms of Contextualization through Various Lenses

Radical (high) Contextualization (Muslim, several *Isai* Muslim groups) with Inside Missiology	Theological Lens by Author	Moderate (low) Contextualization of MBBs (Christian, *Isai*, some *Isai* Muslim group)
Bartlotti's Five Lenses		
Word, Spirit, two or three gathered, simple church, Synoptic Jesus emphasis	Ecclesiology	Word, Sacraments, discipline, order, leadership, Pauline emphasis
Local (contextual) theologies, theologies from majority world church, "Indigenizing Principle"	Doing Theology	Universal truths, Western theological tradition, "Pilgrim Principle"
Continuity, fulfillment, preparation of the way for the gospel	Other Religions	Discontinuity, exclusivism, radical disjunction
"islams" (lower case, plural), culturally embedded, "muslims," "Which Islam?," "Whose Islam?"	Islam	"Islam," historically essentialized, "Muslims," Islamic tradition
Process, belonging, behaving, believing, kingdom of God, centered set, moving toward Christ	Conversion-Initiation	Event, believing, behaving, belonging, people of God, bounded set, clear in/out markers of identity
E04, M04	Representative figures	H01, E02 (*uboi* identity)

Bibliography

Abdulahugli, Hasan. "Factors Leading to Conversion among Central Asian Muslims." In *From the Straight Path to the Narrow Way: Journeys of Faith.* Edited by David Greenlee, 157–66. Waynesboro, GA: Authentic, 2006.

Accad, Fouad Elias. *Building Bridges: Christianity and Islam.* Colorado Springs, CO: Bridge of Peace International, 1997.

Accad, Martin. "Towards a Theology of Islam: A Response to Harley Talman's 'Is Muhammad also among the Prophets?'" *International Journal of Frontier Missiology* 31, no. 4 (2014): 191–93.

Andrews, Colin. "Contextualization in a Glocalizing World." *Evangelical Mission Quarterly* 45 (2009): 314–17.

Asad, Abdul. "Rethinking the Insider Movement Debate: Global Historical Insights toward an Appropriate Transitional Model of C5." *St Francis Magazine* 5, no. 4 (2009): 133–59.

Azad, Anwarul. "Discipling, Identity, and Belonging of M. Heritage Believers in Bangladesh." Presentation Paper (date and location confidential), 2015.

Ayub, Edward. "Observation and Reactions to Christians Involved in a New Approach to Mission." *St Francis Magazine* 5, no. 5 (2009): 21–40.

Babbie, Earl. *The Practice of Social Research.* 11th ed. Belmont, CA: Thomson Wadsworth, 2007.

Baeq, Daniel Shinjong. "Contextualizing Religious Form and Meaning: A Missiological Interpretation of Naaman's Petitions (2 Kings 5:15–19)." *International Journal of Frontier Missiology* 27, no. 4 (2010): 197–207.

Baig, Sufyan. "The Ummah and Christian Community." In *Longing for Community: Church, Ummah, or Somewhere in Between?* Edited by David Greenlee, 69–78. Pasadena, CA: William Carey Library, 2013.

Bartlotti, Leonard N. "Seeing Inside Insider Missiology: Exploring Our Theological Lenses and Presuppositions." *International Journal of Frontier Missiology* 30, no. 4 (2013): 137–53.

Beit-Hallahmi, Benjamin. *Prolegomena to the Psychological Study of Religion.* London: Associated University Press, 1989.

Bernard, Russell. *Research Methods in Anthropology: Qualitative and Quantitative Approaches*. Lanham, MD: AltaMira, 2006.

Brogden, Dick. "Inside Out: Probing Presuppositions among Insider Movements." *International Journal of Frontier Missiology* 27, no. 1 (2010): 33–40.

Brown, Rick. "Biblical Muslims." *International Journal of Frontier Missiology* 24, no. 2 (2007): 65–74.

———. "Contextualization without Syncretism." *International Journal of Frontier Missiology* 23 (2006): 127–33.

Brown, Rick, and Steven C. Hawthorne. "Three Types of Christward Movements." In *Perspectives on the World Christian Movement: A Reader*, 4th ed. Edited by Ralph D. Winter and Steven C. Hawthorne. Pasadena, CA: William Carey Library, 2009.

Central Intelligence Agency. "Bangladesh Religious Population." *The World Factbook*. Accessed on 3 February 2015. https://www.cia.gov/library/publications/the-world-factbook/geos/bg.html/.

Cheong, John. "The Socio-Religious Identity and Life of the Malay Christians of Malaysia." PhD diss., Trinity International University, 2012.

Conn, Harvie M. "Indigenization." In *Evangelical Dictionary of World* Missions. Edited by Scott Moreau, 481. Grand Rapids, MI: Baker, 2000.

———. "The Muslim Convert and His Culture." In *The Gospel and Islam: A 1978 Compendium*. Edited by Don M. McCurry, 97–113. Monrovia, CA: MARC, 1979.

Constitution of Bangladesh. Dhaka: Udoyon Publication, 2012.

Cornille, Catherine. "Introduction." In *Many Mansions?: Multiple Religious Belonging and Christian Identity*. Edited by Catherine Cornill, 1–6. Maryknoll, NY: Orbis, 2002.

———. "Double Religious Belonging: Aspects and Questions." *Buddhist-Christian Studies* 23 (2003): 43–9.

Corwin, Gary. "An Extended Conversation about 'Insider Movements': Responses to the September–October 2005 *Mission Frontiers*." *Mission Frontiers* (January–February 2006): 16–20. https://www.missionfrontiers.org/pdfs/28-1-insider-movements.pdf.

———. "A Humble Appeal to C5/Insider Movement Muslim Ministry Advocates to Consider Ten Questions, with Responses from Brother Yusuf, Rick Brown, Kevin Higgins, Rebecca Lewis, and John Travis." *International Journal of Frontier Missiology* 24, no. 1 (2007): 5–20.

Creswell, John W. *Research Design: Qualitative, Quantitative, and Mixed Method Approaches*. Thousand Oaks, CA: Sage, 2003.

Croft, Richard. "Muslim Background Believers in Bangladesh: The Mainline Church Scene with These New 'Church' Members from Muslim Backgrounds." *St Francis Magazine* 10, no. 1 (2014): 37–59.

Cumming, Joseph. "Muslim Followers of Jesus?" *Christianity Today* (20 November 2009). https://www.christianitytoday.com/ct/2009/december/main.html.

Daniels, Gene. "Saying the *Shahada*: Matters of Conscience, Creed, and Communication." *Evangelical Mission Quarterly* 50, no. 3 (2014): 304–11.

Daniels, Gene, and L. D. Waterman. "Bridging the 'Socio-Religious' Divide: A Conversation between Two Missiologists." *International Journal of Frontier Missiology* 30, no.2 (Summer 2013): 59–66.

Decker, Frank, and Darrell Whiteman. "White Paper: Radical Biblical Contextual (or "Insider") Movements, Including Their Application to Ministry among Muslims." Unpublished in-house paper prepared for The Mission Society Board of Trustees, 2010.

Dixon, Roger L. "Moving on from the C1–C6 Spectrum." *St Francis Magazine* 5, no. 4 (2009): 3–19.

Dutch, Bernard. "Should Muslims Become "Christian"?" *International Journal of Frontier Missiology* 17 (2000): 15–24.

Esposito, John. *Islam: The Straight Path.* New York: Oxford University Press, 1988.

Farah, Warrick. "Emerging Missiological Themes in MBB Conversion Factors." *International Journal of Frontier Missiology* 30, no. 1 (2013): 13–20.

Farrokh, Fred. "Indigenous Perspectives on Muslim Identity and Insider Movements." In *Global Missiology* (January 2015): 1–15. Accessed 23 July 2015. http://ojs.globalmissiology.org/index.php/english/article/view/1757/3897.

Fleming, Dean E. *Contextualization in the New Testament: Patterns for Theology and Mission.* Downers Grove, IL: InterVarsity Press, 2005.

Garrison, David. "Church Planting Movements vs. Insider Movements: Missiological Realities vs. Mythiological Speculations." *International Journal of Frontier Missiology* 21, no. 4 (2004): 151–54.

———. *A Wind in the House of Islam: How God Is Drawing Muslims around the World to Faith in Jesus Christ.* Monument, CO: WIGTake Resources, 2014.

Gaudeul, Jean-Marie. "Learning from God's Ways." In *From the Straight Path to the Narrow Way: Journeys of Faith.* Edited by David Greenlee, 81–92. Waynesboro, GA: Authentic, 2006.

Gefen, Gavriel. "Jesus Movements: Discovering Biblical Faith in the Most Unexpected Places." *Mission Frontiers* (May–June 2011): 7–10.

Geffre, Claude. "Double Belonging and the Originality of Christianity as a Religion." In *Many Mansions?: Multiple Religious Belonging and Christian Identity.* Edited by Catherine Cornill, 93–105. Maryknoll, NY: Orbis, 2002.

Gillespie, V. Bailey. *The Dynamics of Religious Conversion: Identity and Transformation.* Birmingham, AL: Religious Education Press, 1991.

Gilliland, Dean S. "Contextual Theology as Incarnational Mission." In *The Word among Us: Contextualizing Theology for Mission Today*. Edited by Dean S. Gilliland, 9–31. Dallas, TX: Word, 1989.

Goldsmith, Martin. "Community and Controversy: Key Causes of Muslim Resistance." *Missiology* 4, no. 3 (1976): 317–23. doi:10.1177/009182967600400306.

Goosen, Gideon. "An Empirical Study of Dual Religious Belonging." *Journal of Empirical Theology* 20, no. 2 (2007): 159–78. doi:10.1163/157092507X237327.

Green, Tim. "Beyond the C-Spectrum? A Search for New Models." *Evangelical Review of Theology* 37, no. 4 (2013): 361–80.

————. "Conversion in the Light of Identity Theories." In *Longing for Community: Church, Ummah, or Somewhere in Between?* Edited by David Greenlee, 41–52. Pasadena, CA: William Carey Library, 2013.

————. "Identity Choices at the Border Zone." In *Longing for Community: Church, Ummah, or Somewhere in Between?* Edited by David Greenlee, 53–68. Pasadena, CA: William Carey Library, 2013.

————. "Identity Issues for Ex-Muslim Christians, with Particular Reference to Marriage." *St Francis Magazine* 8, no. 4 (2012): 435–81.

————. "Issues of Identity for Christians of a Muslim Background in Pakistan." PhD diss., University of London, 2014.

Greenlee, David. "The "Good News" Is Good News!" In *From the Straight Path to the Narrow Way: Journeys of Faith*. Edited by David Greenlee, 3–10. Waynesboro, GA: Authentic, 2006.

————. "Introduction: Transformed in Christ." In *Longing for Community: Church, Ummah, or Somewhere in Between?* Edited by David Greenlee, xiii–xix. Pasadena, CA: William Carey Library, 2013.

Greenlee, David, and Rick Love. "Conversion through the Looking Glass: Muslims and the Multiple Facets of Conversion." In *From the Straight Path to the Narrow Way: Journeys of Faith*. Edited by David Greenlee, 35–50. Waynesboro, GA: Authentic, 2006.

Haskell, Rob. "Editorial." *Evangelical Review of Theology* 37, no. 5 (Oct 2013): 291–92.

Hedley, Scott. "Helpful for Those Wanting to Understand Why Some Oppose Insider Movements." Review of *A Theological Analysis of the Insider Movement Paradigm from Four Perspectives*. Accessed 23 July 2012. http://www.amazon.com/review/R3ND1C1X0ZZNLD/ref=cm_cr_dp_title?ie=UTF8&ASIN=0865850380&channel=detail-glance&nodeID=283155&store=books.

Hibbert, Richard. "Negotiating Identity: Extending and Applying Alan Tippett's Model of Conversion to Believers from Muslim and Hindu Backgrounds." *Missiology: An International Review* 43, no. 1 (2015): 59–72. doi:10.1177/0091829614541094.

Hiebert, Paul G. *Anthropological Insights for Missionaries*. Grand Rapids: Baker, 1985.

———. *Anthropological Reflections on Missiological Issues*. Grand Rapids, MI: Baker, 1994.

———. "Critical Contextualization." *Missiology: An International Review* 12, no. 3 (1984): 287–96. doi:10.1177/009182968401200303.

———. *The Gospel in Human Context: Anthropological Explorations for Contemporary Missions*. Grand Rapids, MI: Baker Academic, 2009.

———. "Metatheology: The Step eyond Ccontextualization." In *Reflection and Projection*. Edited by Hans Kasdorf, 383–95. Bad Liebenzell, West Germany: Liebenzeller Missions Verlag, 1988.

Higgins, Kevin. "Acts 15 and Insider Movements among Muslims: Questions, Process, and Conclusions." *International Journal of Frontier Missiology* 24, no. 1 (2007): 29–40.

———. "Identity, Integrity, and Insider Movements." *International Journal of Frontier Missiology* 23, no. 3 (2006): 117–23.

———. "Inside What? Church, Culture, Religion and Insider Movements in Biblical Perspective." *St Francis Magazine* 5, no. 4 (2009): 74–91.

———. "The Key to Insider Movements: The "Devoted's" of Acts." *International Journal of Frontier Missiology* 21, no. 4 (2004): 155–65.

———. "Response to Gary Corwin. A Humble Appeal to C5/Insider Movement Muslim Ministry Advocates to Consider Ten Questions." *International Journal of Frontier Missiology* 24, no. 1 (2007): 5–20.

Hirsch, Alan, and Tim Catchim. *The Permanent Revolution: Apostolic Imagination and Practice for the 21st Century Church*. Hoboken, NJ: John Wiley, 2012.

Jaz, Abu. "Clarification." *Christianity Today* (April 2013).

Jennings, Nathaniel Issac. "The Muslim Background Believers Movement in Bangladesh." ThM thesis, Queen's University of Belfast, 2007.

Johnson, Carl. (pseudonym). "Training Materials for Muslim-Background Believers in Bangladesh." DMiss project, Trinity International University, 1999.

Jorgensen, Danny L. *Participant Observation: A Methodology for Human Studies*. Thousand Oaks, CA: Sage, 1989. doi:10.4135/9781412985376.

Jørgensen, Jonas Adelin. *Jesus Imandars and Christ Bhaktas: Two Case Studies of Interreligious Hermeneutics and Identity in Global Christianity*. Frankfurt: Peter Lang, 2008.

———. "Jesus Imandars and Christ Bhaktas: Report from Two Field Studies of Interreligious Hermeneutics and Identity in Globalized Christianity." *International Bulletin of Missionary Research* 33 (2009): 171–76. doi:10.1177/239693930903300402.

Kashem, Chanchul Mahmud. "Actual *Isai Somaj* Should Have Been Established." *Omega* 79 (August 2013): 5–8.

———. "Needs of More Concentration about Preaching the Gospel into the Majority Group." *OMEGA* 92 (October 2014): 8–9.

Kim, John. *Jesus Coming into Muslim Community (무슬림 가운데 오신 예수).* Seoul: Insiders, 2011.

Kraft, Charles H. *Anthropology for Christian Witness.* Maryknoll, NY: Orbis, 1996.

———. "Dynamic Equivalence Churches in Muslim Society." In *The Gospel and Islam: A 1978 Compendium.* Edited by Don M. McCurry, 114–28. Monrovia, CA: MARC, 1979.

Kraft, Kathryn Ann. "Community and Identity among Arabs of a Muslim Background Who Choose to Follow a Christian Faith." PhD diss., University of Bristol, 2007.

———. *Searching for Heaven in the Real World: A Sociological Discussion of Conversion in the Arab World.* Oxford: Regnum, 2012.

Lee, Hyun-Mo. "Response to Kevin Higgins: Does Jerusalem Council Answer the Questions of the Insider Movement?" *(예루살렘 공의회는 무슬림 내부자 운동에도 답을 줄 수 있을까?) Korean Journal of Frontier Missiology* 8 (2009).

Lee, Musa. *Orientation Paper for New Foreign Practitioners.* Dhaka, Bangladesh, 2014.

Lewis, Rebecca. "Insider Movements: Honoring God-Given Identity and Community." *International Journal of Frontier Missiology* 26, no. 1 (2009): 16–19.

———. "Possible Pitfalls of Jesus Movements: Lessons from History." *Mission Frontiers* 32 (May–June 2010): 21–24.

———. "Promoting Movements to Christ within Natural Communities." *International Journal of Frontier Missiology* 24, no. 2 (2007): 75–76.

———. "Response to Brogden. Inside Out: Probing Presuppositions among Insider Movements." *International Journal of Frontier Missiology* 27, no. 1 (2010): 33–40.

Marshall, Catherine, and Gretchen B. Rossman. *Designing Qualitative Research.* Thousand Oaks, CA: Sage, 1995.

Massey, Joshua. "Editorial: Muslim Contextualization 1." *International Journal of Frontier Missiology* 17, no. 1 (2000): 2–3.

———. "His Ways Are Not Our Ways." *Evangelical Mission Quarterly* 35, no. 2 (1999): 188–97.

———. "Misunderstanding C5: His Ways Are Not Our Orthodoxy." *Evangelical Mission Quarterly* 40 (July 2004): 294–304.

Maurer, Andreas. "In Search of a New Life: Conversion Motives of Christians and Muslims." In *From the Straight Path to the Narrow Way: Journeys of Faith.* Edited by David Greenlee, 93–108. Waynesboro, GA: Authentic, 2006.

Meral, Ziya. "Conversion and Apostasy: A Sociological Perspective." *Evangelical Mission Quarterly* 42, April (2006): 508–13.

Mol, Hans J. *Identity and the Sacred*. New York: Free Press, 1976.

Moon, Steve Sang-cheol. "Critical Review to the Insider Movement as a Frontier Mission Strategy (개척선교전략으로서 내부자운동 비평)." *Korean Mission Quarterly* 8, no. 4 (2009): 18–25.

———. "Self-Theologizing (자신학화)." *Current Mission Trends* 15 (August 2013): 5–6.

Moreau, A. Scott. "Contextualization." In *The Changing Face of World Missions: Engaging Contemporary Issues and Trends*. Edited by Michael Pocock, Gailyn Van Rheenen, and Douglas McConnell, 321–48. Grand Rapids, MI: Baker Academic, 2005.

———. *Contextualization in World Missions: Mapping and Assessing Evangelical Models*. Grand Rapids, MI: Kregel, 2012.

———. "Syncretism." In *Evangelical Dictionary of World Missions*. Edited by Scott Moreau, 924–25. Grand Rapids, MI: Baker, 2000.

Netland, Harold. "Evangelical Missiology and Theology of Religions: An Agenda for the Future." *International Journal of Frontier Missiology* 17, no. 1 (2012): 53–59.

Nevius, John. *The Planting and Development of Missionary Churches: His Basic Principles*. Philadelphia, PA: P&R, 1958.

Nikides, Bill. "Evaluating 'Insider Movements': C5 (Messianic Muslims)." *St Francis Magazine* 4, March (2006): 1–15.

Ottenberg, S. "Changes over Time in an African Culture and in an Anthropologist." In *Others Knowing Others: Perspectives on Ethnographic Careers*. Edited by D. D. Fowler and D. L. Hardestry, 91–118. Washington, DC: Smithsonial Institution Press, 1994.

Palash, Samsul Alam, Anwar Hossain, and Edward Ayub. "Isai Fellowship in Bangladesh (IFB)." *Asia Evangelical Alliance*, February (2011): 1.

Parshall, Phil. "Danger! New Directions in Contextualization." *Evangelical Missions Quarterly* (October 1998): 404–10.

———. "Going Too Far?" In *Perspectives on the World Christian Movement: A Reader*, 4th ed. Edited by Ralph D. Winter and Steven C. Hawthorne, 663–67. Pasadena, CA: William Carey Library, 2009.

———. "Lifting the Fatwa." *Evangelical Missions Quarterly* 40, no. 3 (July 2004): 288–93.

———. *Muslim Evangelism: Contemporary Approaches to Contextualization*. Waynesboro, GA: Gabriel, 2003.

Priest, Robert J. "Researching Contextualization in Churches Influenced by Missionaries." In *Communities of Faith in Africa and the African Diaspora*.

Edited by Casely B. Essamuah and David K. Ngaruiya, 299–318. Eugene, OR: Pickwick, 2013.

Sanneh, Lamin O. *Disciples of All Nations: Pillars of World Christianity.* New York: Oxford University Press, 2008. doi:10.1093/acprof:o so/9780195189605.001.0001.

———. *Translating the Message: The Missionary Impact on Culture.* 2nd ed. Maryknoll, NY: Orbis, 2009.

———. *Whose Religion Is Christianity?: The Gospel beyond the West.* Grand Rapids, MI: Eerdmans, 2003.

Schlorff, Sam. "The Translation Model for Mission in Resistant Muslim Society: A Critique and an Alternative." *Missiology: An International Review* 28, no. 3 (2000): 305–28. doi:10.1177/009182960002800304.

Shenk, Wilbert R. "Rufus Anderson and Henry Venn: A Special Relationship?" *International Bulletin of Missionary Research* 5, no. 4 (October 1981): 168–72. doi:10.1177/239693938100500404.

Syrjanen, Seppo. *In Search of Meaning and Identity: Conversion to Christianity in Pakistani Muslim Culture.* Vammala, Finland: Annals of the Finnish Society for Missiology and Ecumenics, 1984.

Stephenson, John. "The Messiah of Honor: The Christology and Atonement of Follower of *Isa Masih.*" PhD diss., Open University, 2012.

Stewart, Alex. *The Ethnographer's Method.* Thousand Oaks, CA: Sage, 1998. doi:10.4135/9781412986144.

Straehler, Reinhold. "Areas of Change in the Conversion Processes of East African Muslims." In *Longing for Community: Church, Ummah, or Somewhere in Between?* Edited by David Greenlee, 125–38. Pasadena, CA: William Carey Library, 2013.

Tan, Kang-San. "Can Christians Belong to More Than One Religious Tradition?" *Evangelical Review of Theology* 34, no. 3 (2010a): 250–64.

———. "Dual Belonging: A Missiological Critique and Appreciation from an Asian Evangelical Perspective." *Mission Studies* 27, no. 1 (2010b): 24–38. doi:10.1163/157338310X497973.

Taher, Abu. "Interview by author. Dhaka, Bangladesh. October 24.

———. "Society of Bangladesh: The Obstacles to Build Up *jama'at/somaj.*" Translated by Md. Golam Rabbani, 1–3. Gajipur, Bangladesh: Education Welfare Trust, 2009.

Talman, Haley. "Is Muhammad Also among the Prophets?" *International Journal of Frontier Missiology* 31, no. 4 (2014): 169–90.

Tennent, Timothy C. "Followers of Jesus (Isa) in Islamic Mosques: A Closer Examination of C-5 'High Spectrum' Contextualization." *International Journal of Frontier Missiology* 23, no. 3 (2006): 101–15.

Terry, John Mark. "Indigenous Churches." In *Evangelical Dictionary of World Missions*. Edited by Scott Moreau, 483. Grand Rapids, MI: Baker, 2000.

Tippett, Alan R. "Conversion as a Dynamic Process in Christian Mission." *Missiology: An International Review* 5, no. 2 (1977): 203–21. doi:10.1177/009182967700500206.

Totire, Alan. "An Investigation into the Identity Theory as Experienced by Immigrant Muslim Background Believers." PhD diss., Trinity International University, 2015.

Travis, John. "The C1 to C6 Spectrum." *Evangelical Missions Quarterly* 34 (1998a): 407–8.

———. "Messianic Muslim Followers of 'Isa: A Closer Look at C5 Believers and Congregations." *International Journal of Frontier Missiology* 17, no. 1 (2000): 53–59.

———. "Must All Muslims Leave 'Islam' to Follow Jesus?" In *Perspectives on the World Christian Movement: A Reader*. 4th ed. Edited by Ralph D. Winter and Steven C. Hawthorne, 668–72. Pasadena, CA: William Carey Library, 2009.

———. "Response to Phil Parshall. Must All Muslims Leave "Islam" to Follow Jesus?" *Evangelical Missions Quarterly* 34 (1998b): 411–15.

———. "Response to Tennent (Followers of Jesus ['Isa] in Islamic Mosques)." *International Journal of Frontier Missiology* 23, no. 3 (2006): 124–25.

Travis, John, and Anna Travis. "Appropriate Approaches in Muslim Contexts." In *Appropriate Christianity*. Edited by Charles H. Kraft, 397–414. Pasadena, CA: William Carey Library, 2005.

Travis, John J., and Dudley Woodberry. "When God's Kingdom Grows Like Yeast: Frequently-Asked-Questions about Jesus Movements within Muslim Communities." *Mission Frontiers* 32, no. July-August (2010): 24–30. http://www.missionfrontiers.org/issue/article/when-gods-kingdom-grows-like-yeast.

Trull, Richard E., Jr. *The Fourth Self: Theological Education to Facilitate Self-Theologizing for Local Church Leaders in Kenya*. New York: Peter Lang, 2013.

US State Department. 2012. Bangladesh 2012 International Religious Freedom Report. *International Religious Freedom Report*. Accessed 7 June 2015. http://www.state.gov/documents/organization/208636.pdf/.

Waterman, L. D. "Do the Roots Affect the Fruits?" *International Journal of Frontier Missiology* 24, no. 2 (2007): 57–63.

Walls, Andrew F. "The Gospel as Prisoner and Liberator of Culture: Is There a 'Historic Christian Faith'?" In *Landmark Essays in Mission and World Christianity*. Edited by Robert L. Gallagher and Paul Hertig, 133–48. Maryknoll, NY: Orbis, 2009.

Whiteman, Darrell. "Contextualization: The Theory, the Gap, the Challenge."
    International Bulletin of Missionary Research 21, no. 1 (1997):
    2–7. doi:10.1177/239693939702100101.
Wilder, John W. "Some Reflections on Possibilities for People Movements among
    Muslims." *Missiology: An International Review* 5, no. 3 (1977): 301–
    20. doi:10.1177/009182967700500305.
Winter, Ralph. "Going Far Enough?" In *Perspectives on the World Christian
    Movement: A Reader*. 4th ed. Edited by Ralph D. Winter and Steven C.
    Hawthorne, 668–72. Pasadena, CA: William Carey Library, 2009.
Woodberry, J. Dudley. "Contextualization among Muslims: Reusing Common
    Pillars." In *The Word among Us: Contextualizing Theology for Mission Today*.
    Edited by Dean S. Gilliland, 282–312. Dallas, TX: Word, 1989.
———. "A Global Perspective on Muslims Coming to Faith in Christ." In *From the
    Straight Path to the Narrow Way: Journeys of Faith*. Edited by David Greenlee.
    Waynesboro, GA: Authentic, 2006.
———. "To the Muslim I Became a Muslim?" *International Journal of Frontier
    Missiology* 24, no. 1 (2007): 23–28.
Yang, Fenggang. *Chinese Christians in America*. University Park, PA: Pennsylvania
    State University Press, 1999.
Yoder, Michael L., Michael H. Lee, Jonathan Ro, and Robert J. Priest.
    "Understanding Christian Identity in Terms of Bounded and Centered Set
    Theory in the Writings of Paul G. Hiebert." *Trinity Journal* 30 (2009): 177–88.
Yusuf, Brother. "Response to Gary Corwin. A Humble Appeal to C5/Insider
    Movement Muslim Ministry Advocates to Consider Ten Questions."
    International Journal of Frontier Missiology 24, no. 1 (2007): 5–20.

Langham Literature, with its publishing work, is a ministry of Langham Partnership.

Langham Partnership is a global fellowship working in pursuit of the vision God entrusted to its founder John Stott –

> *to facilitate the growth of the church in maturity and Christ-likeness through raising the standards of biblical preaching and teaching.*

Our vision is to see churches in the Majority World equipped for mission and growing to maturity in Christ through the ministry of pastors and leaders who believe, teach and live by the word of God.

Our mission is to strengthen the ministry of the word of God through:
- nurturing national movements for biblical preaching
- fostering the creation and distribution of evangelical literature
- enhancing evangelical theological education

especially in countries where churches are under-resourced.

Our ministry

Langham Preaching partners with national leaders to nurture indigenous biblical preaching movements for pastors and lay preachers all around the world. With the support of a team of trainers from many countries, a multi-level programme of seminars provides practical training, and is followed by a programme for training local facilitators. Local preachers' groups and national and regional networks ensure continuity and ongoing development, seeking to build vigorous movements committed to Bible exposition.

Langham Literature provides Majority World preachers, scholars and seminary libraries with evangelical books and electronic resources through publishing and distribution, grants and discounts. The programme also fosters the creation of indigenous evangelical books in many languages, through writer's grants, strengthening local evangelical publishing houses, and investment in major regional literature projects, such as one volume Bible commentaries like the *Africa Bible Commentary* and the *South Asia Bible Commentary*.

Langham Scholars provides financial support for evangelical doctoral students from the Majority World so that, when they return home, they may train pastors and other Christian leaders with sound, biblical and theological teaching. This programme equips those who equip others. Langham Scholars also works in partnership with Majority World seminaries in strengthening evangelical theological education. A growing number of Langham Scholars study in high quality doctoral programmes in the Majority World itself. As well as teaching the next generation of pastors, graduated Langham Scholars exercise significant influence through their writing and leadership.

To learn more about Langham Partnership and the work we do visit **langham.org**

Lightning Source UK Ltd.
Milton Keynes UK
UKHW020637111021
392013UK00009B/365